# SPIRITUAL
# WORKS & JOURNEYS

A. C. Emmerick

# SPIRITUAL
# WORKS & JOURNEYS

## The Nuptial House, Vineyard, Sufferings for Others, the Church, and the Neighbor

*From the Visions of*
ANNE CATHERINE EMMERICH

*Selected, Edited & Arranged*
*With Extensive New Translations from*
*the Original Notes of Clemens Brentano by*
JAMES R. WETMORE

Volume 11 of 12
of the Series: *New Light on the*
*Visions of Anne Catherine Emmerich*

(With 1 Illustration)

Angelico Press

First published in the USA
by Angelico Press 2018
Revised Text, New Text, Translations,
and Layout © James R. Wetmore 2018

For information, address:
Angelico Press
169 Monitor St.
Brooklyn, NY 11222
angelicopress.com


ISBN 978-1-62138-378-9 (pbk)
ISBN 978-1-62138-377-2 (cloth)

Cover Image:
J. James Tissot (French, 1836–1902)
*Samarian Woman at the Well* (detail), Brooklyn Museum,
purchased by public subscription: 00.159.69
Reproduced by permission of the Brooklyn Museum
Cover Design: Michael Schrauzer

# CONTENTS

## Suffering-Works for the Church

## Journeys Undertaken for Her Neighbor

# Preface

ANNE Catherine Emmerich was born on September 8, 1774, at Flamske, near Coesfeld, Germany. From early childhood she was blessed with the gift of spiritual sight and lived almost constantly in inner vision of scenes of the Old and New Testaments. As a child, her visions were mostly of pre-Christian events, but these grew less frequent with the passing years, and by the time she had become, at twenty-nine, an Augustinian nun at the Order's convent in Dülmen, Germany, her visions had become concerned primarily with the life of Jesus Christ, although they encompassed also the lives of many saints and other personages (some unknown as yet to history) as well as far-reaching insights into the creation, the fall, a mysterious mountain of the prophets, the spiritual hierarchies, paradise and purgatory, the heavenly Jerusalem, and much besides.

In the context of Anne Catherine's visions, and related conversations, much was said also of spiritual labors, described symbolically as work in the "nuptial house," the "inner chamber," the "garden," and the "vineyard." In this way many teachings on the inner life and prayer came forward, along with detailed accounts of healing work and journeys for "poor souls" in purgatory or in past epochs. Anne Catherine also showed considerable concern for the souls of those around her, especially her later amanuensis Clemens Brentano, in connection with his initial lack of faith.

Owing to difficult political circumstances, Anne Catherine's convent was disbanded on December 3, 1811, and one by one the nuns in residence were obliged to leave. Anne Catherine—already very ill—withdrew to a small room in a house in Dülmen. By November, 1812, her illness had grown so severe that she was permanently confined to bed. Shortly thereafter, on December 29, 1812, she received the stigmata, a manifesting of the wounds suffered by Christ on the cross, and the highest outward sign of inner union with him. Unable to assimilate any form of nourishment, for the rest of her life she was sustained almost exclusively by water and the eucharist.

As news spread that she bore the stigmata (which bled on Fridays), more and more people came to see her. For us, the most significant of these was Clemens Brentano, who first visited her on Thursday morning, September 24, 1818. He was so impressed by the radiance of her being that he decided to relocate nearby in order to record her visions. Anne Catherine had already had a presentiment that someone—whom she called "the pilgrim"—would one day come to preserve her revelations. The moment Clemens Brentano entered her room, she recognized him as this pilgrim.

Brentano, a novelist and Romantic poet then living in Berlin, was associated with leading members of the Romantic Movement in Germany. He settled his affairs and moved from Berlin to Dülmen early in 1819. Thereafter he visited Anne Catherine every morning, noting down briefly all she related to him. After writing out a full report at home, he returned later the same day to read it back to her. She would then often expand upon certain points, or, if necessary, correct details.

On July 29, 1820, Anne Catherine began to communicate visions concerning the day-by-day life of Jesus. These visions encompassed the better part of his ministry, and she was able to describe in extraordinary detail the places he visited, his miracles and healings, his teaching activity in the synagogues and elsewhere, and the people around him. She not only named and described many of these people with astonishing concreteness, but spoke also of their families, their occupations, and other intimate biographical details.

It seems clear that Anne Catherine was called to relate these day-by-day details of the life and ministry of Jesus, and that Clemens Brentano was called to record all she communicated of her visions. They worked together daily until her death on February 9, 1824, except for one period of six months, during which Brentano was away, and several shorter periods when, mainly due to illness, it was impossible for Anne Catherine to communicate her visions.

⊕

ENCOUNTERING the visions of Anne Catherine Emmerich can raise the question: how is it possible that this woman, who never left the German region in which she was born and had very little education, could describe in such detail not only the story of creation; heaven, hell, and purgatory; the fall of angels and humanity; the spiritual hierarchies and saints; the Promise and the Ark of the Covenant; the apocalypse; spiritual warfare; and the heavenly Jerusalem—but *also* the geography and topography of Palestine and the customs and habits of people living there at the time of Jesus Christ? To at least partially answer this, the researcher upon whose work the *chronological* aspects of this new edition is largely based, Dr. Robert Powell, undertook an exhaustive analysis of her work, gradually laying bare the historical reality underlying the life of Jesus (see "Chronology" below). But his work was not done in isolation, for others had earlier laid some groundwork.

For example the French priest Abbé Julien Gouyet of Paris, after reading an account of Anne Catherine's visions concerning the death of the Virgin Mary near Ephesus, traveled there and searched the region. On October 18, 1881, guided by various particulars in her account, he discovered the ruins of a small stone building on a mountain (Bulbul Dag, "Mount Nightingale") overlooking the Aegean Sea with a view across to the remains of the ancient city of Ephesus. Abbé Gouyet was convinced that this was the house described in Anne Catherine's visions as the dwelling of the Virgin Mary during the last years of her life. He was at first ridiculed, but several years later the ruins were independently rediscovered by two Lazarist missionaries who had undertaken a similar search on the basis of Anne Catherine's visions. They determined that the building had been a place of pilgrimage in earlier times for Christians descended from the church of Ephesus, the community referred to by St. John (Rev. 2:1–7). The building had been known in those days as Panaya Kapulu, the house of the Blessed Virgin, and was revered as the place where she had died. Traditionally, the date of her death, August 15, was the *very day* of the annual pilgrimage to Panaya Kapulu.

That Anne Catherine's visions provide spiritual nourishment had long been the experience of many spiritual seekers, but the discovery of Panaya Kapulu confirmed that her visions could also (at least in part) be corroborated along conventional lines of research.

## Sources

THE visions of Anne Catherine Emmerich have been published in English translation in various editions since late in the nineteenth century. These editions focused primarily on the visions of the life of Jesus Christ and of Mary, with some material drawn from Old Testament times also. However the *original* notes of Clemens Brentano contained material on many other fascinating subjects. Much of this material has not been readily available before now, either in German or in English translation, a gap that this twelve-volume *New Light on the Visions Anne Catherine Emmerich* series is meant at least to begin filling.

Until now the only translations available of some of this latter material appeared in the two-volume biography of Anne Catherine by Rev. Carl E. Schmöger, first published in English in 1885. Rev. Schmöger, who was also instrumental in the selection and arrangement of the visions related to the life of Jesus Christ upon which later English translations were based, included in the biography a selection of the supplemental material mentioned above —but his selection was necessarily limited.

Clemens Brentano himself was only able to compile from his notes a few volumes for publication, and upon his death the notes passed to his brother Christian, who had been an interested participant in Clemens's work with Anne Catherine from the start (in fact, Christian had arranged his brother's first meeting with the visionary). Christian, however, proved unable to coordinate the notes any further. And so the first phase of this seemingly insurmountable task fell in due course to Rev. Schmöger.

Then, in the last decades of the twentieth century, the German publisher Kohlhammer commenced publishing, under the auspices of the *Frankfurter Brentano Ausgabe*, an intended complete edition of Brentano's works, projected to number as many as sixty volumes. Part of this project was the publication of facsimiles of the thirty-eight notebooks of Brentano's notes of the visions of Anne Catherine. (Brentano also noted down details of their conversations in other contexts, as well as his own experiences while attending her.) With the Kohlhammer edition, a wider public would finally gain access to the originals upon which later compilations and translations of the visions had been based. However, this noble project has not been completed, and at present there is no indication whether it will recommence. An additional impediment for researchers in dealing with the facsimiles is the fact that Brentano's notes were penned in a now archaic German script that only specialists can read.

Thus matters stood until Jozef De Raedemaeker, a dedicated Belgian researcher, undertook the enormous task of transcribing the full body of notes from the archaic script into modern German—making it available in printed and digital form in 2009. The combined 38 notebooks exceed 7,300 pages and include many hand-drawn illustrations as well as typographic conventions to identify the contributions of others present at Anne Catherine's bedside, who sometimes took notes or added comments, and sometimes drawings.

⊕

ANYONE who does even minimal research on the visions of Anne Catherine Emmerich as depicted in the works attributed to Brentano's notes will soon discover that there are conflicting opinions regarding their fidelity to the words of Anne Catherine herself. This would be a subject in itself, but some remarks may be offered here. First, Anne Catherine, who had little formal education, spoke in a Low-German dialect that even Brentano, at the outset, had some difficulty understanding. Secondly, the material that was eventually fit together into a connected account in the published versions often represents a collation of as many as a dozen or more passages gleaned from visions separated sometimes by months, or even years. This can be partially explained by the fact that the visions were often related to events in the ecclesiastical year, to feasts of saints, to individuals with specific needs or requests, or to the presence of relics.

And so a great deal of work had to be done to organize and knit together related segments of visions, and to then arrange them in a meaningful sequence. Then again, it was deemed necessary to refine the language sufficiently to render it in a more contemporary idiom. There is, then, a legitimate concern that so famous and gifted a literary figure as Clemens Brentano might, even if unintentionally, have introduced some of his own impressions, interpretations, and sensitivities into his renditions. And a similar concern could be raised concerning Rev. Schmöger's subsequent arrangements, as well as those of later editors and translators working at yet a further remove.

Much of the debate on this subject, however, took place without ready access to the original notes, a defect that has now been remedied. At certain points in his transcriptions De Raedemaeker addresses this issue by comparing fragments of the original notes with versions of these same fragments as they appear in Rev. Schmöger's edition, after he in turn had worked, in some instances, with Brentano's own compilations from his original notes—and in some cases there are non-trivial discrepancies. This is an area that requires further research.

Perhaps I myself may be permitted to chime in here, as there are not many who have entered into this vast field, and I can at least appeal to many years of engagement with the visions of Anne Catherine, *including* examining De Raedemaeker's transcriptions of all thirty-eight notebooks. While thus occupied, I inevitably began to identify for myself many of the original sources upon which Rev. Schmöger based his versions well over a century ago, and in such cases could assess the fidelity of the latter to the former. Although such details do not lie within the scope of this series, I can say that, with very rare exceptions—especially allowing for the frequent need to splice together disparate fragments—Rev. Schmöger's renderings remain remarkably true to the original, and any minimal divergences are for the most part quite trivial, insofar as I have been able to investigate.

During this process, however, I *was* struck by the fact that considerable material had been *omitted*. This may well have been owing to the enormity of the task, as also to pagination limits set by the publisher; or also, partly a measure of Rev. Schmöger's personal judgment and concerns. Perhaps some of the excluded material seemed unintelligible to him, or even scandalous. However that may be, in this current series as much as possible of this neglected material has been extracted, translated, and incorporated in the relevant volumes.

It needs to be said also, in response to assertions (made mostly without benefit of access to his actual notes) that Brentano misrepresented Anne Catherine, or, even worse, took advantage of his notes to compile an independent literary work that might embellish his reputation, that in fact, in his notes, Brentano *candidly* reports *exactly* what he heard Anne Catherine say, *no matter* how extraordinary, puzzling, or even apparently contradictory. He himself offers many instances where only later—sometimes years after Anne Catherine had died—he (often with the help of academic experts) finally began to understand previously incomprehensible passages in the visions. He steadfastly refused—according to his own account and that of others—to edit out "difficulties," feeling himself, rather, under a sacred obligation to preserve his record intact and unaltered for posterity. And when the notes passed to his brother Christian, the latter adhered to the same policy.

Even without the benefit of access to the original notes on the part of most researchers, and even in face of an undercurrent of scepticism as to the authenticity of the visions, it may be worthwhile, in drawing this matter to a close for our present purposes, to note that on October 3, 2004, Anne Catherine was beatified by Pope John Paul II, who remarked: "Her example opened the hearts of poor and rich alike, of simple and cultured persons, whom she instructed in loving dedication to Jesus Christ." And in the Vatican's biography of Anne Catherine we read: "Her words, which have reached innumerable people in many languages from her modest room in Dülmen through the writings of Clemens Brentano are an outstanding proclamation of the gospel in service to salvation right up to the present day."

## Chronology

PERHAPS the most surprising feature of this new series on Anne Catherine Emmerich will be the inclusion of *historical dates*—and so a brief discussion of this feature is offered below.

As described earlier, Anne Catherine was so attuned to the life of Jesus Christ as a mystical-historical reality that her comprehensive visions encompassed even minute details of time and place—testable "coordinates" in fact. This degree of precision was made possible by the many temporal as well as geographical descriptions and references contained in the visions—as mentioned earlier in connection with the discovery of the house of the Blessed Virgin.

Many chronologies of the life of Jesus Christ have been put forward over the centuries, but the dates offered in this current series differ from previous efforts in that they derive from the application of modern chronological and astro-chronological science to the whole of Anne Catherine's visions—which latter constitute a vast body of data internally consistent as to time and place to an extraordinary degree, so that, taking the generally agreed upon time period of Jesus's life, results of a high degree of reliability can be determined.

Naturally, the overriding value of the visions lies in the additional insight they offer into the life of Jesus Christ, so that for some the dating may represent no more than a convenient framework for study and meditation. Such readers need not trouble themselves about the specific dates, although they may nonetheless find that the chronology offers a useful way to maintain their orientation within any given volume, as also when referring to events in volumes already read. Some, however, will wish to assess for themselves the method by which specific dates have been thought reliable enough to include here. They may read elsewhere[1] the story of the determination of the chronology of the life of Jesus Christ included in these volumes.

---

[1] *The Visions of Anne Catherine Emmerich*, Book III, Appendix I (Kettering, OH: Angelico Press, 2015), which is based on the work of Dr. Robert Powell.

# *The* New Light on the Visions
# of Anne Catherine Emmerich *Series*

THE present book is one of the twelve volumes of the "New Light on the Visions of Anne Catherine Emmerich" series published by Angelico Press. This series supplements two earlier Angelico publications: *The Visions of Anne Catherine Emmerich*, Books I–III (1,700 pages in large format, with 600 illustrations and forty-three maps); and the smaller-format, slightly abridged edition: *Life, Passion, Death, & Resurrection of Jesus Christ (A Chronicle from the Visions of Anne Catherine Emmerich)*, Books I–IV (1,770 pages with 150 illustrations and 43 maps). As described earlier, in 2009 Clemens Brentano's original notes of Anne Catherine's visions became readily available for reference. At that time the above texts were already nearing completion. With the appearance of these notes, however, the editor resolved to pause, and, to the extent possible, research this vast body of notes to ascertain what further light they might shed on what had by then been prepared for publication. While the better part of another decade was devoted to the task, much research, of course, remains to be done (see "Future Prospects" below). But at some point one must call a halt, and so, after the insertion of relevant new translations into the two sets mentioned above and their publication in 2015–2016, the present series was conceived as a means to present in various contexts such new material as has since then been selected and translated from the notes.

In general, the content of each volume of this series consists (1) of material selected by individual or theme from earlier translations—reviewed, supplemented, and revised where necessary, especially for consistency of usage; and (2) of newly selected and translated material germane to the content of that volume. With regard to both individuals and themes, the procedure was to extract every reference thus far located in the notes and in prior translations and weave them together into a connected account. The reader can thus find in one place almost all of what Anne Catherine had to say about any given individual or theme.

Virtually every individual in the biblical visions (approximately 250 in total) is referenced in the five *People of the New Testament* volumes (which include also some figures from earlier and later times). A separate volume, *The Life of the Virgin Mary*, is dedicated to Mary and her ancestry (including much on the Essenes); and another volume, *Scenes from the Lives of the Saints*, treats of fifty-nine saints. Separate volumes cover events prior to the appearance of the holy family: *First Beginnings* and *Mysteries of the Old Testament*. Two further volumes cover a multitude of separate themes: *Inner Life and Worlds of Soul & Spirit* and *Spiritual Works and Journeys*. A final volume represents a condensed, edited, rearranged, supplemented, and retypeset edition of Rev. Carl E. Schmöger's exhaustive biography of Anne Catherine, first published in English in 1885. For clarity of organization, much of this biography in its original form has been redistributed among other volumes of this series. What remains has also been enriched with newly-translated material. A list of all twelve volumes of this series appears at the conclusion of this preface.

## *Practical Considerations*

IN view of the sometimes extensive wealth of material presented concerning certain individuals—especially major characters—a judicious essentializing of scenes has sometimes been resorted to. In some cases, especially those of closely related apostles and disciples (or others regularly treated together in the visions), rather than duplicating material, the expedient adopted was to disentangle scenes to the extent possible, so that the full story could be garnered gradually by reading the separate accounts of each. Nonetheless, since readers may jump around in their selection of individuals to study, some repetition was unavoidable in order to provide enough context to keep the separate accounts reasonably sequential and unified. Put another way, these volumes are conceived primarily as reference works to which one turns for particulars on specific persons or themes rather than as connected narratives to be read cover to cover. Of course, the volumes may be read in the latter fashion also, in which case the occasional repeated material will be more noticeable.

Another consideration was that some individuals play so great a role in the visions (e.g., John the Baptist, St. Joseph, Peter, Matthew, Judas, and the Virgin Mary) that it would be impractical to include every mention in a chronological itinerary. Emphasis in such cases has been placed primarily on more general and newly-translated material. Inquisitive readers can of course turn to the index of the large-format, three-volume *The Visions of Anne Catherine Emmerich* to expand their research on such individuals.

It must be well understood that all the editor could do was work with what Anne Catherine actually said. Some little-known (or even totally unknown) individuals may enjoy longer accounts in these volumes than other, very well known, figures from the gospels or later Christian tradition! There can be no question of assigning relative importance to any individual based solely upon how extensive Anne Catherine's visions of that person may have been. Likewise, stories may have gaps, or sometimes end abruptly. It is indeed unfortunate that (as Brentano repeatedly laments in his notes) so much was lost owing to Anne Catherine's considerable suffering, household distractions, and the many obligations laid upon her—all of which interfered with her visions and her capacity to recall them. And yet withal, how much we have to be grateful for!

To streamline as far as possible a complex text, these usages were established: The voice of the narrator (Rev. Schmöger) is put in italics. Direct citations from Brentano (and a few others) are put in quotes. Anne Catherine's text bears no quotation indicators *except* where references to her words are embedded in the two contexts just mentioned. Parentheses enclose supplemental material from Anne Catherine or Brentano; brackets enclose material from Rev. Schmöger or the present editor. Footnotes from the hand of Brentano are followed by CB; those consisting of further visionary content from Anne Catherine are—for clarity in this context—enclosed in quotation marks; all other unattributed footnotes have been supplied by the present editor, sometimes incorporating what seemed worth retaining from notes by others in earlier editions.[1]

---

[1] The most useful material of this sort has been integrated from notes to a version of *The Life of the Virgin Mary* provided by Rev. Sebastian Bullough, O.P., to whom we express our gratitude.

For convenience, especially in itineraries of individuals, dates are incorporated in what is otherwise purely Anne Catherine's visionary text. It must, however, be well understood that these dates are derivative, as mentioned in "Chronology" above, *not* from the hand of Anne Catherine. As another help, for many major figures, summaries are provided at the outset. These are often in the third person—as they represent a condensation by the editor—but are nonetheless derived directly from the visions.

In such a context as these visions represent, capitalization (a topic upon which there are many and various usages, and often passionate opinions) represented a particular challenge. In the end, after experimenting with progressively increasing degrees of simplification, it was determined—in order not to overly fatigue the reader of what essentially amounts to an extended narrative rather than devotional reading properly speaking—to implement a very spare policy indeed, reserving capitalization to the Deity, and to certain terms that in Anne Catherine's visions assume a unique significance, such as the Ark of the Covenant, and what she calls the Promise, or sometimes the Holy Thing, the Mystery or Sacrament (in this special sense), or even the Germ or Seed. Finally, in cases where more general considerations are followed by chronological extracts forming a connected itinerary, the break is signaled by a row of five typographic crosses.

## Prospects for the Future

AS editor of this series I am only too aware of my limitations in the face of the awe-inspiring magnitude of the task. My initial inspiration was solely the *spiritual value* of Anne Catherine's visions as a means to help seekers find their way *back* to a faithful connection with Jesus Christ; or, in the case of so many in our time, find their way *for the first time* to a dawning awareness of what they may thus far have failed to see. Further, there are great, resonant depths in the visions, like choirs of symbolism. As time went on I could only go deeper, entering upon the work that has led now, finally, to completing this series. Along with spiritual benefits and guidance, it was and will ever remain also a thrilling journey of discovery. Now, with Brentano's original notes available thanks to the efforts of Jozef De Raedemaeker, there are further depths to explore, as alas—despite so many years of work—the rich sod has only been broken.

In the visions will be found fascinating indications and hints for archeologists, historians, linguists, theologians, students of comparative religion, chronologists, specialists in symbolism, and more. Over and above the *primary element* of spiritual inspiration, it is my hope that such specialists may in due course take up these visions (including the entire corpus of Brentano's notes) and press further forward. How one would love to see a foundation, a university, a religious sodality, or some private individual or group sponsor so important and propitious a project. If the largely solitary results presented here serve to advance such future research, if hearts and souls are moved and enriched by *The Anne Catherine Emmerich Series* as a whole, the effort will have achieved its primary purpose.

JAMES RICHARD WETMORE

## Acknowledgments

IT is difficult to sift out elements from earlier translators of these visions, but our main debt of gratitude for much of the English text taken as a foundation in the current work is owed to Sir Michael Palairet. Incalculable thanks are owed to Jozef De Raedemaeker for his past and present work with the original handwritten notes of Clemens Brentano. Occasional assistance with translation was received from Mado Spiegler, James Morgante, and especially Harrie Salman. A special thanks goes to Robert Powell, who has been a companion at every stage of this journey owing to his dedication to Anne Catherine in every respect: researching, translating when necessary, and, preeminently, applying his skills to the task of establishing the chronology that has been incorporated in this edition (in which connection Fr. Helmut Fahsel should also be mentioned). Most line drawings in the volumes are taken from Brentano's notes; the occasional paintings included are from the hand of James J. Tissot, as are all but one of the cover illustrations.

# The New Light on the Visions
## of Anne Catherine Emmerich Series

# Spiritual Works

## The Nuptial House—Action in Vision

IN *November, 1820, Anne Catherine remarked: "It is now twenty years since my Lord led me into the covenant house and laid me upon the hard nuptial bed on which I still lie." Thus did she designate her labors for the Church, labors imposed upon her from her entrance into the convent at Agnetenberg. No account had ever been demanded of this hidden operation, no director had even been willing to listen to her on the subject, and it is only now, toward the close of her career, that she testifies to the ways by which God had led her for the good of the church. Now for the first time she raises the veil concealing that mysterious action which, though operated in contemplation, derives its origin and merit, its importance and results, from the divine virtue of faith.*

*Before her entrance into religion, her principal task consisted in expiatory sufferings referring to the religious vocation and vows. But when she had embraced the conventual life, her action was extended to the whole Church. What this task embodied she characterized by these striking words: "My heavenly Bridegroom brought me into the covenant house," for such is the relation that the Church holds with Jesus Christ, her spouse and head—a relation that was shown to Anne Catherine as an immense sphere, embracing the most varied and opposite states, for whose individual failings she was to supply by her sufferings.*

*Jesus is continually renewing his indissoluble union with the Church, his spouse, and that he may present her spotless to his Father, he incessantly pours out upon her the torrents of his graces. But every grace must be accounted for, and few among those who receive them would be found ready for this if the heavenly Spouse did not at all times prepare chosen souls to gather up what others waste, to utilize the talents that others bury, and to discharge the debts contracted by the negligent.*

*Before manifesting himself in the flesh, in order to ratify the New Covenant with his blood, he had by the immaculate conception of Mary*

1

*prepared her to be the immaculate Type of the Church. He had poured upon her the plenitude of his graces, that her prayers might hasten the messiah's advent, her purity and fidelity retain him among the very men who received him not, who resisted and persecuted him.*

*When Jesus, the good shepherd, began to gather his flock together, it was Mary who cared for them, particularly for the poorest, the most abandoned, in order to lead them into the way of salvation. She was the faithful stewardess, she was the support of all. After the return of her son to his eternal Father, she remained many years upon earth to strengthen and protect the infant Church. And until the second coming of her son, the Church will never be without members who, following in her foot-steps, will be so many sources of benediction to their brethren. It is Mary, the mother of mercy, who assigns to these privileged souls their tasks for the ecclesiastical year. And in accordance with this order, Anne Cathe-rine received—in what she denominates the nuptial house—her yearly portion of expiation for the Church. Every detail was made known to her, all was to be finished in a certain time, for choice and duration of suffering are at the option of none.*

*This order was indicated by the different parts of the nuptial house, which had both a symbolical and historical signification. It was the house of Jesse near Bethlehem, the house in which David was born, and in which he had been trained by God Himself for his future career as a prophet. It was from this house also that the divine Spouse himself had sprung in his holy humanity. It was the house of the royal race of the immaculate Virgin Mother of the Church, and the paternal house of Joseph. It was fitting that Anne Catherine should contemplate therein the present state of the Church and receive her mission for it, since its former holy occupants had hailed in spirit the advent of the Redeemer, had gazed upon the Church's career through coming ages, and had received their share in the good works that were to hasten redemption.*

*This house—with its numerous apartments, its spacious surround-ings of gardens, fields, and meadows—was a symbol of the spiritual gov-ernment of the Church. With its various parts, its functionaries, the intruders who laid it waste, it presented to the soul allowed to contem-plate it a perfect representation of the Church in her different relations with the state and the country, with certain dioceses and institutions, in fine, with all the affairs connected with her government.*

*The wrongs done her in her hierarchy, rights, and treasures, in the integrity of her faith, discipline, and morals, by the negligence, slothfulness, and disloyalty of her own children; all that intruders (that is, false science, pretended wisdom, irreligious education, connivance with the errors of the day, with worldly maxims and projects, etc.) endanger or destroy—all were shown to Anne Catherine in visions of wonderful depth and simplicity. The scenes of these visions were the nuptial house and its dependencies, and thither was she conducted by her angel to receive her expiatory mission.*

*Before considering the details of this action-in-vision let us first glance at its hidden nature and signification. We have already remarked that what Anne Catherine did and suffered in contemplation was as real and meritorious, in itself and its results, as were the actions and sufferings of the natural waking state. This double operation sprang from one common source. But for the perfect understanding of it we must study her gift of contemplation. Her own communications throw the greatest light upon the question, since they are both numerous and detailed. We can compare them with the testimony of others favored with the same graces, with the decisions of the holy doctors, and with the principles that guide the Church in her judgment of such phenomena.*

*Anne Catherine tells us that the gift of contemplation had been bestowed upon her in baptism, and that from her entrance into life she had been prepared in body and soul to make use of it. On one occasion she denominated this preparation "a mystery of a nature very difficult for fallen man to comprehend, one by which the pure in soul and body are brought into intimate and mysterious communication with one another."*

*The undimmed splendor of baptismal grace is then, according to her, the first and chief condition for the reception of the light of prophecy— for the developing of a faculty in man obscured by Adam's fall—that is, that capability of communicating with the world of spirit without interrupting the harmonious and natural relation of body and soul. Every human being possesses this capability; but if we may so speak, it is hidden in his soul. He cannot of himself overleap the barrier separating the regions of sense from those beyond. God alone, by the infusion of superior light, can remove this barrier from the path of his elect. But seldom is such light granted, for few there are who rigorously fulfill the conditions exacted.*

*Before considering Anne Catherine's physical training in preparation for her action in vision, let us glance at St. Hildegarde, that great mistress of the mystical life, since there exists so striking a resemblance between the two. The latter, being directed by Almighty God to commit her visions to writing, heard these words:*

*"I who am the living light enlightening all that is in darkness, have freely chosen and called you by my own good pleasure for marvelous things—for things far greater than those shown by me to men of ancient times. But, that you may not exalt yourself in the pride of your heart, I have humbled you to the dust. The world shall find in you neither joy nor satisfaction, nor shall you mingle in its affairs, for I have shielded you against proud presumption. I have pierced you with fear; I have overwhelmed you with pain. You bear your sorrows in the marrow of your bones, in the veins of your flesh. Your soul and your senses are bound, you must endure countless bodily pains, that false security may not take possession of you, but that on the contrary you may regard yourself as faulty in all you do. I have shielded your heart from its wanderings, I have put a bridle upon you that your spirit may not proudly and vaingloriously exalt itself, but that in all things it may experience more fear and anxiety than joy and complacency. Write, then, what you see and hear, O creature, who receives not in the agitation of delusion, but in the purity of simplicity, what is designed to manifest hidden things."*[1]

*How strikingly do not the above words characterize Anne Catherine also! Her body was from her birth a vessel of sufferings, and like Hildegarde, she too was told by the celestial Spouse why she endured them: "Your body is weighed down by pain and sickness, that your soul may labor more actively, for he who is in good health carries his body as a heavy burden." And when, during the investigation [of her stigmata], the vicar-general expressed astonishment that Anne Catherine could have received a wound in the breast unknown to herself, she replied simply: "I did feel as if my breast had been scalded but I never looked to see what it was; I am too timid for that. From my childhood I have always been too timid to look upon my person. I have never seen it, I never think of it, I know nothing about it."*

---

[1] *Scivias*, L. I. Proefatio. Edit. Migne.

*This was literally true, for Anne Catherine had never thought of her body, excepting to mortify it and burden it with suffering. In vain do we strive to understand her great love for penance and mortification. We may form some idea of it as witnessed in a monk in all the vigor of manhood, or in one advanced in years to whom but little sleep and food are necessary, or in the cloistered contemplative; but in a young and delicate child, lively and ardent, employed in hard labor from her earliest years, having no example of the kind before her, it is truly astonishing! How powerful must have been the strength infused into her young heart by the grace of the Holy Spirit!*

*We are prone to represent the saints to ourselves at immeasurable heights above us, and not amid weakness and miseries such as our own. We see their sanctity without reflecting on their heroic efforts in its attainment. We forget that the nature of these valiant conquerors was the same as our own, that they reached the goal only by patient struggling. And so, by pain and mortification did Anne Catherine's body became in a measure spiritualized, dependent on the soul for its support, and endued with the capability of serving the latter as an instrument in the labors accomplished in vision.*

*If we now consider the spiritual and supernatural preparation of a soul to dispose her for the reception of prophetic light, we shall see that, besides sanctifying grace, it is the infused virtue of faith that renders her capable of receiving and making use of this gift. And yet, infused faith is not a simple condition, it is the proper cause and end by virtue of which God bestows the gift of contemplation. For man to attain beatitude, the first and most necessary of God's gifts is the light of faith. All extraordinary gifts of grace relate to faith as the inferior to the superior, the means to the end, although the visible effects of these gifts are often more striking, more wonderful, than the invisible, which are however incomparably more elevated. Faith, and not visions, is the source, the root of justification.*

*No one can draw near to God or be pleasing to Him without faith. It is by faith that Jesus Christ dwells in the heart—and it is faith, not visions, that seizes upon and appropriates the salvation offered with him. St. Paul, in his Epistle to the Hebrews, calls faith the substance—that is, the real and essential possession—of things hoped for, the real sign of invisible goods. Although faith gives not a clear, precise intuition of the facts and mysteries of our redemption, yet does it exclude even the possibility of error or doubt, enabling the believer to acquire the immense treasures contained in God's revelations and promises to His Church.*

*The believer, by virtue of his faith, possesses actually the goods acquired for him by the redemption, however multiplied or admirable they may be. But owing to his imperfect intelligence, they are veiled from him—just as the appearance and form of the future plant are concealed in the seed. To arrive at a clear perception of his treasures, to appreciate them as they deserve, he needs light to penetrate what is hidden, to read at a glance the history of bygone ages, or the unfulfilled promises of the future. This almighty God communicates by the angel-guardian of the soul, who sustains its weakness and renders it capable of supporting its brilliancy.*

*The angel's assistance is necessary. Without it the soul could never rise to the marvelous regions of contemplation. The first effect of the angelic teaching is an awakening to the practices of the theological virtues. For the soul receives this light, not to find in it a source of joy, but an increase of intelligent faith. Therefore, in Anne Catherine, faith was never inactive. From her very baptism it manifested itself in uninterrupted acts of love, so much the more perfect as her soul never rested on sensible goods.*

*Thomas Aquinas teaches that faith holds the first rank in the spiritual life since it is by faith alone that the soul is bound to God—the foundation and source of its life. As the body lives by the soul, so does the soul live by God, and that which gives life to the soul is that which binds it to God—namely, faith. This light made known to Anne Catherine—through the angel—the signification of the twelve articles of the Creed, which is a summary of the mysteries of salvation hidden in God from all eternity, revealed first as a Promise, and then, in the fullness of time, accomplished in Jesus Christ.*

*The whole history of redemption, with all its circumstances of time, place, and actors, passed before Anne Catherine's soul in pictures. Thousands of years could not separate her from these different events. She saw all by faith, and penetrated into the interior and mutual relation between the most remote and the most recent facts connected with our redemption, standing face to face with one another—the Promise and the fulfillment.*

*Every outward sign of faith renewed its effects in her soul. If she wit-*

*nessed the administration of a sacrament, its supernatural effects were revealed to her by floods of light that either flowed in upon the soul of the recipient or were repelled in their course, thus making known to her his spiritual disposition. Were a pious picture placed under her eyes, she instantly perceived a representation infinitely more faithful than the one before her, since faith awakened in her soul a perfect image of the original. Pious reading, holy conversation, the breviary, the chanting of psalms—everything, in fine, connected with religion—awoke in her emotions so strong and lively that, to resist absorption in vision, she was often obliged to use violence with herself.*

*Anne Catherine tried several times to give the pilgrim some idea of her contemplation, but in vain; she could never satisfactorily explain the spiritual activity of her visions. We quote below what the pilgrim was able to write on different occasions.*[1]

⊕

I SEE many things that I cannot possibly express. Who can say with the tongue what he sees not with the bodily eyes?

I see it not with the eyes. It seems as if I saw it with my heart in the midst of my breast. It makes the perspiration start! At the same time I see with my eyes the objects and persons around me; but they concern me not, I know not who or what they are. I am in contemplation even now while I am speaking.

For several days I have been constantly between the state of vision and the natural waking state. In the middle of a conversation I suddenly see before me other things and pictures, and I hear my own words as if proceeding from another, as if coming out of an empty cask. I feel as if I were intoxicated and reeling. My conversation goes on coolly and often more animatedly than usual—but when it is over I know not what I have said, though I have been speaking connectedly. It costs me an effort to maintain this double state. I see passing objects dimly and confusedly, like a sleeper

---

[1] See also "Interiority" in *Inner Life and Worlds of Soul & Spirit*, for a different contextualizing of several of the paragraphs that follow.

awaking out of a dream. The second sight attracts me more powerfully, it is clearer than the natural, but it is not through the eyes.

*After relating a vision one day, she laid aside her work, saying*: All this day have I been flying and beholding; sometimes I see the pilgrim, sometimes not. Does he not hear the singing? It seems to me that I am in a beautiful meadow,[1] the trees arching over me. I hear wondrously sweet singing, like the clear voices of children. All around me here below is like a troubled dream, dim and confused, through which I gaze upon a luminous world perfectly distinct in all its parts, intelligible even in its origin, and connected in all its wonders. In it the good and holy delight more powerfully, since one sees his way from God to God; and what is bad and unholy troubles more deeply as the way leads from the demon to the demon in opposition to God and the creature. This life in which nothing hinders me—neither time nor space, neither the body nor mystery, in which all speaks, all enlightens—is so perfect, so free, that the blind, lame, stammering reality appears but an empty dream. In this state I always see the relics by me shining, and sometimes I see little troops of figures floating over them in a distant cloud. When I return to myself, the boxes and caskets in which the shining relics lie reappear.

*Once the pilgrim gave her a little parcel into which (without her knowledge) he had slipped a relic. She took it with a significant smile, as if to say she could not be so easily deceived, and laying it on her heart, she said*:

I knew directly what you were giving me. I cannot describe the impression it produces. I not only see, I *feel* a light like the will-o'-the-wisp—sometimes bright, sometimes dull—blowing toward me as if directed by a current of wind. I feel also a certain connecting link between the light and the shining body, and between the latter and a luminous world, itself born of light. Who can express such things?

The light seizes me, I cannot prevent it from entering my heart. And when I plunge in deeper it seems as if I pass through it into the body from which it emanates, into the scenes of its life, its

---

[1] A *meadow*, symbol of a *festival*.

8

struggles, its sufferings, its triumphs! Then am I directed in vision as is pleasing to God. There is a wonderful, mysterious relation between our body and soul. The soul sanctifies or profanes the body. Otherwise there could be no expiation, no penance by means of the body. As the saints, while alive, worked in the body, so—even when separated from it—do they continue to act by it upon the faithful. But faith is essential to the reception of holy influences.

Often while speaking with others on quite different subjects I see far in the distance the soul of a deceased person coming toward me, and I am forced to attend to it at once. I become silent and thoughtful. I have apparitions also of the saints in the same way.

I once had a beautiful revelation on this point, in which I learned that seeing with the eyes is no sight, that there is another —an interior sight—that is clear and penetrating. But when deprived of daily communion a cloud obscures my clear inward sight. I pray less fervently, with less devotion. I forget important things, signs, and warnings, and I see the destructive influence of exterior things that are essentially false. I feel a devouring hunger for the blessed sacrament, and when I look toward the Church I feel as if my heart were about to escape from my breast and fly to my Redeemer.

When I was in trouble—because in obedience to my guide's orders I refused to be removed to another abode—I cried to God to direct me. I was overwhelmed with trials, and yet I saw so many holy visions that I knew not what to do. In my prayer I was calm. I saw a face, a countenance, approach me, and melt as it were into my breast, as if uniting with my being. It seemed as if my soul—becoming one with it—returned into itself and grew smaller and smaller, while my body appeared to become a great massive substance large as a house.

The countenance,[1] the apparition in me, appeared to be triple—infinitely rich and varied, but at the same time always one.

---

[1] This face, this countenance was the gift of vision, the light of prophecy proceeding from God, by which Anne Catherine conversed with the saints and angels and received their communications.

It penetrated (that is, its beams, its regards) into all the choirs of angels and saints. I experienced joy and consolation from it, and I thought: could all this come from the evil spirit? And while I was thus thinking, all the pictures, clear and distinct like a series of bright clouds, passed again before my soul, and I felt they were now out of me, at my side, in a luminous sphere. I felt also that although I was larger, yet was I not so massive as before. There was now, as it were, a world outside me into which I could peer through a luminous opening. A maiden approached who explained this world of light to me, directed my attention here and there, and pointed out to me the vineyard of the holy bishop in which I had now to labor.

But I saw too on my left a second world full of deformed figures, symbols of perversity, calumny, raillery, and injury. They came like a swarm, the point directed toward me. Of all that came to me from this sphere I could accept nothing, for the just, the good, were in the pure, luminous sphere on my right. Between these two spheres I hung by one arm, poor and abandoned, floating so to say between heaven and earth. This state lasted long and caused me great pain. Still, I was not impatient.

At last, St. Susanna[1] came to me from the luminous sphere with St. Liborius, in whose vineyard I had to work. They freed me, and I was brought again into the vineyard, which was uncultivated and overgrown. I had to prune the wild, straggling branches on the trellises, that the sun might reach the young shoots. With great trouble I worked at a gap in the lattice. I gathered the leaves and decayed grapes into a pile, wiped the mould from others, and, as I had no fine cloth, had to use my kerchief. This labor tired me so that I lay on my bed next morning all bruised and sore. I felt as if not a bone were left in my body. My arms still ache.

The way in which a communication from the blessed souls is received is hard to explain. What is said is incredibly brief. By one word only from them I understand more than by thirty from others. I see the speaker's thought, but not with the eyes. All is clearer, more distinct than in the present state. One receives it

---

[1] Anne Catherine had this vision on August 11, 1821, the feast of St. Susanna.

with as much pleasure as when one hails a breeze in summer. Words cannot well express it.

All that the poor soul said to me was, as usual, brief. To understand the language of the souls in purgatory is difficult. Their voice is smothered, as if coming through something that dulls the sound. It is like one speaking from a pit or a cask. The sense also is more difficult to seize. Closer attention is required than when Our Lord—or my guide, or a saint—speaks to me, for their words penetrate like a clear current of air: one sees and knows all they say. One of their words says more than a lengthy discourse.

## Knowledge of the Thoughts of Others

LATE *one evening in the winter of 1813, Father Limberg returned tired and worn out after a whole day spent in sick calls. As he sat down in Anne Catherine's room, breviary in hand, the thought occurred to him: "I am so tired and I have so many prayers to say—if it were no sin, I would let them go." Hardly had he conceived the thought, seated at some distance from her than she cried out: "O do say your prayers!" He asked: "What prayers do you mean?" "Your breviary," she answered, "why do you ask?" "This was the first time," remarked the Father, "that I was struck by anything extraordinary in her."*

*On July 25, 1821, Anne Catherine spoke thus to the pilgrim: "The pilgrim has no devotion, he prays nervously, mixing things up quickly. I often see all kinds of bad thoughts chasing one another through his head. They peer around like strange, ugly, wild beasts! He checks them not, he does not drive them away promptly; it is as if he were used to them, they run about as over a beaten path." The pilgrim remarked: "It is unhappily only too true!" She continued:*

From the lips of those that pray I see a chain of words issuing like a fiery stream and mounting up to God, and in them I see the disposition of the one who prays, I read everything. The writing is as varied as the individuals themselves. Some of the currents are all aglow, others are dull; some of the characters are round and full, some running, just like different styles of handwriting.

*When Anne Catherine characterized her contemplations as "not seen with the eyes but with the soul, the heart being, so to say, the organ of* sight," she intended to indicate not only its beginning and development, but also its supernatural and meritorious character. Every good work originates in the heart; there it is that the faithful soul receives the impulse of grace to produce meritorious acts, either interior or exterior. It is in the heart that the Holy Spirit dwells; there he pours out his gifts, there is formed that bond of charity which unites the faithful together, and binds them to their invisible head, Jesus Christ, as the branches to the vine. Man's value before God is estimated by the dispositions of his heart—its uprightness, good will, charity—and not by keenness of intellect or extent of knowledge.

Thus it was that Anne Catherine saw in her heart the visions vouchsafed her by her God. There it was that she heard her angel's voice and her confessor's commands, whether expressed in words or only mentally and at a distance. She obeyed instantaneously in either case, returning promptly from ecstasy to consciousness. In her heart also did she hear the distressed cries of those whom she was appointed to succor, even though seas and continents lay between her and them. There too did she feel the agony of the dying whom she was to assist in their last moments by her own sufferings and prayers. It was her heart that warned her of impending danger either to the Church or individuals. She often endured distress of mind long before she clearly understood the cause. In her heart she saw the thoughts, the dispositions, the whole moral character of those with whom she treated either actually or in spirit. There she heard impious words, blasphemy, etc., for the expiation of which God was pleased to accept the torments of his innocent creature. Finally, it was in her heart that she heard the voice that called her to ecstasy. She promptly obeyed the call, and collected together all the powers of her soul to accomplish whatever was demanded of her. She had never known an attachment to perishable goods. Apart from God and his service she desired nothing, knew nothing. Her soul, delighted by heavenly visions, sought no earthly gratification. Faith and the commandments were her only measure of created things.

Anne Catherine also was, like Hildegarde, taught by her angel in infancy how to practice faith as the foundation of the spiritual life:

When in my sixth year I meditated on the first article of the Catholic Creed—"I believe in God, the Father almighty, Creator of heaven and earth"—pictures of the Creation passed before my soul. I saw the fall of the angels, the Creation of earth and paradise, of Adam and Eve, and the fall of humankind. I thought everybody saw them just as we see other things around us. I spoke of them freely to my parents, my brothers and sisters, and to my playmates, until I found that they laughed at me, asking if I had a book in which all these things were written. Then I began to be more reserved on such subjects, thinking I ought not to mention them, though why I could not tell. I had these visions by day and by night, in the fields, and going about my different occupations.

One day at school I spoke with childish simplicity of the resurrection, using other terms than those taught us. I thought every one knew the same; I never suspected that I was saying anything strange. The children wondered and told the master, who gravely warned me not to indulge such imaginations. I still had visions, but I kept silence concerning them. I was like a child looking at pictures, explaining them in its own way without thinking much upon their meaning. These visions represented the saints or scenes from sacred history, sometimes in one way, sometimes in another. They produced no change in my faith; I thought them my picture-book. I gazed at them calmly and always with the good thought: "All to the greater glory of God!"

I have never believed anything in spiritual things but what God, the Lord, has revealed and proposed through the Catholic Church for our belief, whether written or not; never have I believed so firmly what I saw in vision. I looked upon them as I devoutly regard, here and there, the various cribs at Christmas, without annoyance at their different style. In each I adore only the same dear little infant Jesus, and it is the same with these pictures of the Creation of heaven, of earth, and of humankind. I adore in them God, the Lord, the almighty Creator. I never studied anything from the gospels or the Old Testament, for I have myself seen all in the course of my life. I see them every year; sometimes they are alike, or again they are attended by new scenes. I have often been present with the spectators, assisting as a contemporary—even taking part in the scene, though I did not always remain in the same place. I was often borne up into the air and I beheld the scene from on high. Other things—mysteries especially—I saw interiorly. I had an inward consciousness of them, pictures apart from the outward scene. In all cases I saw through and through, one body never hid another, and yet there was no confusion.

While a child, before I entered the convent, I had many visions, principally from the Old Testament, but afterward they became rare and the life of our Lord took their place. I knew the whole life of Jesus and Mary from their very birth. I often contemplated the Blessed Virgin in her childhood and saw what she did when alone in her little chamber; I even knew what she wore. I saw that the people of our Lord's time had sunk lower, were even more wicked than those of our day; still, there were a few more simple, more pious than now. They differed as much from one another as tigers do from lambs. Now reign general tepidity and torpor. The persecution of the just in those days consisted in delivering them to the executioner, in tearing them to pieces; now it is exercised by injury, disdain, raillery, patient and constant efforts to corrupt and destroy. Martyrdom is now an endless torment.

## Religious Balloons

ANNE *Catherine's communications with the pilgrim furnished her many opportunities for combating his religious errors and prejudices. One day he maintained in specious arguments that the institution of the feast of Corpus Christi was unnecessary, since on Holy Thursday and in the daily mass the holy eucharist is celebrated. She listened in silence, but next day she said to him:*

I have received a severe reproof from my guide. He says I should not have listened to the pilgrim's words, I should not countenance such talk, it is heretical. All that the Church does, even if there should glide in through human weakness views not altogether pure, is done under the direction of the Holy Spirit of God, and for the wants of the times. The feast of the Blessed Sacrament had become a necessity, since, at the time of its institution, the adoration due to Jesus therein was neglected: therefore, the Church proclaimed her faith by public worship. There is no feast, no worship, no article of faith established by her that is not indispensable, not absolutely requisite at the time for the preservation of true doctrine. God makes use of individuals, even with

14

views less pure, to serve His own designs. The Church is founded on a rock; no human weakness can ravish from her her treasures. Therefore I must never again listen to such denials of necessity in the Church's decisions, for they are heretical. After this severe lesson, I endured cruel sufferings for my condescension.[1]

*Anne Catherine expressed herself as follows on the "Illuminati," who, rejecting the holy usages of the Church, seek to introduce in their stead empty formulas and high-sounding phrases:*

If the Church is true, all in her is true; he who admits not the one believes not the other. Whoever attributes things to chance, denies the effects of cause and makes them the result of chance. Nothing is mere ceremony, all is substantial, all acts through the outward signs. I have often heard learned priests say: "We must not ask people to believe everything at once; if they only get hold of the thread, they will soon draw the whole ball to themselves." Such a speech is bad, erroneous. Most people take very fine thread and wind until it breaks or is scattered in shreds around. The whole religion of either laymen or priests who speak thus is, in my opinion, like a balloon filled with holy things and sent up into the air, but which never reaches the sky. I often see the religion of whole cities floating over them like a balloon.

I have often been told that God has attached to the holy cross of Coesfeld, and to all places in which sacred objects are venerated, the power of resisting evil; but miracles depend on the fervor of prayer. I often see the cross venerated in processions and those that receive with faith the graces flowing from it, preserved from evil, and their petitions heard, while their neighbors are shrouded in darkness. I have also been told that lively, simple faith makes all things *real* and *substantial*. These two expressions gave me great light on the subject of miracles and the granting of prayer.

*With such words as the above she strove to combat the pilgrim's inclination to laud the "piety" of the Moravians[2] while he bitterly decried the "miseries of the Church":*

---

[1] Here Brentano adds this note: "This is a warning to me of how wrong it is to speak lightly of what concerns the Church."

[2] The Moravian Church (its name means "Unity of the Brethren") is one of the oldest Protestant denominations.

I was sternly rebuked by my guide when I listened silently to such remarks. He pointed out the rashness of such judgments, saying that one falls thereby into the same faults as the first apostates. He told me that I had to supply what is neglected in the Church, otherwise I shall be more guilty than they to whom it is not given to see what I see. I saw the Moravian settlement. They are as restrained in their movements as a person who tries to avoid waking one who is asleep. It is all so formal, clean, and quiet; they appear so pious, but they are inwardly dead and in a far more deplorable state than the poor Indians for whom I have now to pray. Where there is no struggle there is no victory. They are idle, therefore they are poor; their affairs go badly enough in spite of their fine talk and fair appearance. I saw this in the nuptial house. Under the picture of two invalids I saw the difference between souls, and their interior state before God. I saw the Moravian community under the appearance of a sick person who conceals her maladies, who is very agreeable and pleasing in the exterior; opposite to her, as in a far-off vision, I saw another invalid covered with ulcers that sparkled and shone like pearls. The bed on which she lay was bright; the floor, the ceiling, the whole room, were dazzlingly white like snow. As the sick Moravian drew near this room she left stains wherever she stepped though she pretended not to see anything of it.

# Spiritual
# Undertakings and Travels

ANNE *Catherine's manner of acting was even more significant than her words. Though so highly privileged; though in almost continual contemplation of the highest mysteries and truths of religion, the life of our blessed Lord and his saints; though admitted to a corporal participation in his sacred passion; yet her greatest happiness, her most earnest desire, was to assist at the celebration of the feasts and ceremonies of the Church in company with the faithful. Her infirmities cut her off for years from this consolation, and she felt the privation most deeply; no ecstasy, no vision could indemnify her for the loss. In this she resembled Magdalene di Pazzi, who, though in constant communication with her guardian angel, knew no greater pleasure when a child than to lis-*

16

ten to the devout conversation of her mother, whom she sometimes embarrassed by her questions; nothing seemed to her comparable to the happiness of possessing the true faith. As St. Hildegarde could say: "In contemplation I am more like a child than an old woman," so too did Anne Catherine in vision often become again a child of five or six years old.[1] This puzzled her, and she once asked her angel what it meant. He replied: "If you were not really a child, that could not happen." He wished to imply that, if she were not in soul and body as pure as a flower in the morning dew, she never could return to the innocent simplicity of childhood. Here we discover the secret of these privileged souls: no earthly image ever dimmed the mirror of their soul, which should reflect alone the bright beams of prophetic light. And by this also we understand why the Church, when passing judgment on extraordinary graces, seeks proofs of their reality in those virtues attained only by constant mortification and detachment. It would be in contradiction with the sanctity of God for the supernatural light of contemplation to dwell in a soul not wholly dead to itself and creatures; therefore is this gift so rare, for in very few are found that purity and humility which characterized Anne Catherine.

We need no more convincing proof of the latter virtue than the pilgrim's own testimony. From close observation he had drawn the conclusion that her unaccountable maladies arose from causes in the spiritual order quite foreign to her own physical condition; and great was his disappointment, not to say disgust, when he saw her attach no importance whatever to their supernatural origin, and pay little attention to their intimate connection with certain evils of the spiritual order that she was called upon to expiate. His journal contains such lines as the following: "All goes to waste, the greatest graces are not understood! Her carelessness deprives me of the most important revelations concerning the inward workings of her privileged life, etc."

---

[1] One day, Anne Catherine lay in ecstasy, when suddenly she began to gesticulate like a little child, stretching out her arms and exclaiming: "Good-day, little mother! It has been a long time since you came with your child. Oh! give him to me! I have not had him for so long!" Returned to herself, she said joyously: "I saw the Mother of God coming to me with the child Jesus. It made me so glad! I wanted to take the child, but she disappeared, and I called after her."

17

*The pilgrim failed to reflect that her patient sufferings had obtained for her an increase of fortitude, which proves that her childlike simplicity in receiving them without seeking for a cause was infinitely more agreeable to God than those around her dared to suspect. Three years previously, when struck by her unalterable peace of soul, the pilgrim had recorded:*

She is extraordinarily courageous, full of childlike peace and simplicity. She is always in contemplation, although she tries to resist it. She rejoices only in this, that she lives to suffer. It is impossible to repeat her words, her transition from outward realities to the state of vision, her childlike joy, patience, courage, abandonment, the charm and candor of her whole demeanor. Only they who see her can know it. In this state she is the picture of an innocent, trusting child full, not of faith, but of that certainty that sight gives. What we believe by God's grace, she knows; it is as real to her as is the existence of her parents and family. She is, consequently, free from all returns upon self; she exhibits no discontent, no irritation. She has no enemy; she is full of peace, of joy, and of love. There is no assumption of false gravity about her. They are a little disappointed who expect to find in her exterior some striking confirmation of extraordinary graces. Such persons attend rather to the emblems of dignity than to the dignity itself.

*When the pilgrim visited her she had a book before her, though indeed she was not reading—she made use of it to prevent her mind's becoming absorbed in vision, but such efforts were often useless:*

At times she joyfully thanked God for letting her live to suffer for her neighbor, for in eternity she could no longer do so. She knows no sadness. Many scenes, forgotten during the past days, have returned to her mind; for instance, these last cold nights she saw all the people in the neighborhood who were without beds. The sight touched her, and she immediately supplied their need. She saw also a poor widow, her own relative, in the same want. She turned to her angel, begging him to get her brother's angel to inspire him to send the poor woman a bed, and next day she had the consolation of learning that her brother had done so.

*False sanctity, as we may easily believe, knows no such consolations, since it turns good into evil and has its root in spiritual pride. It can aspire only to the recompense offered by the father of lies; viz., the satis-faction springing from gratified vanity, the praise of men, and sensual joys. True contemplation grounds the soul in obedience and self-con-tempt. Its chief characteristic is a disinclination to reveal the graces received, deference to spiritual authority alone being able to break the seal of silence in which it shrouds itself. On the other hand, boasting, vainglory, and publicity are the marks of a deluded soul; and, as the effects of grace are an increase of light, and of all the theological and moral virtues, so the inevitable consequences of spiritual pride are hypocrisy, heresy, and superstition.*

*One day Anne Catherine, overwhelmed by suffering, entreated Our Lord to withdraw those visions in which she beheld so much that was incomprehensible to her. But she received the following reply:*

I give you visions not for yourself, but that you may collect and communicate them. The present is not the time for sensible mira-cles; therefore I give you visions. I have done the same at all times to show that I am with my church to the consummation of ages. But *visions alone secure not anyone's salvation. You must practice char-ity, patience, and the other virtues.*

*At another time she related what follows:*

I begged almighty God to withdraw my visions, that I may not be forced to communicate them, but I was not heard. As usual I was told to relate all that I could recall, even if I should be laughed at, or even if I do not see any use in it. I was again told that no one has ever seen all that I have seen or in the same way, but that that is not my affair, it is the Church's. So much being allowed to go to waste will entail great accountability and do much harm. They who deprive me of leisure, and the clergy who have no faith and who find no one to take down my visions, will have to render a severe account of their negligence. I saw too how the demon raises obstacles.

Long ago I was ordered to tell all, even if I should be looked upon as a fool. But no one wanted to listen to me, and the holiest things that I had seen and heard were so misunderstood and derided that through timidity I shut all up in my own heart, though not without pain. Then I used to see in the distance the figure of a stranger who was to come to write by me. I have found him. I recognize him in the pilgrim.

19

From childhood I have had the habit of praying every evening for all who are in danger from accidents, such as violent falls, drowning, fire, etc., and I see pictures of such things turning out happily. If I should happen to omit this prayer, I always see or hear of some great disaster; consequently, I understand by this not only the necessity of special prayers, but also the advantage there may be in making it known, since it may incite others to this loving service of prayer, though they see not its effects as I do. The many, many wonderful communications from the Old and the New Testament, the innumerable pictures from the lives of the saints, etc., have been given me, through God's mercy, not for my instruction alone (for there is much that I cannot understand), but that I may communicate them, that they may revive what is now forgotten.

This duty has again been imposed upon me. I have explained this fact as well as I could, but no one will take the trouble even to listen to me. I must keep it to myself and forget much of it. I hope God will send me what is necessary.

*The following communication shows that it was with the shield of faith that Anne Catherine combated the tempter when he dared approach her in vision:*

I endured such pain in my wounds that I was forced to scream. I could hardly bear it. The blood flowed in a jerking way toward them. Suddenly satan stood before me as an angel of light and said: "Shall I pierce your wounds? In the morning all will be well. They will never again give you pain, you will never suffer more from them." But I recognized him at once and said: "Begone! I want nothing from you! You did not make my wounds! I shall have nothing to do with you!" Then he withdrew and squatted like a dog behind the cupboard. After a while he came out and said: "Do not think yourself so well off with Jesus, because you imagine you are always running around with him. It all comes from me! I show you all those pictures. I, also, have a kingdom!" I chased him again by my reply. After a long time he came again and said boldly: "Why torment yourself with doubts? All that you have, all that you see, is from me. Things are in a bad state, I have you. What need of worrying yourself?" Again I cried: "Begone! I will belong only to Jesus, I

20

will love him and curse you! I shall endure such pains as he wills me to suffer!"

My anguish was so great that I called my confessor. He blessed me and the fiend fled. But this morning as I was saying my *Credo* he again appeared and said: "What use is the *Credo* to you? You do not understand a word of it; but I will teach you all things clearly—then shall you both see and know." I replied: "I want not *to know*, I want *to believe*." Then he recited a passage from holy scripture; but there was one word in it that he could not pronounce, and I said again and again: "say that word, say it distinctly, if you can!" I trembled in every limb, and at last he disappeared.

When I see the communion of saints in the light of vision—their actions and their love, their interpenetrating one another, how each is in and for the others, how each is all and still one in unending brilliancy of light—I feel unspeakable joy and lightsomeness. Then I see far and near the dark figures of living beings; I am drawn to them by irresistible love. I am urged so sweetly, so lovingly, to pray for them, to beg God and the saints to help them, that my heart beats with love. I feel, I see, more clearly than day that we all live in communion with the saints, that we are in constant relation with them. Then I grieve over men's blindness and obduracy. I cry out confidently to the Savior: "Thou art all-powerful, Thou art all love! Thou canst do all things! Suffer them not to be lost! Think of thy precious blood!" Then I see how he labors for them so touchingly. "Only see," he says, "How near I am to help them, to heal them, and how rudely they repulse me!" And then I feel that his justice is full of sweetness and love.

My guide often takes me in spirit through all sorts of human miseries: sometimes to prisoners, sometimes to the dying, to the sick, the poor, to the homes of sin and discord. I see bad priests, I see bad prayers, the profanation of the sacraments, and of holy things. I see disdained by miserable creatures the graces, the helps, the consolations, the eternal nourishment of the most holy sacrament that the Lord offers them. I see them turning away, driving the Lord violently from them. I see all the saints in a sweet, loving readiness to help them; but lost to them are the graces poured upon them from the treasure of Christ's merits confided to the Church. That afflicts me. I gather up all these lost graces into my heart and thank Jesus for them, saying: "Ah! pity thy blind, miserable creatures! They know not what they do! Ah! look not at their offences, keep these graces for poor, blind sinners! Lord, give them at another time that they may be helped by them. Ah! let not thy precious blood be lost to them!" The Lord often hears my prayer, and to my great consolation, I see him again bestowing his graces.

When I pray in general for the most needy, I usually make the way of the cross at Coesfeld, and at each station I pray for a different necessity. Then I have all sorts of visions that show me in pictures—right and left of the station, far off in the distance—the distress, the assistance given, and the places in which the scenes are enacted. Today as I knelt at the first station, I prayed for those who were going to confession before the feast, that God would grant them sincere repentance, and the grace to declare all. Then I saw in various regions people praying in their homes or otherwise occupied, while thinking of the state of their conscience. I saw their hearts and I urged them not to fall again into the sleep of sin. Then I saw those that would come to my confessor, and I was directed to say to him, but in general terms, how to treat this or that person.

At the second station I prayed for those whom poverty or misery deprived of sleep, that God would give them hope and consolation. And then I saw into many wretched huts in which the residents tossed on their straw beds, thinking that morning would find them no better off than the evening had done, and I saw my prayer procuring them rest.

At the third station I prayed against strife and quarrels, and I saw in a cottage a man and wife very angry with each other. I prayed for them; they grew calm, mutually forgave, and joined hands.

At the fourth station I prayed for travelers, that they might lay aside their worldly thoughts and go in spirit to Bethlehem to do homage to the dear Christ child. I saw around me many journeying along with bundles on their shoulders, and one in particular more thoughtless than his fellows. I prayed for him, and suddenly

I saw him fall over a stone in his path. He exclaimed: "The devil put that stone there for me!" But, recovering himself, he took off his hat and began to pray.

At the fifth station I prayed for prisoners who, in their misery, think not of the holy season and deprive themselves of its divine consolations. Here too I was consoled. The rest has escaped my memory…

⊕

AS I lay one day thinking: "In what a miserable state I am! What a fate is mine! Others can work and do good, while I lie here like a cripple," I begged God to give me something I could do. Then I saw an inn in which some men were quarrelling. I prayed with all my heart for them to cease their strife. They became calm, and peace was restored. I thought of poor, helpless travelers, and saw a sorrowful-looking man dragging along the road, not knowing where to turn for food or lodging. I was filled with pity. I prayed for him, when there rode up a horseman who, as he passed the poor man, asked whence he came and in what direction he was going. The man mentioned the cities (but I forget the names). The rider gave him some money and galloped on. The poor man stood in wonder gazing at the money, four whole thalers! He could hardly realize his good fortune; he exclaimed: "How wonderful is God! Had I reached the city, I should not have received this money." Then he began to think of all that he would do with it. I can still see him. My guide then took me to about twenty sick people whose ulcers I drained.

When my guide calls me on such errands, I follow blindly. We pass through walls and doors to the sick, and he tells me what I have to do. I see all distinctly, and even if there be a crowd around the sick-bed, that does not hinder me, there is always room for me. While I assist the invalids, they seem to sleep or to be unconscious, but they get better.

I give such assistance only in Christian countries. In far-off infidel lands I float above the darkness, earnestly praying for the inhabitants to be enlightened. I think that everyone who prays from his heart for such unhappy creatures, earnestly desirous of helping them all he can, really gives such assistance.

I have to heal spiritual maladies also. My guide took me to a spiritual hospital full of sick, of every age and condition, men and women. There were numbers whom I knew; others were strangers. I had no help excepting my guide, who blessed the water that I carried in a little kettle. I had relics also, but I only used them in secret. All the inmates were sick in soul through sin and their passions, their maladies appearing exteriorly in the body. The degree of sin was indicated by their greater or less poverty, especially shown forth in their beds. The poorest lay on the ground on straw, others in beds, either clean or filthy, which bespoke their good or bad surroundings; some were lying on the bare ground, while others were sitting up, etc. I spoke not to them, nor they to me; but when I bandaged their wounds or drained their sores, sprinkled them with the blessed water or secretly touched them with the relics, they were relieved or cured.

They who had sinned through sloth, had sore or lame hands; they who were given to theft and suchlike practices, had convulsions, cramps in their limbs, and ulcers. Secret evils had their seat in internal ulcers, which had to be dissolved by poultices, or drawn out by blisters. Some were not quite right in their mind from having tormented themselves with useless researches. I beheld them staggering around and suddenly striking their heads against something, which brought them to their senses. I had to attend to many, natives and foreigners, also to Protestants. There was a girl who was suffering from obstinacy. Hard and livid welts ran through her whole body like veins; they looked like the red strokes of a lash. I cured her with holy water. I also raised the dead. They were in a third place and differed from the others in this—that they lay quite patient, but utterly incapable of helping themselves. Among them, also, the evil to be cured manifested itself in corporal maladies. I bandaged them.

Toward the close of my task I was assisted by some maidens, and then I was brought home by my guide, who gravely reproved me for thinking myself useless; for, he said, I had done a great deal. God makes use of every one in a different way.

Again I was taken to a large military hospital. It seemed as if it were under a shed—but where, I know not. Some of the patients were Germans, and there were others who looked like prisoners who had been brought thither in wagons. Many of the drivers were in rags and wore gray smock-frocks. Some of the sick seemed to be a little elevated in the air; they had moral evils represented, as in the other hospital, by corporal sickness.

I went all around relieving, curing, putting on bandages, making lint. Some saints accompanied me, helping me, hiding from my eyes whatever was not decent and throwing a veil of darkness over many of the unfortunate beings who were quite naked. At last I came to some who had bodily wounds; they were not suspended in the air, they lay on the ground. The wounds of the morally sick were the most offensive, for their source is in the depths of the heart; exteriorly they do not seem so hideous, though they are really far more horrible. Bodily wounds are not so deep, they have a more healthful odor; but they who do not understand such things think them the more frightful. Moral wounds are often healed by patient endurance. I gave all I had, I cut up my bed-clothes, used all my white linen, and Abbé Lambert's too, but the more I gave away the more need there was. I never had enough. Many good people brought me things. There was a room full of officers, and for them something better was necessary. There lay my enemies, and I rejoiced that I could do them good. There was one whom I could not relieve. He wanted a physician according to his own ideas and such could not be found. His state was fearful. Later I had other patients, my own acquaintances, peasants, citizens, ecclesiastics, and also a particular priest I knew. I had been commissioned a long time before to tell him something; his state grew daily worse. He sought honors and neglected souls.

It was given me to see all whom I had cured by draining their sores, both really and spiritually. My Spouse told me again that such spiritual assistance is *real* assistance, that I do it in *spirit* only because I am now not capable of doing it corporally.

When I worked as a child in the fields, or as a religious in the garden, I used to feel myself urged to beg God to do for men what I could do only for the plants. I often have a clear idea of the mutual relations and resemblances between creatures which, like emblems, can explain one another; so also in prayer and communion with God one can do *really* in desire and affection what he could not do *actually* on account of external hindrances. As a portrait can make me know the original, so can I exercise charity, render services, bestow care upon the picture or image of the object for whom I can do nothing personally and directly. If I do it in Jesus and for Jesus, he transmits it to the person for whom I do it by virtue of his merits; therefore, the merciful God grants to my earnest prayers and longing to assist my neighbor those lively pictures in which I supplicate for the welfare of this or that person.

I have also been shown how unspeakably good it is in God to give such visions, to accept the labor done in them as a full and perfect work, and to reckon it as an increase in the treasury of the Church, but—that it may profit the Church—it must be done in union with the merits of Christ. The needy members of the Church can receive help only from the Church herself. The healing power must be awakened in the Church as in a body, and here it is that the cooperation of her members comes in; but this is more easily felt than expressed.

It used to seem strange to me to have to travel so far every night and engage in all sorts of affairs. I used to think: "When I am on a journey, when I help others in spirit, all seems so real, so natural! And yet all the time I am lying sick and miserable at home!" Then I was told: "All that a person earnestly desires to do and suffer for Jesus Christ, for his Church, and for the neighbor, *he really and truly does in prayer.* Now you can understand!"

*These last communications throw light upon Anne Catherine's action-in-spirit, or in the symbolical pictures shown her in vision. It is action by prayer accompanied by suffering and sacrifice, and applied by God to determinate ends. It is always heard, and its fruits applied to him for whom it is offered through the instrumentality of him who suffers and entreats. Such prayer is infinitely more efficacious than any other, it is certain of success; it gathers, so to say, fruit already ripe. It is a prayer active, expiatory, and propitiatory in and through Jesus Christ. Anne Catherine was like to a tree by the side of running waters, upon whose boughs daily hung fresh fruits for the needy; she was like the nursing mother supplying nourishment to multitudes of spiritual chil-*

*dren. She often tried to explain in what such prayer consists. The pilgrim's journal records, for July 7, 1820:*

She has suffered intensely for days. Last night she was steeped in perspiration and the wound in her side bled abundantly. She wanted to change her linen herself, so she took a few drops of St. Walburga's oil, which gave her the strength necessary for so painful an effort. She looks like a martyr today. She acknowledges that her pains were so great last night that she cried aloud to God to help her, not to let her suffer beyond her strength. "These pains," she said, "are my greatest torment, for I cannot bear them in silence, I must groan; and then I always think that, as I have not borne them lovingly, they have not been pleasing to God. It was as if fire had been applied to my person, sending fine currents of pain through my breast, my arms, and my hands." As she spoke, the tears flowed down her cheeks, not so much from her own sufferings, as from those of her Savior which she constantly contemplated.

*Anne Catherine continued*: No human intelligence can comprehend what Jesus endured from his birth to his death, even if it were seen as I see it. His infinite love is manifest in his passion, which he bore like a lamb without a murmur. I was conceived in sin, a miserable sinner, and life has ever been a burden to me from the pain sin causes me; but how much more must the incomprehensible perfection of Jesus suffer, insulted on all sides, tormented to death?

Last night in the midst of my own pains I saw again all he endured from his conception till his death. I saw, also, his interior sufferings, I felt their nature—so intelligible did his grace render them to me. I am so weak, I shall only say what comes to my mind:

I saw under the heart of Mary a glory, and in the glory a bright, shining child. While I gazed upon it, it seemed as if Mary floated over and around it. I saw the infant increasing in size and all the torments of the crucifixion accomplished in him. It was a frightfully sad spectacle! I wept and sobbed aloud. I saw him struck, pushed, beaten, crowned with thorns, laid on the cross, and nailed to it, his side pierced. I saw the whole passion of Christ in the child. It was fearful! As the child hung on the cross, he said to me: "I suffered all this from my conception till my thirty-fourth year, when it was accomplished exteriorly." [The Lord died at the age of thirty-three years and three months.] "Go, announce this to men!" But how can I announce it?[1]

I saw him, also, as a newborn babe, and I saw how many children abuse the infant Jesus in his crib. The Blessed Virgin was not there to protect him. The children brought all kinds of whips and rods and struck his face until it bled. He tried gently to parry the blows with his little hands, but even the youngest children beat him most cruelly, their parents even trimming and preparing the rods for some of them. They used thorns, nettles, scourges, switches of all kinds, each had its own signification. One came with a fine switch like a cornstalk, which broke when he tried to strike with it. I knew many of these children. Some strutted about in fine clothes which I took away from them. I corrected them soundly.

Then I saw the Lord walking with his disciples. He was thinking of all he had endured even in his mother's womb, of all that men had made him suffer in his infancy and his public life by their blindness and obduracy. But above all he thought of what he had undergone from the malice, the envious spying of the Pharisees. He spoke to his disciples of his passion, but they understood him not. I saw his interior sufferings like colors and heavy black shadows passing over his grave, sad countenance, through to his breast, and thence to his heart, which they tore to pieces. This sight is inexpressible! I saw him grow pale, his whole being agonized, for the sufferings of his soul were far sharper than those of his crucifixion; but he bore them silently, lovingly, patiently.

After this I beheld him at the Last Supper, and saw his infinite grief at Judas's wickedness. He would willingly have undergone still greater torments, could he have kept Judas from betraying him. His mother also had loved Judas, had often spoken with him, had instructed and advised him. The fall of Judas grieved

---

[1] The pilgrim here remarks: "She forgot that she was then fulfilling her commission. Her question reveals the way in which she always acted in such cases. She has often been directed to tell even what seemed absurd."

Jesus more than all the rest. I saw him washing his feet sorrow-fully and lovingly, and looking at him affectionately while pre-senting to him the morsel. Tears stood in the Lord's eyes and his teeth were clenched in pain. I saw Judas approach. I saw Jesus give him his body and blood to eat and I heard him say with infi-nite sorrow: "That which thou dost, do quickly." Then I saw Judas slink behind and soon after quit the supper room.

I saw all the sufferings of the Lord's soul under the form of clouds, colored rays, and flashes of light. I saw him going to the Mount of Olives with his disciples. He ceased not to weep on the way, his tears flowing in torrents. I saw Peter so bold and self-con-fident that he thought himself able to crush all his enemies. That distressed Jesus, for he knew Peter would deny him.

I saw him leave his disciples, excepting the three whom he loved most, in a kind of open shed near the garden of Olives. He told them to sleep there. He wept all the time. Then he went fur-ther into the garden leaving behind the apostles who thought themselves so valiant. I saw that they soon fell asleep. I saw the Savior overwhelmed with sorrow and sweating blood, and I saw an angel presenting him the chalice.

*On this evening the pilgrim records*: She still shudders and trem-bles with pain; but she is all patience and love, sweetness and gen-tleness. There is something noble about her in the midst of her pains.

*In another entry, on August 30, 1820, the pilgrim writes*: She has been racked by inexpressible sufferings. It was shown her that each has a special signification according to which some particu-lar members are tormented, also that every kind of pain, pierc-ing, tearing, or burning has its own meaning. She knows that each one patiently borne in the name of Jesus, in union with his passion, becomes a sacrifice for the sins and negligences for which it was imposed. She thereby regains for the Church that of which man's perversity deprives her.

# Forms of Active Prayer

## (Or, Labors in the Nuptial House)

THE *forms under which Anne Catherine exercised her action in prayer, or her labors in the nuptial house, were not optional; they were conformable to the nature of the tasks imposed—which were as varied as the gospel parables in which Christ's union with the Church is represented. There he shows us the Church as his spouse, his body, his vine, his garden, his field, his flock—while he himself is the bridegroom, the head, the vinedresser, the gardener, the sower, the shepherd. The priesthood he denominates the salt of the earth, etc.*

*These parables are not empty figures. They symbolize the union existing between Christ the Savior and the objects of his purchase. So also were Anne Catherine's labors in vision neither vain nor arbitrary—but truly necessary inasmuch as they corresponded to the nature and end of her task. Had she for instance to repair the omissions of negligent servants in the Church—the vine of the Son of God—her action in vision partakes of that nature; that is, it has the same form, the same results, as labor expended on a real vine. An evident proof that this labor in vision is real are the physical effects it produces—fatigue, bruises, wounds, and so forth.*

*Anne Catherine relates the following June 20, 1820:* I was taken by my guide to a miserably neglected vineyard west of the nuptial house. Several of the vines were strong and healthy, but the branches lay unpruned and straggling, the soil neither dug nor manured. The whole place was overrun with nettles that grew high and thick where the stock was most vigorous, though they were not so sharp. Where the branches hung half-dead, they were almost buried under small stinging nettles.

*On June 22, 1820, the pilgrim writes: "She is constantly engaged in these labors of suffering. In whatever position she is placed, she feels that she is lying among nettles and thorns":*

In the vineyard were many beautiful houses, all in the very best order inside, although on the outside the weeds grew up to the doors and almost as high as the windows. I saw in them ecclesiastics—dignitaries of the Church—reading and studying all sorts of useless books. But no one took the least care of the vineyard. In the middle of the latter stood a church with several farmhouses around it, but there was no way to get to it—all was covered with rank weeds, even the church was as it were tapestried with green. The blessed sacrament was in the church, but no lamp hung before it.

The bishop appeared to be away. Inside the church—even there —was no clear passage. All was overgrown with weeds. It made me sad. I was told to set to work, and I found a two-edged bone knife like a reaping-hook with which to prune the vine, a hoe, and a basket for manure. The work to be done was all explained to me. It was hard at first but afterward became easier. I was told how to gather and press the grapes, but now I have forgotten it. As soon as I began to work in the vineyard my sufferings changed. I felt as if I were being pierced with a three-edged knife. The pain darted through every member, intolerable shootings in my bones and joints, even in my fingertips.

I was at work in the wild vineyard, and besides, I was over-whelmed by a swarm of new torments. I knew nothing of what was going on around me. I was worn out and I felt as if I were lying, not in my bed, but among nettles. Nearby was a corner that I had weeded, and I begged to be laid there. My attendants pitied me, saying they would put me where there were no thorns, and lifted me to my bed. But I groaned: "Ah! You have deceived me, you have laid me among still sharper nettles," for so it seemed to me.

I thought I was in the vineyard. The tearing-up of the stinging nettles was very painful, and I ached all over from pruning the vine with the bone knife. I had already done up to the first house—the wildest part of the vineyard. In my intense pains I made use of the relics of St. Ignatius and St. Francis Xavier and I found relief. I saw the two saints on high. A beam of light from them passed through me like a shock, and I was instantly relieved.

When I reached the church, St. Frances of Rome appeared to me, haggard and emaciated; she looked like a skeleton. "See," she said, "I also had to labor like you, I was just as miserable as you now are, but I did not die."

*Her words encouraged Anne Catherine. Her pale face began to glow; she looked like one who had received fresh incentive to exertion, and her*

31

*hands began to clutch and pull, the middle fingers stiff and bent. Suddenly she laughed and exclaimed*: There, I have hurt my knee! I struck the bone. I am always so eager, in such a hurry; I struck it against a great root in the vineyard and the bone knife has hurt my hand. *Her right hand is swollen, her arms covered with scratches.*

*June 26, 1820*: Now I have only a few days' work before me. Through self-victory my task has doubly succeeded. Now I must grind the weeds to dust. The hardest part of the work was in a presbytery in which a bad servant was the mistress. St. Clare of Montefalco appeared to me and said: "The worst is over."

*July 2, 1820*: The work in the vineyard is done. Still I have to pray and help with the young shoots. Nettles signify carnal desires. My guide said, "You have labored hard, you must have a little rest,"—but I do not think I will get it!

*July 15, 1820*: Last night I had a labor in prayer. A good man whom I know has for a long time been shown me as having fallen into sin, and I prayed that his heart might be touched. He does not know I am aware of his state. I have not seen him for some time. Last night I prayed for him earnestly; he is changed, he will go to confession. This morning he came unexpectedly to see me and I tried to be kind to him. He does not suspect that I have any idea of his state, nor that I have converted him by prayer. He is about to return (to God). What I said to him, God inspired.

*July 29, 1820*: I was in an apple orchard around which lay hills covered with vineyards, some in the sun, others in the shade. In it was a round building like a storehouse, full of casks and vats, and a great press with holes in the bottom. The little old nun who often helps me took me into the orchard, and I gathered the apples from a high tree until my arms ached. When my apron was full I emptied it into the press. I was told not to put in any that were unripe, and when I answered that the few I had gathered were hardly worth the trouble, I was shown how much juice they would yield. I understood neither the vision nor its signification, but it is the beginning of a new task.

*July 30, 1820*: The pilgrim says: The vision of laboring under the direction of deceased religious was again repeated. She was wearied with carrying fruit to the press, and her arms ached violently.

*July 31, 1820*: There is only one large apple tree in the orchard. I gathered no apples today, but I straightened up the plants around the tree, transplanting some, tying up others, pulling up the dead ones, watering and shading the drooping. All has reference to sectarians (false mystics). There are some overripe, worm-eaten apples on the tree—the first decayed from an excess of juice, and the worms in the others indicate pride, self-love, and bad company. They fall and crush the plants below, filling them with worms. But when gathered and pressed they yield juice that may be used. They signify teachers in parishes that have gone astray. My companions were the holy old nuns of the convent. Then I had another vision on the state of these people. I saw that most of those who had gone north followed dangerous ways and separated more and more from the Church; and I saw the necessity of importuning God that the proud, exuberant plants may be rooted out of those parishes, in order that the others may not be lost to her.

*August 2, 1820*: I worked hard in the garden last night. After I had picked out the blemished apples, I had to go to a neighboring vineyard. I had a little tub with me and gathered bunch after bunch of decayed grapes and threw them into it, that the green ones might ripen and no more be spoiled. When it was full, I emptied it into a press smaller than the apple press. I prayed all the time and had visions of the good resulting from my labor. It refers to the new sect. Only my guide was with me.

*August 3, 1820*: For a long time I have gathered and sorted the grapes, filled and emptied the tub, my guide alone with me. I have already accomplished a good deal and I have been told that it bears fruit.

*August 5, 1820*: I am very tired, for I worked so hard in the vineyard last night. Some bunches were enormous, almost as large as myself, and so heavy! I knew not how I should carry them. I was told that it was the vineyard of bishops, and I saw the bunch of each one. I had to attend to about ten. I remember our vicar-general, the bishop of Ermeland, and one who has not come (*a future one*). I had to pick out the spoiled grapes. I was puzzled how to carry those huge bunches, but I remembered that when a child I used to put great bundles of fodder far larger than myself on my head, and bending under their weight run along with them. So I slipped under the bunch, and as I was afraid of bruising it, I spread leaves and moss over it. I succeeded in getting it into the tub, but to my dismay I found that it had not escaped a bruise. I was reassured, however, on being told that it was to be so. I did it all in constant prayer. I was allowed to eat three grapes from three different bunches; the vicar-general's was one of them, but I know not what it means.

*August 8, 1820*: Last night I did some troublesome work on the vines at Coesfeld; they were in a miserable condition, almost all the fruit half-decayed. I found few truly pious Christians, and the ecclesiastics were in a tavern. In one place I passed some people who insulted me, though at the same time they sent me to do their work. I saw old N. who is always in the clouds while things go to ruin around him.

*August 10, 1820*: I had to work hard last night in the vineyard on account of the want of charity among the clergy. I had to endure the same fatigue as St. Clare of Montefalco in her garden. She was with me and showed me a bed full of plants. In the center were mignonette and an aromatic plant that flourishes in warm countries; outside were smooth-leaved herbs with long thorns. I knew not how to get across this hedge. Clare told me to dash bravely through it and I should have all the plants in the center as a reward. She related many incidents of her own life. I saw her as a child kneeling in prayer by a rosebush. The infant Jesus appeared and gave her a written prayer that she wanted to keep, but it was taken from her. I know some of this prayer: "I salute thee, O Mary, through the sweet heart of Jesus! I salute thee, O Mary, for the deliverance of all the poor souls! I salute thee, O Mary, through all the seraphim and cherubim!"—between each of these invocations she kissed the ground. The last part was beautiful, but I have forgotten it. One of Clare's practises was to kiss her hand when in company, and recall to mind that she was but dust and ashes.

I crossed the hedge, but not without scratches; the pain was so acute that I cried aloud. Then Clare left me and Frances of Rome appeared. She told me what horrible torments she had endured, but, as St. Alexis had helped her, she was going to help me. Her malady had been the same as that of the Canaanite woman who touched the hem of Our Lord's robe. Alexis threw his mantle over her and bade her read that passage in the gospel that related to the miracle. She promised that I should soon be relieved.

*Anne Catherine had earlier (July 17th) the following vision of this wonderful cure at the same hour it had actually been wrought in St. Frances:*

I saw St. Frances of Rome. She was married, but still young. She was lying in bed praying, for she had been ill a long time. An elderly woman slept nearby. It was early dawn, when suddenly her room was lit up and St. Alexis, in the garb of a pilgrim, approached her bed, holding a book like the golden book of the gospels that his mother had given him. I am not certain that it was the same book or only one like it. I think the latter more probable. The saint called Frances by name. She started up in bed, and he told her that he was Alexis and that he had come to cure her, adding that he had found salvation in the book he had in his hand. Then he held it open before her and bade her read. I do not remember distinctly what followed, but Frances was cured and the saint vanished. She arose, awoke the woman— who was amazed to see her up and well—and they went at day-break to the Church of St. Alexis to bless God in His saints.

*August 11, 1820*: Last night again I lay all alone in the thorns of the vineyards, which signify priests void of charity. I awoke, thanks to God, about three o'clock.

## Vineyard, Tree of God, Herbal Remedies

LAST night (*August 12, 1820*) I toiled in the vineyard. St. Clare was there encouraging and consoling me as I lay upon the slanting branches that gave me great pain. She told me that every sharp knot in them signified the rector of a parish and that grapes would grow out of them if I lovingly offered for those priests my sufferings in union with Jesus. Then I saw numerous parishes profiting by it.

*On September 5, 1820, while in ecstasy, Anne Catherine said*:

From Mary's nativity till the feast of St. Michael I shall have to labor and travel. Angels from all parts have come for me. I am

needed in so many places! I was told last night that in many parishes in which I had pulled up the weeds and nettles, tied up and
pruned the vine branches, the fruit had begun to ripen—but that
robbers and wild beasts were roaming through the vineyards and
that I must enclose them by my labor in prayer. I saw the vintage
flourishing by my labor, the grapes ripening, and the red juice
flowing to the ground from the wine-presses—which signified
that when good people aspire to holiness they have to struggle
and endure persecution and temptation. I was told that I had
weeded and manured, but that I must now raise a hedge, that
they (these struggling souls) may not fall prey to temptation and
persecution. It is time for the grapes to ripen, and they must be
protected. Then I saw innumerable parishes for which I had to do
the same between Mary's nativity and Michaelmas.

I was taken to my vineyard (*September 7, 1820*) and reproved for
not having hedged it in. I carried weeds to the mill[1] and then left.
I was so glad to be well again, and I did not continue my prayer. I
had to pile up the rubbish and make a hedge with thistles to protect the vineyard. By prayer, I had to enclose the vineyards with
dense hedges.

God has mercifully shown me the signification of the vine and
its fruits. The vine is Jesus Christ in us. The wild branches must be
pruned in a certain way, that they may not absorb the sap that is
to become the grape, the wine, the sacrament, the blood of Jesus
Christ—a blood that has purchased our sinful blood, that will
cause it to rise again, to pass from death to life. This pruning of
the vine by certain rules is, spiritually, the cutting away of super-
fluities and the mortification of the flesh, that what is holy in us
may increase, flourish, and produce fruit. Otherwise, corrupt
nature will bring forth only wood and leaves.

The pruning must be done by rule, because only the superflu-
ous elements of human nature—of which I was shown an almost
infinite number—are to be destroyed. Anything more would be
sinful mutilation. The stock itself is not retrenched. It was planted

[1] Regarding this mill, see "Return to Purgatory" in *Inner Life and Worlds of Soul & Spirit.*

in humanity in the person of the Blessed Virgin, and it will last till the end of time: yes, eternally—for it is with Mary in heaven.

The signification of many other fruits was shown me. I saw a spiritual tree of colored light. The soil on which it stood was like a mountain in the air, or a rock of colored crystal. The trunk was a stream of yellow light. The twigs, the branches—even the fibers of the leaves—were threads of light, more or less delicate, of various forms and colors, and the leaves were green and yellow light. It had three rows of branches—one below, one in the middle, and one above—surrounded by three angelic choirs. On the top stood a seraph veiled with his wings, who waved his scepter in different directions. The highest choir received through the seraph effusions of light and strength from God, like a heavenly, fruitful dew. This uppermost choir and the one below it labored, acted, without stirring from their places. They transmitted directions to the lowest choir at the foot of the tree, whose angels bore spiritual gifts into innumerable gardens—for every fruit had its own garden in which it was propagated according to its variety. This tree was the Tree of God, and the gardens were the different kinds of fruit produced by it.

Below on the earth were the same kinds of fruits, but tainted in their fallen nature, more or less poisoned because the guilty use made of them had subjected them to the influence of the planetary spirits. In the center of each garden I saw a tree covered with all the varieties of its kind, which grew around it. I saw pictures indicating the essence and signification of the plants. I saw the meaning of their name in universal language. Wonderful is the saints' influence over plants! They seem to deliver them from the curse and power of the planetary spirits and—by certain religious invocations—render them remedies in sickness. As they become antidotes against diseases that I see as corporal sins in this lower, earthly region, so in the heavenly gardens are they antidotes against faults and sins I there see as spiritual sickness.

In each garden there stood a small house or tent that had also its signification. I saw that bees here play an important part. Some were very large, others quite small, their members transparent, as if formed of light, the legs like rays, the wings silver—I cannot describe it. There were hives in the orchards in which they worked

—all was transparent. I have received information on the bees, their work, and its signification morally and physically, but I have forgotten it.

I was taken into several orchards and saw wonderful things. I knew and understood everything before I was tormented. I was told for instance that nuts signify combat and persecution in vision, as well as in everyday life; therefore, I often see them growing around the Church and even gathered and given to others. I saw around the nut-gardens visions of strife, single combatants, and whole armies struggling. I saw two men beating each other, neither gaining any advantage until one threw sand into the other's eyes, and so won the victory, though not without a final effort on the part of the vanquished—the whole scene was ridiculous! The men were dressed as at the present day. I knew what it all meant and its relation to the several kinds of nuts. I learned that the mystery of strife and persecution signified by the nuts in the spiritual garden became—after the fall of humankind and by the power of the evil spirit—the combat of hatred, the origin of homicide.

In each garden I was taken into the house, as if I were sick, and shown how the nature and secret virtue of fruits—gathered in certain states, with certain consecrations, and mingled with other ingredients—were very efficacious in such or such ailments. Unfortunately I can remember only a little of it. For instance I understood why on St. John the Baptist's day the green nuts should be marked with a cross and allowed to remain on the tree until after a rain, when—preserved in honey—they are excellent for weak stomachs. This preparation was explained to me in detail, but I have forgotten it. At the time I understood it all clearly, but now it is incomprehensible to finite intelligence.

Again, I learned that the oil of nuts is hurtful, and I knew the reason—but it loses its poisonous qualities if we cook a morsel of bread in it. I saw a secret relation between it and John the Baptist: the cross made on the nuts, their exposure to the rain, and the power they thus acquire to cure the stomach, refer to the saint's baptism and his labors as precursor, the oil to the anointing and sacerdotal consecration.

I understood all about apples, and I saw that, like nuts, they refer to different things. I saw something about one with six red pips, one of which—administered in a certain way and in certain maladies—could restore health to the dying. Before the apple orchard I had a vision referring to fruit that looked like lemons; perhaps they really were lemons. I saw in Rome a holy person lying ill, and by her one of these fruits. I think she had had a vision on the subject. A slave, for some fault, had been thrown into a pit full of venomous serpents. The saint gave the fruit to her physician to give to the poor slave for his cure, and by virtue of the same he was healed of the serpents' bites. I saw him afterward led before the emperor.

I saw something of the same kind concerning another of these fruits which, cooked in milk and honey, was a cure for the most violent fevers. I saw something about a feast of the Blessed Virgin—I think the Immaculate Conception—and also the way in which the knowledge of it was spread. I saw something about figs, but I cannot remember what it meant. They are an excellent remedy when used with a certain kind of apple, but by themselves they are hurtful. When so used, the apple must be weighed. The fig and apple hung side by side on the celestial tree which, under the angelic choirs, was covered with all kinds of spiritual fruit.

I saw many things concerning the fruit of the tree of original sin in paradise. The tree had a huge trunk and arose in a sharp, tapering point; but after the fall it inclined toward the earth. The branches took root and sent forth new shoots whose branches did the same, until the tree soon formed a whole forest. In warm, Eastern countries, people live under them. The boughs have no branches, they bear great shield-like leaves that hide the fruit, growing five together in a bunch—one has to hunt for them.

They are tart, not pleasant as they used to be, and yellow, streaked with blood-red veins.

I had a vision of peaches. I saw that in the country to which they are indigenous they are accursed, deadly poisonous. The people, by the aid of witchcraft, extract from them cursed juice to excite lust. They bury them in the ground with dung, then distill them with certain ingredients. I saw that by its use they fall into the most abominable practices, and all who eat of the fruit became raving maniacs, because it is accursed. I saw some unsuspecting strangers entering the country. The Persians offered them some of it in order to destroy them, but God rendered it harmless. I saw these fruits taken to foreign lands for evil purposes, but they were hurtful only in their own country. I saw two kinds, one grew like osiers with delicate branches.

I was also in a cherry orchard, and I was shown that cherries signify ingratitude, adultery, and treason—for that is the nature of sweet fruit with a hard, bitter kernel. Of the laurel tree I saw that a certain emperor always wore a laurel crown during a storm, that he might not be struck by lightning. And I was told—yes, and I saw it too—that the perfume of this tree possesses a virtue against storms. I saw some reference to the Blessed Virgin in it.

All was distinct and wonderful. I saw the secret virtue of plants before humankind's fall. But Adam's sin infected all nature, for plants as well as men then fell under the influence of the planetary spirits. I saw many of the secret properties that paganism used and abused; but they were afterward regenerated and purified by Jesus Christ and his Church in their struggle against the planetary spirits.

*In August and September, 1821, Anne Catherine's labors introduced her to wheat fields. One day she said:*

I am worn out and bruised by the rough work I have done in the fields of some people I know. I had to sow and plough. I had no horses, and the plough no handle. They were fields belonging to the Church; some had grain, others none. I had to gather seeds from the best fields and prepare the others to receive it.

*Then, in the rustic dialect of her country, she described farming and farm utensils, which the pilgrim could not understand, and she related besides the enemy's attempts to hinder her work:* Satan struck me so violently, as if with a trowel, that I screamed aloud, and next morning I found my chemise stuck to the wound the blow had made just above the sign on my right side.

*She was not discouraged by the enemy's artifices, but boldly undertook a still more severe labor. She had to stow away the harvest in numberless barns, the immensity of the labor being greatly disproportioned to the time allotted for it. And she was obliged to reap the grain so hurriedly that she thought every moment she would sink from fatigue. Still, she reached the end of her task. She had to reap, bind, and thresh the wheat, put the grain into sacks, separate the seed-corn from that for present use. She worked fast, as if in dread of a heavy storm that would destroy the whole crop. The labor succeeded, but she was too exhausted to explain its signification. She only said:*

I saw so many ears that had not been reaped, that I ran to help. I saw all clearly: the people, the task imposed, the neglect, all that was wanting. The vision gave me a clear and rapid perception of the case, because I know all about field labors, having been so engaged when a child. I prayed while I worked, for by prayer I knew who were suffering and struggling with me, and it seemed as if I often sent my angel to obtain their help. I had visions in which were shown me the cowardly, the slothful, the negligent, the wavering—whose place I had to take. I saw here and there some weak ecclesiastics on the point of spoiling everything by hesitating to sign, to regulate, something either good or bad. And by prayer I had to force them, as it were, to choose the right, to defend the good, to repudiate evil. It was all clear and natural at the time, but now I cannot recall it.

*Anne Catherine's task often took the form of repairing and cleaning all kinds of church ornaments. Sometimes she had to gather up the linen from the neighboring parishes, carry it to the cathedral cloister, and there in the midst of constant interruptions wash, bleach, iron, and mend it, that it might be ready for the service of the altar. At other times her attention was given to chasubles, maniples, and stoles that had to be made over: "Such a task," she said, "is a symbolical image of prayer for the clergy. It has the same signification, the same effect, as these sacred vestments have for the Church and her ministers." At the end of a most painful task of the kind, she received the following instruction upon it:*

I must not wonder at my sufferings. I had a great, indescribable vision of sin, the reparation through Jesus, and the state of the priesthood; and I understood how with infinite toil and pains all that is spoiled, destroyed, or lost must be restored and turned again into the way of salvation. I have had an immense, connected vision of the fall and redemption. It would take a year to relate it, for I saw and understood all mysteries clearly and distinctly; but I cannot explain it. I was in the nuptial house and I saw in its numerous apartments all forms of sin and reparation. I saw sin from the fall of the angels and Adam down to the present, in its numberless ramifications; and at the same time I beheld all the preparations for its reparation to the coming of Jesus and his death on the cross. I saw his power transmitted to priests in what related to the remedy, and how every Christian shares in Jesus Christ. I saw the imperfections, the decay, of the priesthood, and their cause; also the chastisements awaiting them and the efficacy of expiatory sufferings. And I felt by my pains the strict bond existing between the fault and its atonement. I saw a future war, many dangers and sufferings in store for me.

All these varied instructions and revelations of history, nature, and the mysteries of God's kingdom upon earth appeared to me in perfect order, following one another, arising from one another clearly and intelligibly. All were explained to me in parables of labor and tasks—while suffering, satisfaction, and reparation were shown me under the form of sewing. I have had to rip others' work, as well as my own, and do it over with great pains and trouble. I had to examine what was crooked, see how it had happened, and patiently fix it straight. In the shape of different articles, in the various kinds of sewing, in the trimming—and the careless way in which it was all done—I saw the origin and consequence of every sin. In the repairing of it I saw the effect of spiritual suffering and labor in prayer.

I recognized work belonging to deceased persons, my former acquaintances—work that had actually been done and that was now brought to me to do over again. I had also to rip some of my own sewing: for example, an undergarment I had embroidered too richly to gratify a vain woman, and other things of the kind. But my work for the Church and the poor was good. I went into the nuptial house as if to a school, and there my Lord explained everything to me, showing me in great historical pictures all he had done to repair the sin of Adam. I saw all as going on under my eyes. And yet at the same time it seemed as if I beheld it in a mirror, which mirror was myself.

My Affianced explained to me how all things had deteriorated since the fall, all had become impure—how, when the angels fell, innumerable bad spirits came upon the earth and filled the air. I saw many things infected by their malice and possessed by them in various ways.

The first man was like heaven. He was an image of God. In him was unity, and his form was a reproduction of the divine model. He was to receive and enjoy creatures, accepting them from God and returning thanks for them. He was free, and therefore was he subjected to trial.

The garden of Eden, with all it contained, was a perfect picture of the kingdom of God. So too was the Tree of Knowledge. Its fruit—on account of its essence, its properties, and effects—was not to be eaten by humankind, since he would thereby become an independent being, having his principle of action in himself. He would abandon God to concentrate himself in himself, so that the finite would compass the infinite. Therefore was he forbidden to eat its fruit—I cannot explain how I saw this.

When the shining hill upon which Adam stood in paradise arose, when was hollowed out the bright flowering vale in which I beheld Eve, the corrupter was already near. After the fall all was changed, divided, dispersed. What had been one became many. Creatures looked no longer to God alone, but each was concentrated in self. At first there were two, they increased to three, and finally to an infinite number. They wanted to be one like unto God, but they became a multitude. Separating from God, they reproduced themselves in infinite varieties. From images of God, they became images of themselves—bearing the likeness of sin.

They entered into communication with the fallen angels; participated in the fruits of the earth already tainted by these spirits. This indiscriminate blending of things—this division in humankind and fallen nature—gave birth to endless sins and miseries. My Lord showed me all this clearly, distinctly, intelligibly—more clearly than one sees the ordinary things of life. I thought at the time that a child might comprehend it, but now I am unable to repeat it.

I saw the whole plan of redemption from the very beginning. It is not perfectly correct to say that God need not have become Man, nor died for us upon the cross, that He could have redeemed us otherwise in virtue of His omnipotence. I saw that He did what He did in His infinite goodness, mercy, and justice. There is indeed no compulsion in God. He does what He does. He is what He is!

I saw Melchizedek as angel, as symbol of Jesus, as priest on earth. Inasmuch as the priesthood is in God, he was like an angel, a priest of the eternal hierarchy. I saw him prepare, found, separate, the human family—and serve them as a guide. I saw too Enoch and Noah—what they represented, what they effected.

On the other side, I saw the influence of the kingdom of hell, the infinitely varied manifestations and effects of an earthly, carnal, diabolical paganism, corrupting virtue through a secret, inborn necessity.

In this way I saw sin and the foreshadowing—the prophetic figures—of redemption, which in their way were the images of divine Power, as humankind itself is the image of God. All were shown me from Abraham to Moses, from Moses to the prophets, all as symbols of our own time, as connected with our own time.

Here followed an explanation why priests no longer relieve or cure, why it is either not in their power or why it is now effected so differently from what it used to be. I saw this same gift possessed by the prophets and the meaning of the form under which it was exercised. For instance I saw the history of Elisha giving his staff to Gehazi to lay upon the dead son of the Sunamitess. Elisha's mission and power lay spiritually in the staff, which was his arm—the continuation of his arm, that is, his power.

In connection with this I saw the interior signification and effects of a bishop's crozier and a monarch's scepter if used with faith, which in a certain way binds them together, separating them from all others. But Gehazi's faith was weak, and the mother thought her prayer could be answered only by Elisha in person. Between the power bestowed by God upon Elisha and his staff there intervened human doubts, so that the latter lost its efficacy. But I saw Elisha stretch himself hand to hand, mouth to mouth, breast to breast upon the boy and pray, and the child's soul returned to his body. This form of healing was explained to me as referring to and prefiguring the death of Jesus.

In Elisha—by faith and the gift of God—were all the avenues of grace and expiation opened again in humankind that had been closed since the fall in Adam: that is, the head, the breast, the hands, the feet. Elisha stretched himself as a living, symbolical cross upon the dead, closed, cross of the boy's form—and through his prayer of faith, life and health were restored. He expiated, he atoned for the sins his parents had committed by their head, heart, hands, and feet—sins that had brought death to their boy.

Side by side with the above I saw pictures of the wounds and death of Jesus, as also the harmony, the conformity, existing between the figure and the reality. After the crucifixion of Jesus I saw in the priesthood of his Church the rich gift of repairing and curing. In the same proportion as we live in him and are crucified with him, are the avenues of grace, his sacred wounds, open to us.

I learned much of the imposition of hands, the efficacy of a benediction, the influence exerted by the hand even at a distance—all was explained by the staff of Elisha. That priests of the present day so seldom cure and bless was shown me in an example significant of the conformity to Jesus upon which all such effects depend:

I saw three painters making figures in wax. The first used beautiful white wax very skillfully and intelligently, but he was full of himself—he had not the likeness of Christ in him—and so his figures were of no value. The second used bleached wax, but he was indolent and self-willed—he did nothing well. The third was unskillful and awkward, but he worked away earnestly on common wax—his work was good, a speaking likeness, though with coarse features. And so did I see renowned preachers vaunting their worldly wisdom but doing nothing, while many a poor, unlettered man retains the priestly power of blessing and curing.

It seemed all the time as if I were going to the nuptial house to school. My Lord showed me how he had suffered from his conception till his death, always expiating, always satisfying for sin. I saw it also in pictures of his life. I saw that by our prayer and suffering many a soul who labors not during life can be converted and saved at the hour of death.

I saw the apostles sent over the greater part of the earth to scatter benedictions and to cast down satan's power, a power that by his full atonement Jesus acquired and secured forever to such priests as had received or who would receive his Holy Spirit. The countries in which they labored were those that had been most contaminated by the enemy, and I was shown that the power of withdrawing various regions from satan's dominion by the sacerdotal benediction is signified by these words: "You are the salt of the earth." It is for the same reason that salt is put into holy water.

That these countries did not persevere in Christianity, that they are now lying uncultivated, I saw also as a wise dispensation of divine providence. They were only to be blessed, prepared for a future time, in order that—being again sowed—they might bring forth magnificent fruits when other countries shall lie desolate, when other lands shall lie uncultivated.

I saw that David understood the plan of redemption, but that Solomon did not—for he took too much complacency in his wisdom. Many prophets, especially Malachi, comprehended the mystery of Christianity.

I saw innumerable things, all inwardly related, all following one another naturally. While I was thus instructed I saw about twenty other persons in various positions, some walking, others lying down, who seemed to be taking part in the same instruction. They were all far distant from me and from one another, and there were more women than men. Communicating rays from the pictures fell upon them, but each one received them differently. I wanted to speak to them, but could not reach them. I thought: "Now, I should like to know if they receive this light in its purity," when I saw that, unfortunately, all changed it in some manner. I thought: "I do not mix anything with it"—when, on a sudden, a tall female appeared to me, one long deceased, and showed me a garment of her own making. Around the neck and sleeves the sewing was beautiful, but the rest was very badly done. I thought: "See, what work! No, no, I never sewed like this!"— when I was made to feel that I too mixed things up, that I was vain, and that this very work—some parts good, others bad—was symbolical of the manner in which I had received this instruction. The thought troubled me.

I saw too in this vision that the punctilios of sensual, worldly life are most scrupulously observed, that the malediction (the so-called benediction and miracles in the kingdom of satan)—the worship of nature, superstition, magic, mesmerism, worldly art and science, and all the means employed for smoothing over death, for making sin attractive, for lulling the conscience—is practiced with rigorous exactitude, even to fanaticism, by those very men who look upon the Church's mysteries as superstitious forms for which any others may be indifferently substituted. And yet these men subject their whole life and all their actions to certain ceremonies and observances. It is only of the kingdom of the God-Man that they take no account. The service of the world is practiced in perfection, but the service of God is shamefully neglected! Ah! If souls should ever claim what is owed them by the clergy, through whose carelessness and indifference they have lost so much, what a terrible reckoning there would be!

*The nearer the ecclesiastical year drew to its close, the more painful and multiplied became Anne Catherine's spiritual labors. As each different period approached its term, the heavier became her task of satisfying for the offences offered to God by the omissions and negligence of His servants. This was plainly visible in her increase of fatigue and suffering, since she had to expiate for the whole mass of the faithful not only their abuse of the means of salvation within their reach, but also their culpable loss of time. There is no created good so lightly esteemed, so carelessly trifled away, by an immense majority of human beings, as the fugitive moments of this short life so rapidly flying toward eternity. For this blindness Anne Catherine did sharp penance, expiating for many who without her aid would never have attained salvation. The following vision presents a symbolical picture of the abundant blessings flowing from her labors in prayer:*

Last night I was in the nuptial house. I found there three wild cows, plunging and raging. I had to milk them. With immense fatigue I had to draw milk from my own face, hands, feet, and side, and put it into a large pail for people of all ranks. I was told: "These people have dissipated their gifts and now they are in want, but you have laid up so many treasures from the Church that you can indemnify them for what they have lost."

I went again with my guide to the nuptial house and again I was told to milk the three cows. They had now grown quite gentle, and their litter was so clean that one might have slept on it. I milked first from the middle one, and then from the other two, three large pails full, which I had to carry to a place where it was measured out by priests into small vessels, which they counted. Many received it: priests, schoolmasters, and mistresses. It even flowed around outside of the house. I asked my guide why none was kept in the house and why I always had to do the milking. I was told not to ask questions, but to do as I was bid; that I should obey like Isaac, whom Abraham answered not when questioned regarding the sacrifice; that the milk will be otherwise distributed because the female is not fitted for it—it receives, preserves, fosters—that the fruits of my labor were to be propagated by the priesthood. "You must milk, and not question. The priests will distribute it, for through them it becomes fruitful."

They brought me a poor, miserable cow that I thought was about to die. It stuck up close to me. I could not get it away. Not knowing what to do with it, I invoked Mary, who instantly appeared and said to me: "Take care of the poor animal. It comes alone because its keeper, who ought to work and pray for it, demands not for it any one's assistance." Then she told me with what I should feed it—prayers, sufferings, self-victories, alms, etc., all shown under the form of plants and fruits. I had so miserable a night from colic and other pains that I cried. At last, when quite worn out, I took some blessed oil, which relieved me.

Again I had to busy myself in the stable of the nuptial house, cleaning and feeding the cows. My feet were bare and I dreaded the dirt. The stable was so crowded that I had to push my way through, holding on to the cows. But they did not hurt me, and I had many souls to help me. It was always the Mother of God, however, who gave advice and directions, pointing out this or that herb for this or that cow, and showing me a bitter one for a cow that was too fat. I milked none today, but I had—in my bare feet among stones and briers—to gather all kinds of herbs, for all had to be done with suffering and love.

When I invoke her, the Mother of God always appears as an apparition in the air—tall, majestic, white as snow, her light robe unconfined at the waist and formed from top to bottom of pure rays or folds. Although no corporal figure is visible, nevertheless this apparition impresses one with its majestic, supernatural bearing.

I went into the vineyard of the nuptial house and found there all the children for whom I had worked, whom I had clothed. They were entwined among the vines and growing with them. The boys were just above the knots of the vine, their hands and feet twisted in the branches, their arms extended in the form of a cross. From them grew branches laden with grapes. The girls bore no grapes, but great ears of wheat.

Here I had to work hard, for entangled around the wheat and grapes were two kinds of weeds against which the Lord had warned the bridegrooms of Sichar to guard in the cultivation of the fields and vineyards. They can easily be cleared from the vines, but not from the wheat.

I took what the girls produced, crushed the grains between my hands, ground them with a stone, sifted the flour—which seemed too coarse—through very fine gauze, and took it to the sacristy of the Church along with a whole cask of wine that I had made from the grapes. I was told what it all signified, but my pains were so great that I forgot it.

Then I saw religious going out of the vineyard into the different houses of their order. Among them were many for whom I had made clothes, whom I had prepared for school, for confession and communion. The girls from whom I had taken the wheat to grind and to make into bread became nuns. The boys, who bore the grapes for the Church—that the wine should be changed into the blood of the Lord as the bread into his body—entered the priesthood. Wheat is heavier, more material, and signifies nourishment; it is flesh. Wine is spirit. Wine is blood.[1]

When later I returned to the nuptial house I found in two separate halls the youths and maidens who were to enter different orders. They were the children of the vine. They had already been replaced by others. In both halls I saw an apparition of the Mother of God seated on a throne. The halls were full of magnificent, shining, heavenly fruits, which the future religious took with them when they left the house, and scattered throughout

---

[1] As Anne Catherine related the above, she spoke also of the great dangers that menaced the Church, urging the pilgrim to unite with her in prayer, renunciation, and mortification, and to endeavor to overcome himself—saying: "It often happens that I cannot approach the pilgrim. I am held back, my soul is restrained. It certainly comes from our sins."

the Church. The children of the vine are all those whom I clothed and directed during my life.

*Anne Catherine's labors, as we have already remarked, were accompanied by uninterrupted physical sufferings, the most excruciating and varied. To encourage herself, she used often to say: "Now is a holy time, the new ecclesiastical year is approaching, and the old one bears with it many faults that must be redeemed by suffering. I have much work to do, and so I must suffer." She often lay as if at the point of death. One day, feeling a chilly sensation around her heart, she requested her sister to apply a warm cloth; but the latter did so only after having steeped it in hot wine which brought on most painful vomitings.*

*On November 27, 1820, Anne Catherine awoke from ecstasy with a cry of pain, the blood gushing from the wound in her side, and said:*

I saw high above me a resplendent figure from which streamed rays of light: they met in a sharp arrow and pierced my side. I cried out with the pain. For some days I have constantly had before me a double picture of the Church, the Church Triumphant treating with the Church Militant. The former I see as a beautiful, heavenly Church on a mountain of precious stones. In it are holy pastors and angels making entries on tablets and rolls of parchment, which seem to be the accounts of the Church Militant—the faults and omissions of the clergy and the faithful, faults and omissions that abound everywhere.

Then I have pictures of the innumerable shortcomings of priests and their neglect of their flocks. I see people ill-prepared kneeling at the communion table; others left without consolation in the confessional; negligent priests and soiled altar ornaments; the sick not consoled, or receiving the holy viaticum too late; relics disrespectfully thrown around, etc. Then I sigh ardently to remedy these evils. I implore God to satisfy His justice on me, to accept my good will in reparation for the faults of weak members of the Church, and I unite my sufferings to the inexhaustible, superabundant sufferings of Christ. I see sin effaced by the angels and saints, and the omissions of priests in the service of God and the salvation of souls supplied in most wonderful ways...

The Mother of God has divided the task among seven persons, most of them females. I see among them the stigmatisee of Cagliari and Rosa Maria Serra, as also others whom I cannot name. I see too a Franciscan in the Tyrol and a priest in a religious house among the mountains; the latter suffers unspeakably from faults committed in the Church. I too received my share. I know my pains, their cause and effect. I shall have to suffer the whole week.

*Till noon today (December 2, 1820), says the pilgrim, Anne Catherine suffered intensely throughout her whole person. Her hands were icy-cold, she looked like one who had died on the rack. The pains in her head were the most violent, but she endured all with loving patience. She said:*

Last night I saw St. Bibiana. She did not help me, but she was so kind, and the sight of her sufferings gave me strength for my own. I had a vision of the different kinds of martyrdom. I saw the holy martyrs piling up all sorts of instruments of torture until they formed a high and wonderful tower on the summit of which appeared the cross. Then with the Blessed Virgin Mary at their head they surrounded this trophy of their victories. I saw too all who had suffered like myself and all who now, at the close of the ecclesiastical year, are sharing with me the task of expiation. I saw myself pierced from head to foot with thorns.

I have constant visions of the two churches, Triumphant and Militant, and I must labor for three places in which all goes wrong. My last work was to gather honey from thistles—a heavy, painful task. I began by gathering figs from thorns, I ended with honey from thistles. There is a small, white worm in the large ripe thistle-heads that possesses virtue against fever and rheumatism, and especially incurable earaches. It is to be bound on the pulse of children, but taken internally by adults.

*This worm Anne Catherine had mentioned before. She described it as solitary and not found in all thistles. Toward evening her pains ceased at the same hour they had commenced eight days previously. She fell into a state of utter prostration, and sank as if without consciousness into a light slumber of a few instants. Her whole appearance had in it something singularly sweet, lovely, and childlike. The water that was offered her she refused with a smile, saying "No, I dare not pour water on my pains. They might return. I see them going."*

# At the Close
## of the Ecclesiastical Year

ON *December 3, 1820, Anne Catherine was exhausted by pain and tormented by domestic cares; nevertheless she made an effort to relate a vision she had had the preceding night. She lay prostrate and miserable after her labors and sufferings of the last eight days with continual vomiting of blood, bleeding of her side, and bloody sweats—though she never ceased, day or night, making caps for poor children. The greater part of several nights she passed in a sitting posture, her head resting on her knees. She was unable to lie down and still too weak to sit upright. Her heart and breast were torn with racking pains and the hot tears flowed copiously from her eyes, greatly aggravating her misery. Another vision showed her the Church—after being purified with im-mense trouble and fatigue—again degraded and dishonored by faithless ministers. St. Barbara appeared and consoled her, reminding her that she too had labored and prayed in vain for the conversion of her own father. Then she had a vision on the state of several individuals among the clergy who fulfilled not their duty toward the souls entrusted to them. She saw that they would have to render an account for all the love, all the consolation, all the exhortations, all the instructions upon the duties of religion that they do not give their flock; for all the benedictions they do not distribute, although the power of the hand of Jesus is in them; and for all they omit to do in imitation of Jesus. They will have to give a strict account to Jesus for their neglect of souls. For such pastors she had to undergo great trouble and fatigue, carrying them in spirit through water, and praying for such of them as were tempted.*

*St. Hildegarde and St. Catherine of Sienna often saw the Church under the form of a virgin or a matron, sick, persecuted, struck with leprosy, their spiritual labors assuming an analogous form. And so too did Anne Catherine find in the nuptial house and its dependencies the Church symbolized under the form of a matron in various positions. In the last week of Advent, 1819, she related the following:*

As I was going to Bethlehem, I found on the road to the nuptial house an old matron covered with ulcers that she tried to conceal under her soiled mantle. I invoked St. Francis Xavier to overcome my repugnance and I drained her sores, from which immediately streamed forth rays of light that shed their brilliancy all around. The draining[1] of these wounds was wonderfully sweet and pleasant. A resplendent lady floated down from on high, took from the matron—who was now almost well—her old stiff mantle, threw around her her own beautiful, shining one, and disappeared. The matron now shone with light and I took her into the garden of the nuptial house, from which she had formerly been driven. It was while wandering around that she had fallen sick. I have never been able to get her any farther than the garden, which I found overrun by weeds and the flowers nearly all dead, because the gardeners were not united. Each one gardened for himself alone. They did not consult the old man placed over them, they gave themselves no trouble about him. The poor old man was sick; he knew not of the spreading weeds until the thistles and brambles mounted up to his very windows. Then he gave orders for them to be rooted out.

The matron who had received the mantle from the Mother of God carried a treasure in a box, a Holy Thing that she guarded without knowing clearly what it was. It is the mysterious spiritual authority of the Church, with which they in the nuptial house no longer want to have anything to do, which they no longer understood. But it will again silently increase, and they who resist will be driven from the house. All will be renewed.

*During the above recital, Anne Catherine had assumed a listening attitude, as if in expectation of someone's approach. Suddenly she was rapt in ecstasy. She was with her Spouse, whom she tenderly conjured to allow her to suffer for the matron and for "those three homeless women, wandering about with their poor children"—symbols of the various denominations separated from the Church, wandering out of the sheepfold. "There," she exclaimed, still in ecstasy, "there I can suffer no more, there all is pure joy! Ah! leave me here a while longer, leave me here to be of service to my neighbor!" At this moment one of her fellow-religious, with whom she had previously made an appointment, appeared at the door; but seeing her in ecstasy she was about to retire when Anne Catherine called out: "Here is a person who wants something. This is for her,*

---

[1] The word "sucking" is used in the original notes, a term used at the time in connection with medical treatment of ulcerated tissue.

*and this for her landlady!"—and so saying, she took from the closet near the bed some packages of coffee and handed them to her former companion. When the latter withdrew, Anne Catherine began to thank God with signs of delight. "By this alms," she exclaimed, "I have obtained the deliverance of a poor soul from purgatory. I wanted as many as there were grains of coffee; however, I got one!" And she gazed in rapture on the glory of the ransomed soul.*

*On Christmas she related the following:*

I was in the garden of the nuptial house. The matron there was sick, but trying to put things here and there in order. The sheepfold I had seen earlier had become a church, the nut-hedges around the stable were withered, the nuts dried up and empty.[1] I saw blessed souls in antique priestly robes cleaning out the church, taking down the spider webs. The door stood open and all was becoming brighter and brighter. It seemed as if the masters were doing the work of their servants, for the people in the nuptial house, though making a great bustle, did nothing—they were disunited and dissatisfied. They all expected to enter the church when in order, but some were to be excluded. The church continued to grow cleaner and brighter. Suddenly there spouted up a beautiful fountain. Its water, pure as crystal, flowed out on all sides, through the walls and into the garden, refreshing everything—all was blooming and joyous. Above it rose a shining spiritual altar, a pledge of future increase. The church and everything in it kept growing larger and larger, the saints continued their work, and the bustle in the nuptial house became greater.

*Of separate denominations, Anne Catherine spoke as follows:*

I came across the house with the weathercock. People were going in and out with books in their hands; there is no altar in it, all looks bare. I went through it. It is like a public highway, benches and seats thrown here and there—some have been stolen; the roof is in a bad state, and through the rafters can be seen the blue sky. I saw two mothers covered with ulcers wandering around with two children by the hand. They seemed to be lost; a third, the most wretched of all, lay with a little child near the

---

[1] Nuts signify discord.

dilapidated meeting-house, unable to move. These three women were not very old and not dressed like common people. They wore long, narrow garments which they seemed to draw around them in order to hide their sores. I saw that the children derived no strength from them; but that on the contrary all the mothers' strength came from the children. The mothers were not what they ought to be, but the poor children were innocent. Homeless, they tottered along one after the other, tramping about everywhere, lodging miserably and thus contracting disease.

I saw them again later on in the night. I drained their sores and bound them up with herbs. I wanted to take them to the Church, but they were as yet too timid and they turned away. These Christians separated from the Church have no place near the holy sepulcher, although they now try to introduce themselves into such places. They have lost the priestly ordination and rejected the holy sacrifice of the mass to their own great misfortune.

I spoke to the poor wanderers and their children. Surely they will soon be better off! They are like old trees sending up new shoots, for which reason they are not cut down. The children represent souls making efforts to return to the Church and to draw after them their famished mothers who are weak and wholly governed by them. The women nearest the Church (the Catholic Church) have each two sprightly children by the hand whose every wish they follow; the third, lying sick on the road near the ruined meeting-house, has only one child, smaller than the others, but it is still a child, and she too will come.

Again I met the two women with their four children nearer to the nuptial house. The children would not be quieted. They dragged their mothers after them, but they would not go into the garden—they stood outside timid, frightened, and quite amazed at what they saw; they had never thought of such things. I prayed again before the crib for the poor mothers that they might at last enter the garden of the nuptial house, and I saw the matron go out to look for them and coax them in. But she behaved so mysteriously, pretending to be only taking a walk; she looked so furtive and timid that I became anxious, especially when I saw that she wanted to go first to a shepherd not of the fold. I feared she had not her box with her, that consequently she was weak and the shepherd would be able to prevent her returning to the nuptial house. I was so anxious for her to go straight up to the women! I went out to meet her and found to my great relief that she had her box with her, but I was sorry to see that she was not quite cured. Some of her wounds had healed too quickly, corruption was still within, and that was what had prevented her giving the invitation to the mothers properly; her timidity proceeded from it. She went not straight on in the name of Jesus.

I spoke a great deal with her and I found that she was not full of charity. She was so emphatic with regard to her rights, her privileges, her possessions, that one could easily see she was not animated by that virtue. I asked her what she had in the box. She answered: "It is a Mystery, a Holy Thing." She knew not what it was nor what use to make of it, but kept it locked up. She was displeased at my not curing her perfectly. I led her past the shepherd to the vagrant mothers whom the four children were dragging to meet her. She accosted them a little stiffly at first, and tried to persuade them to be reconciled with her and go into the garden of the nuptial house. The children wanted to do so, but the mothers insisted on speaking first to the shepherd—so they went all together to see him. When they found him, the matron addressed him. I was in dread lest, dissatisfied at not being entirely cured, she would manage things badly. This really was the case. She made indiscreet assertions, saying that she owned everything, all belonged to her—grace, strength, goods, rights, etc.

The shepherd wore a three-cornered cap and was not very gracious. He said: "What is in that box you are carrying around with you?" She answered that it was a mystery, and one might readily perceive that it was indeed a mystery even to herself. He replied disdainfully: "Indeed! If you come again with your mystery, I'll hear nothing of it. It is on account of your traffic in mysteries that we are separated from you. Whatever will not bear the light of day, the scrutiny of all, is worth nothing," and so they parted. The mothers would not now go with her, and she and I returned to the garden alone. But the children could not be prevented from running after us. They seemed to have a special attraction for the matron and went with her into the garden when, after examining everything, they ran back to tell their mothers all they had seen. They were very much impressed.

*During the last week of the ecclesiastical year (November, 1820) Anne Catherine saw the result of her labors for the conversion of schismatics:*

In my sufferings I invoke the dear Mother of God, that all hearts drawing near to the truth may be converted and enter the Church. Mary appeared to me in the nuptial house and told me I would have to cook for two hundred and twenty different guests. I had to gather all kinds of fruits and vegetables upon which dew from the heavenly gardens had fallen. My task resembled that of a pharmacist, for I had to prepare mixtures against spiritual evils. It was quite different from ordinary cooking. By the fire of charity something earthly had to be destroyed and the ingredients intimately mixed together—it was a troublesome work. Mary explained to me all I had to do, as well as the signification and effect of the various spices which, according to the spiritual state of this or that guest, were to be added to the food. All these symbolical operations in vision were most painful to my earthly nature. During my work I saw the hard and difficult points in some natures softened; and, according to the different defects of character, was my task more or less difficult. At last, I saw the guests arriving at the nuptial house and partaking of the food prepared for them, and at the same time I saw in far-off countries many hurrying with the children of the Church to the banquet of the Lord.

## Conversion of an Ancient Sect (*Maronite*)

I WENT to Bethlehem. I went in reality, with great fatigue and rapidity. Near the nuptial house I met an old woman, so old that one might think she had lived at the birth of Christ. She was so tightly enveloped in a black robe from head to foot that she could hardly walk. She begged my aid and accepted also some alms and clothing; but she persisted in hiding something from me—of which however I had an instinctive knowledge that had chiefly attracted me to her. It was an infant that she kept concealed under her mantle as if she were ashamed of it, or feared I would deprive her of it. She seemed to own nothing but this child, to live for it alone, and she hid it as if she had stolen it. But she had to give it up to me.

Ah! it was pitiful to see how tightly and painfully it was swathed; it could not move a limb. I loosened some bandages that were injuring its health, bathed it, and wanted to take charge of it, to which however the old woman would not consent. I thought if the little thing, which loved me and clung to me with its hands now free, were allowed to run around the nuptial house, it would grow very fast. I thought also that if I had the old woman in the garden of the nuptial house, she could help me clear away the weeds.

I told her that I would soon return, and that if I found her behaving more reasonably toward the child she should receive more help from me. The poor, feeble creature is proud of her origin and the perfect preservation of the customs of the Primitive Church among her people. It is on this account she is so closely enveloped and so solitary, and that the sect lives scattered in little isolated groups. She really means nothing bad, but she has become horribly stubborn and ignorant.

So it always happens when the wife separates from the husband and wants to preach.[1] She goes apart into the mountains, and swathes her child tightly that it may not grow. She conceals it to preserve its innocence. But while the old swather thinks thus to guard her child, she has nothing for her pains but her miserable obstinacy and helplessly drags herself here and there through the wilderness.

With heartfelt pity and in all charity I represented to her her unreasonableness, her poverty, her obstinacy that drove her even to starvation, her pride, and her misery. Again and again I conjured her to have pity on herself, to turn from her absurd isolation to the source of life, to the holy sacraments of the Church. But she was hardened in her self-will. She spurned me haughtily, saying that Catholics practice not what they teach. I replied that to turn away from the teacher of truth on account of the faults of

---

[1] This and what immediately follows is of course meant as a parable or allegory.

individuals would be as unreasonable as to abandon virtue on account of the wicked. She had nothing to reply, though she still persevered in her obstinacy.

The poor woman has been driven from the holy sepulcher, to which she no longer has a right. But in the spiritual church that I see above the grotto of Bethlehem, prayer is still offered for her. It is her good fortune to possess still a living fiber by which she derives a little strength. Ah! I hope she will yet return!

*In the Advent of the preceding year Anne Catherine had already had dealings with this sect, the Maronites, and their chief. She then received a task that was to continue for the next five years, ending in October, 1822, by a mission given to bring about their reunion with the Church of Rome.*

*She said in December, 1818:* Among those whom I met on my way to the nuptial house there were more women than men. This surprised me. They wore long robes, their heads bound with linen, one end hanging down behind. Near them was one of their priests, a poor helpless fellow, not like a priest. He scarcely knew how to read or pray!

A fiery wild horse was brought to him to tame, but he ran away in fright, followed by all his people. Then my guide ordered me to mount the animal. He helped me upon his back himself. I sat sideways, the horse becoming quite gentle. I was ordered to ride five times around the place where the people were gathered, each time widening the circle, to keep off the impure beasts I had already driven away but that were doing their best to return. I chased them away at last, and on my fifth round discovered a sheepfold. I thought, "You must make a turn around it in order to unite it with the Church." Then I returned to the priest with the horse, which had become quite gentle. It had no saddle, only a bridle.

*This horse of the desert is a symbol of wild, uncurbed nature that the weak priest could not master. But Anne Catherine mounted and tamed him to prove that it could be subdued by the discipline of the True Church clothed with strength and authority from God. The five turns on the horse signified the five ecclesiastical years at the end of which the stray sheep would return to the fold.*

*Anne Catherine also described the Greek schism:*

On my way from Bethlehem to the garden of the nuptial house

I met a distinguished looking gray-haired man wandering around sick and covered with wounds. I understood that he had lost or wasted something belonging to his family and that he was looking for it, unconscious that it lay quite near him. He appeared to belong to a matron whom I saw wrapped in a mantle near the garden of the nuptial house, but he did not want to go to her. He has apparently more repugnance to her than she to him. He always carries with him an old black wooden cross, about as long as one's arm and in shape like a Y. It struck me that he must have had it a long time, for it is well-used and quite polished. He holds on to it most tenaciously.

Ah! you dear old man, of what advantage is the wooden cross to you if it makes you forget your Savior! The poor man is so hardened, so obstinate, so full of his own ideas. One cannot make him move, and he himself advances not a step. He has been separated from his wife a long time and he will not be reconciled to her because she cannot grant him what he demands. I fear great evils will yet follow from their disunion!—I cured something in the perverse old man.

*When the pilgrim heard the above, he expressed his admiration at the merciful dispensations of almighty God, who deigned not only to relieve the corporal wants of the poor by means of His faithful servant, but also to grant spiritual assistance to the stray children of the Church. Anne Catherine replied:*

It would indeed be a matter of astonishment if one lived only in one's self, but the love of Jesus makes all his members One. Every work of mercy performed for his wounded members goes to the Church as to the Body of Jesus. The perverse old man with the cross has no child. He will not listen to reason, he will never come round, he will yet cause many miseries and troubles. The sick matron with the Holy Thing in the box has no child either. She is the Church Herself with the various diseases existing in her members, and like her she is ill-treated and repulsed by her children. After all, she is now once more in the garden.

# A Comparison With
# the Visions of St. Hildegarde

ANNE *Catherine's visions, as well as her whole mission upon earth, bear a striking analogy to those of St. Hildegarde, as may be seen by a perusal of the magnificent epistle the latter addressed in 1170 to the Provost Werner of Kirchheim. The saint, in obedience to a divine command, had undertaken a journey into Swabia in order to portray the state of the Church before the clergy of Kirchheim. The impression produced by her words was so powerful that after her return home the provost wrote to her begging in his own name and "that of his fellow-laborers," that they might meditate constantly upon a copy of what, under the inspiration of the Holy Spirit, she had said on the negligence of priests in offering the holy sacrifice. The following is a copy of Hildegarde's reply:*

✝ ✝ ✝ ✝

Confined to my bed by sickness, I had in the year of the Lord, 1170, a beautiful vision of a lady more lovely and attractive than the human mind can paint. Her form reached from earth to sky, her countenance shone with splendor, her eyes were fixed on heaven. She wore a shining robe of white silk and a mantle embroidered with precious stones: emeralds, sapphires, pearls, and flowers of gold. On her feet were shoes of onyx.

But her face was soiled with ashes, her robe torn on the right side, her mantle stained, her shoes covered with mud. In a clear, plaintive voice she cried: "Hear, O ye heavens! My face is disfigured! Be afflicted, O earth, for my vesture is rent! And thou, O abyss, tremble, for my shoes are soiled! The foxes have holes and the birds nests, but I, I have none to assist or console me. I have no support on which to lean! I was hidden in the bosom of the Father until the Son of Man, conceived and born of a Virgin, shed his blood, in which He espoused me and endowed me with His grace—that in the pure regeneration of spirit and water I might bring forth those anew whom the serpent's venom had infected.

"But my nurses, the priests—who should have preserved my countenance resplendent as the aurora, my robe brilliant as the lightning-flash, my mantle glittering as precious stones, my shoes white as snow—have sprinkled my face with ashes, torn my robe, soiled my mantle, and stained my shoes. They who should have adorned me have allowed me to perish. They sully my countenance when they handle and eat my Bridegroom's flesh and blood in spite of the impurity of their life, their fornications, their adulteries, and their rapacity in selling and buying—a thing unlawful for them. Yes, they cover his flesh and blood with opprobrium. It is like casting a newborn babe to swine.

"As man became flesh and blood at the very instant that God formed him from the slime of the earth and breathed into him the breath of life, so the same power of God, at the words of the priest, changes the offering of bread, wine, and water upon the altar into the true flesh and true blood of Christ, my Spouse—which however, on account of the blindness occasioned by Adam's fall, man cannot see with his corporal eyes.

"The wounds of my Spouse remain fresh and open as long as those of sinful man are not closed. They are outraged by those priests who, instead of preserving me pure and serving me in holiness, seek with insatiable avidity to heap up riches, and benefice on benefice. They tear my vesture by their infidelity to the law, to the gospel, to the priesthood. They stain my mantle by their neglect of the precepts laid down for them instead of fulfilling them joyfully and perfectly by continence like unto the beauty of the emerald, by alms-giving like unto the sapphire, and by the practice of all other good works that honor God as so many precious stones. They soil my shoes by walking not in the right path—the rough and difficult path of justice—and by failing to give good example to their inferiors; but in my shoes I perceive the hidden light of truth among a few.

"The false priests deceive themselves; they crave the honor attached to their functions while dreading the trouble. But it is impossible for them to have one without the other, since to no one who has not labored will wages be given. When God's grace touches a man, it urges him to labor for the reward. God now punishes man by raining evils upon him. He covers the earth with them as with a mist until its verdure disappears and it is clothed in darkness. But the abyss will tremble when He will come in His wrath, making heaven and earth the instruments of His vengeance and man's destruction. Arrogant princes and nations will rise up against you, O ye priests who have hitherto neglected me! They will drive you forth, they will rob you of your wealth, because you have neglected your sacred ministry. They will cry: 'Cast out of the Church these adulterers, these robbers full of iniquity!' In so doing they think they render God a service, saying that you have polluted His Church; therefore the scriptures say, 'Why have the nations raged and the people devised vain things? By God's permission the nations will rise up against you; they will have vain thoughts of you; they will esteem as naught your priestly dignity and consecration. The princes of the earth will unite to cast you down. Your rulers will drive you from their territories, since your crimes have driven the innocent lamb far from you.'"

And I heard a voice from heaven saying: "This vision represents the Church—wherefore, O daughter of man, who dost see these things and hear these lamentations, announce it to the priests who have been instituted and ordained to guide and instruct the people, for to them in the person of the apostles it has been said: 'Go into the whole world and preach the gospel to every creature.' When God created man, He delineated in him *every creature*, as are written upon a scrap of parchment the seasons and numbers of a whole year; therefore it was that God named man *every creature*."

And I, poor woman, saw again a drawn sword floating in the air, one edge toward heaven, the other toward the earth. And it was raised above a spiritual race that the prophet foresaw when he exclaimed in astonishment: "Who are these, that fly as clouds, and as doves to their windows?" (Isaiah 60:8); for they who are raised above the earth, separated from ordinary men, they who should live holily, showing forth in their actions the simplicity of doves, are evil in their works and manners. And I saw the sword strike the priestly race in many places as Jerusalem was destroyed after the Savior's passion; and I saw also that in the time of tribulation God will spare many pure and upright priests who fear Him, even as He said to Elijah that he had left in Israel a thousand men who had not bent the knee to Baal. May the inextinguishable fire of the Holy Spirit be enkindled in you to convert you to better things!

# Further Spiritual
# Works and Travels

## Renewed Labors in the Nuptial House

ANNE *Catherine saw in the nuptial house not only the state of the Church in general but also that of individual dioceses. Münster in particular was shown her. In numerous symbolical pictures she saw its special necessities and how she was to aid it. Her first vision, recounted in December, 1819, clearly tended to the reawakening of piety throughout the country by devotion to the Blessed Virgin and the restoration of religious communities. In one of the chambers of the nuptial house called the "bridal chamber," she had to arrange the dowry and spiritual wedding garments for those for whom they were destined. This symbolized the effects of her sufferings and prayers, by which she obtained for many souls the grace of vocation to the religious life and the means of corresponding thereto. She had, besides, to avert dangers menacing the faith from foreign influences, to atone for the betrayal of the rights and privileges of the Church, for the cowardice of her children who tried to serve two masters—God and the world—and to wrestle with the consequences resulting therefrom. The following is what she relates on this point:*

I went to Bethlehem to meet Mary and Joseph and prepare a lodging for them. I took with me linen and coverings and also my sewing—for I had not yet finished all my work. I entered a house at which I thought they would arrive that night. It was like one of the large farmhouses of our own country, the roof not flat. The people were rough and uncouth. They had a large establishment, and when I asked them to prepare lodgings for Mary and Joseph, they answered that there was no room, that they expected many guests. And in truth, crowds of young and ill-bred people did begin to arrive. They set to work to prepare a repast. They spread the table, cooked, and danced about like mad people.

Again I asked a lodging for the Mother of God, but all the

answer I received was to be trodden upon and pushed from side to side. Then appeared the child in green, *Patience*, whom St. Cecilia had brought to me once before, and with his help I bore their ill-treatment calmly. These rude people did not seem wholly unknown to me; among them were many who had persecuted me. While they were refusing a lodging to the holy travelers, I had discovered a little unoccupied room that, however, they did not want to let me enter. They seemed to have something hidden in it. But I succeeded in getting in, and to my great surprise I found an old woman all covered with spider webs, whom they had imprisoned. I brushed her off and took her out to the wedding, but the guests were greatly agitated when they saw her. I reproached them with their treatment of her, when they all fled from the house and the old woman set about preparing another repast. Then I saw other young persons, mostly girls, who I knew wanted to lead a spiritual life, and I discovered another room that constantly and wonderfully increased in size and brightness. I saw in it the holy deceased of our own country—among them my mother, the lady of Vehme, and their guardian angels. They wore the old Franconian costume, and I kept thinking that my mother in her magnificent dress would never notice me.

I prepared the room for the holy family. Joseph and Mary arrived and were received most cordially. But they paid no attention to anything. They retired in the dark and sat down against the wall, when the whole place was instantly flooded with light. I knelt in veneration. Their stay was short. The old people of the house gazed curiously at the holy travelers through the open door and then withdrew—I thought through humility. In the meantime the old woman whom I had set free had grown quite young and beautiful. She was the most honorable person in the house, indeed she was the betrothed.[1] She was very lovely and dressed in the old peasant style. By degrees the whole house turned into a church, and where the fireplace had stood arose an altar.

As I went over the sea to the promised land, a sudden storm

---

[1] The old woman typifies the piety and faith of former times, the ancient religion of the country that was to be rejuvenated. The costume of the souls referred to the age in which that fervor reigned that was now to be renewed.

arose and I saw an open boat full of wicked, clamoring people. The thought occurred to me: "Those people use a boat, for the waters are deep. How does it happen that I can walk over them?"—and immediately, just like doubting Peter, I sank in the waves up to my neck. But my guide caught me by the arm, bore me to the shore, and reproached me with my want of faith. When I reached the nuptial house near Bethlehem I was going to pass it, but my guide made me go in, and he took me all through it. I saw many strangers in it, men and women. A fine-looking youth in blue uniform seemed to be in command, and there was also a tall, imperious woman strutting around with an important, insolent air. She was attending to everything, and pretending to know everything better than others. But ecclesiastics seemed to be banished from the premises. Although the bridal chamber was locked, still I was able to enter it. I found the walls hung with cobwebs, but the nuptial robes in good condition. There were four unfinished and twenty finished wax tapers, also twenty full sacks and four empty ones.

The youth followed me all over the house, astonished at all I did and said. He showed me a hole into which he and his people had swept—though not without difficulty—swarms of unclean animals, such as toads, etc. He tried to prevent my removing the stone that covered it, saying that I would run a risk in so doing. I replied that I had nothing to fear, having often cleaned the place out, and after peeping at the ugly things, I replaced the cover. Then he told me that his people could not cast these reptiles out. I replied that our priests could do it, and I bade him reflect upon it as a proof of their power. I found also a sealed package of writings whose seal, the youth told me, his people were absolutely unable to break—and I again directed his attention to their weakness. He replied that if they were indeed so weak, it was very imprudent in them to drag that great, imperious woman into the house. The latter was very bitter against me and exceedingly displeased at the young man's being with me. She had already tried to quarrel with me, scoffing at the brides, whom she called old maids, and at the woman with the box, etc. But, as she feared that the young man would put her out, she began to render herself necessary and important. She gathered up the linen of all in the house and prepared for a grand washing [general confession]. But the tub kept tipping over, first on one side, then on the other, so that she could get nothing done; all had to be taken out again wet and dirty. Then she got ready to bake a batch of bread which, like the washing, was another failure. But, not at all discouraged, she made a great fire, hung over it an enormous kettle containing something to be cooked, and spread herself out before it so that no one could approach, keeping up all the time for my benefit her tiresome prattle on the pope and antichrist. Suddenly the pot hook, the kettle, the whole chimney fell with a crash, the fire flew in all directions, and she and her companions scampered from the house, leaving the young man alone. The latter expressed his desire of returning to the Church in the garden of the nuptial house (that is, of becoming a Catholic). He typifies the views (modern pietism) that Protestants entertain of the Church. His uniform signifies the secular dress; his authority in the nuptial house, the pressure of the civil power on the Church in our country; and the insolent female is symbolical of the old Lutheran leaven.

I was in the nuptial house and I swept from the room of the stern superior straw, scraps of charred wood, and some kind of black mould, into a deep hole on the very edge of which I had to stand. The old Lutheran woman stood over in a corner enraged at my return and doing all she could to annoy me. She scattered, as if in defiance, a quantity of dirty trash around where I was. In sweeping it up, my broom happened to touch where she stood. She cried out that I need not sweep near her, she could do it herself. I replied that then she should not have thrown the dirt toward me.

Her daughter (shallow rationalism) was always occupied in adorning and beautifying herself, hiding her filthiness so as to catch the eye of the unwary and entice them to her, for she was not chaste. The odious, crafty boy was among the ecclesiastics, but the stern superior now saw more clearly into his intrigues and labored seriously to baffle them. I swept the filthy room that the Dean occupied when he came there, and he seemed a little confused. The schoolmaster (Overberg) had another bride whom he wanted to hand over to the Protestants. I saw too that the stern superior still wanted to remove me to Darfeld; but I had a vision that showed me how miserable I should have been there lying as if on a bed of state, and that Miss Soentgen would have played a role, if I had gone.

*Another time (Sunday, February 6, the Gospel of the Sowers) Anne Catherine spoke as follows:*

I saw three gardens or territories. The first was covered with rocks, mountains, and stones. The second with brushes, brambles, and weeds, abd here and there flowerbeds. The third, which was the largest and best cultivated, was full of seas, lakes, and islands—everything flourished, for it was fertile ground. I was in the middle one.

First I went—or rather, I gazed—into the rocky garden, which at the first glance looked like a mere scrap of land, but when considered attentively turned out, like all such pictures, to be indeed a little world. Here and there sprang up good grain among the stones, and the people wanted to transplant it to a bed. But a man came along, saying they should not do so because without the support afforded the plantlets by the thorns they would fall to the ground.

The best land was in the garden on the island. The grain there flourished and produced a hundredfold, but in some places the plants were entirely rooted up. The seed was in good condition, the little fields fenced in. I recognized in this garden other parts of the world and islands in which I so often see Christianity spreading.

In the central garden, the one in which I was, I saw by the weeds, by its neglected condition, that its gardeners were slothful. It had everything to make it productive, but it was neglected, choked with weeds, briars, and thistles. I saw in it the state of all the parishes in Europe, and the garden of the pope was not among the best.

In the part symbolical of my own country I saw a lord filling a deep pit with money, the produce of all the fields. Over the pit sat the devil. I saw to my amazement—and it made me laugh—a half-dozen sly, nimble little fellows cutting underground passages to the pit and dragging off with the greatest ease all the produce that had been so laboriously stowed away from above. At last the master spied one stealing off with a sack full of gold. He gazed down into the treasure-pit over which the devil watched so well and expressed his surprise at seeing it almost empty. But his servants told him that the fields produced no more, that they were badly cultivated, insufficiently manured, etc.

In the garden in which I live, I saw many fields attended by gardeners and workmen whom I know, and many beds in charge of under-gardeners. But very few of them sowed and cultivated even tolerably well. I saw it all overgrown with weeds, dry, and parched. I went from bed to bed, recognized all, and understood their condition. I saw people in perilous positions, running on the edge of a black abyss, others sleeping, others wasting their labor over crops of empty ears of corn, and among them some men going around like masters, giving orders, etc., although they really had no business there.

The poor creatures worked hard, digging and manuring, but with little success. Suddenly they dragged in a child stealthily. The place was shown me as the city of Münster, for I recognized most of the people. There was something repulsive, something that inspired horror, about the child. I saw that it was illegitimate: it knew not its father, and its mother had sinned with many. At first it only played around, but it soon showed itself in all its ugliness. It looked old, sick, pale, pock-marked. It was bold, proud, scornful, and servile. It never went to church, but ridiculed everything, dragging itself along laden with books and manuscripts. One ecclesiastic sent it to another. It insinuated itself everywhere, and to my surprise I saw some French priests whom I knew letting themselves be cajoled by it. Few opposed it, for it could perform wonders. It was so insinuating: it understood everything, spoke all languages. I saw it aiming chiefly at schoolmasters. The mistresses it either passed by or ridiculed, but it avoided me altogether. I feared it would do much harm, for wherever it went the garden was still more neglected, bearing rank weeds, but no fruit.

I saw that the pious schoolmaster (Overberg) would have nothing to do with it; the stern superior (Droste) let it go its way; another amused himself talking to it; but the dean gave it a particularly flattering reception, even wanting it to lodge in his house.

The child worried me the whole day. It introduced itself so readily everywhere, so quickly extended its influence, that it seemed to me a real pest. It is always before me with its old, insolent, unchildlike ways. I know that it signifies the new, rationalistic school system.

I have had a frightful vision of persecution. I was in the hands of a masked enemy who tried to drag me away secretly. I was already out of the house and was abandoning myself to the will of God when a dove flew around screaming so that it attracted a crowd of other birds. They kept up such a racket that my enemies hurried me back into the house. It was a perfect tumult. I recognized the birds as my old friends: a lark that my confessor had taken away from me in order to mortify me; a pigeon that I used to feed at my window in the convent; and some finches and redbreasts that used to light upon my head and shoulders in the cloister garden.

*Anne Catherine's frightful visions were repeated in proportion to the encouragement given to the illegitimate boy in the diocese of Münster, for as the representative of its spiritual interests, now so seriously endangered, she had to endure the wrong offered to the diocese by the ecclesiastical patrons of the boy. She saw, also, her enemies forming a project to get possession of her as soon as fresh effusions of blood should furnish them a pretext to remove her from Dülmen (at Dean Rensing's instigation), and for this to arm themselves with the authorization of ecclesiastical superiors. The sight filled her with such compassion for her persecutors that, although in ecstasy, she sprang up on her knees to say a rosary for them, and being in a profuse perspiration she suffered for several days from frequent and violent spells of coughing. Again it seemed to her that she was lying unprotected in a field and set upon by dogs, while twenty-four children whom she had clothed since Christmas stood around her, keeping them at bay. St. Benedict also came to her aid and helped her wonderfully. She exclaimed:*

I had to endure so much that, if it had not been for St. Benedict, I should surely have died. The saint appeared to me, promised me relief, but warned me not to be too discouraged if it were not accorded at once. Then I had a vision in which I saw myself under the form of another, seated on a stool and resting against the wall in a dying state unable to speak or move. Around stood priests and laymen conversing ostentatiously of this, that, and the other thing, but taking no notice whatever of me—that is, of the person who represented me. As I gazed on the scene I was filled with pity for the poor creature, when suddenly I saw St. Benedict indignantly making his way toward her through the throng of ecclesiastics,[1] and as he spoke to her I became conscious that she was none other than myself. He said he would send me holy communion. He introduced to me a gentle-looking young priest and martyr in alb and stole, who gave me the holy eucharist. Benedict said: "Be not surprised at the presence of this youth. He is a priest and martyr, my pupil Placidus." I felt, I tasted, the blessed sacrament, and I was saved. The gentlemen seemed to notice by my attitude what had happened, and they became more reserved. A stranger appeared wrapped in a mantle; he addressed them sternly and put them to shame. Benedict said: "Behold these priests! They strive after offices, but pass by the needy, saying: 'I have not time; or: It is not my duty, it is not customary, I have received no order to attend to it.'" Placidus showed me the parable of the Samaritan and how it applied to me—priest and Levite pass by, a stranger comes to my aid.

*From Quinquagesima Sunday the pains in Anne Catherine's wounds were so violent as frequently to deprive her of consciousness, but she received in vision many sweet consolations. All the poor old people to whom she had given alms in her youth passed before her one after another, displaying the gifts they had received from her. Even in the midst of her intense pains she could not restrain a smile at the sight of the multifarious articles produced for her amusement. The old people themselves seemed to be rejuvenated, while the clothes, food, and other alms she had once bestowed upon them bore no trace of time—indeed they too presented an improved appearance.*

*Here was an aged woman of Coesfeld, for whose sake she had years ago in a retired corner, in broad daylight, deprived herself of a skirt. There was a poor sick man to whom she had sent clothes, a package of the best tobacco and some cracknels (pretzels), since—being sick herself—she had nothing else in her cupboard. The sight of the cracknels amused her much, for they were over twenty years old. Instead of the tobacco, the old man laid on the table a fragrant bouquet (symbol of*

---

[1] The apparition of St. Benedict, the great teacher of the West, is connected with Anne Catherine's sufferings on account of the young schoolboy.

*sufferings). Then came an old woman, now rejuvenated, of whom Anne Catherine said:*

I had almost forgotten her. She had a daughter who turned out badly and whom, as she told me, she could not reclaim. She had vowed, if God would convert her daughter from her sinful life, to make the way of the cross on her knees; but it was quite impossible for her to do so, as she was old and weak. It would have taken three hours to perform the devotion, which would certainly have been too much for her. She told me of her vow and her great anxiety at not being able to fulfill it. I comforted her and promised to make satisfaction for her through the intervention of others. I went on my knees by night several times around a cross in a neighboring field for her intention.

I went to the holy land and saw our Lord on the banks of the Jordan. He said: "Now the time approaches for me to save my sheep. The lambs must be led up the mountain, and the sheep ranged around them." And seeing him so careful of his flock, I thought of my persecutors, who were instantly shown me running through a wilderness. Then the Good Shepherd said: "When I approach them, they injure me, they maltreat me," and I began to pray for them with all my heart, whereupon I obtained the gift of prayer—and I hope it will do some good. I saw that by means of my enemies I had advanced in the spiritual life. As I prayed for them, I saw, to my great surprise, the dean engaging in a plot against me.[1]

I had to carry many sick, lame, and crippled to a church in which all was in good order. Among them was Rave, whom I saved from drowning; the Landrath, whom I bore over a swamp; and Roseri, whom I found lying all bruised as if from a fall—he gave me much trouble. I found myself in vision near a wheat and rye field that lay very high. Around it were ditches, swamps, and deserts full of wild beasts that lay in wait to tear travelers to pieces, and had to be fed in order to keep them out of the fields.

---

[1] The pilgrim added these words: "This seems a little exaggerated." But from the fact of Dean Rensing's subsequent attempt to brand her an impostor, we know that Anne Catherine saw the truth.

For every one of them I had to procure—at the cost of great fatigue and amidst their incessant assaults—a different kind of food, plants, and berries. I had, besides, to carry and feed cats, tigers, swine, and a savage dog. The perspiration poured off of me. These animals signified the passions of the men who tried to get possession of me. I have imposed upon myself a heavy task. I have undertaken to obtain by my prayers this Lent the conversion of my enemies and the liquidation of their debts. I have already obtained this much—that they will not be punished for what they have hitherto done against me, if they only enter into themselves. I know what it is to bear sins and expiate by sufferings.

I have averted many dangers by prayer. I received a special instruction on this point, and I saw how much I am indebted to the protection of holy relics, for it is to the saints that I owe the failures of the project formed against me. I was not deceived. I saw for a certainty that it originated with the dean. Again I was to have been carried off by six men, among them two ecclesiastics, and subjected to a new investigation, but the vicar-general would not give his consent.

*Anne Catherine was so confident of her prayers being heard that she did not hesitate to announce to Dean Rensing the fact of her wounds having bled on the 9th of March. The pilgrim's notes on this occasion are as follows:*

On the evening of March 9th, all her wounds bled, those of her head the most copiously. But she is perfectly calm in spite of the uneasiness of those around her as to whether or not, or when or how, this fact of her bleeding again would be repeated. She lay immersed in contemplation. She knew all that was being done or said about her in different houses, even at a distance. Finally, she became ecstatic and looked fresh and young without a trace of age or pain. Her countenance wore a peculiarly bright expression, and she smiled with mingled devotion and gravity.

On the night of March 9th–10th, her wounds again bled, and next morning she sent word to the dean by her confessor. She believed she had thus discharged her obligation to the Landrath Boenninghausen. The bleeding lasted till three PM, and yet the dean came not to verify the fact. She had to engage her confessor to inform either the vicar-general or the Landrath of it.

*Good Friday, March 30th: Anne Catherine's sufferings up to this time have been steadily on the increase, and although in almost continual contemplation she has to receive the visits of her friends. But this increase of pain, and the terrible violence she endures in the transformation by which she renders testimony to the death of the Man-God, combine to diminish the effects of exterior distractions, and she is entirely absorbed by her task of expiation.*

*At ten that morning the pilgrim found her forehead, hands, and feet bleeding. He tried to remove the blood, but with little success on account of the intense pain any such attempt produced. She was also in dread of some new investigation. She hid the effusions as best she could from both the doctor and Abbé Lambert, fearful of the effect the fact might have upon the latter, himself sick and weak. Dean Rensing was again informed of her state, but he paid as little attention to the second announcement as to the first, merely sending her word not to trouble herself about the Landrath, that he, the dean, would take all upon himself.[1] She endured intolerable agony up to six pm, although, as she remarked, Jesus gave up the ghost at about one o'clock.*

*When contemplating the descent from the cross and Mary holding the body of her Son in her arms, the thought occurred to her: "How strong she is! She has not fainted once!"—whereupon she heard her angel's voice saying: "Well then, do thou feel what she felt!"—and on the instant she fainted away from the violence of her grief, for Mary's sword had pierced her soul.*

*The pilgrim had placed under her feet some relics wrapped in linen, which soon received a few drops of blood from her wounds. That evening he applied the little parcel to her shoulder, from which she was suffering acutely. She exclaimed, though in ecstasy:*

Strange! Here I see my Spouse alive surrounded by thousands of saints in the heavenly Jerusalem, and yonder I see him lying dead in the tomb! And what is this? Among the saints I see a person, a nun, whose hands, feet, side, and head are all bleeding, and the saints standing near her hands and feet, her side and shoulder!

---

[1] And yet before a year had passed, Dean Rensing accused Anne Catherine of imposture!

*The following year, 1821, she was told*: Take note, thou wilt shed thy blood with thy Lord not on the ecclesiastical, but on the real anniversary of his death.

*Good Friday of this year fell on April 20th. The pilgrim records: What has never before happened since Anne Catherine has had the stigmata, occurred today. Her wounds bled not, although it is Good Friday, and for the last few days they have even wholly disappeared, a circumstance for which she cannot account. She lay, however, in ecstatic contemplation of the passion when, at the instant of the Savior's crucifixion, the burgomaster suddenly entered her room, gazed sharply around, asked a few questions, and took his departure as unceremoniously as he had come. Strange sight! The poor, ignorant man and the helpless ecstatica face to face! He had come, as he said, by orders of superiors.*

*The pilgrim's journal of March 30, 1821, explains the above phenomenon respecting the date of her bloody effusions*: Anne Catherine celebrates Good Friday today. At ten this morning her face was covered with blood and her whole person bore the marks of the cruel scourging. About two PM the blood gushed from her hands and feet, but she was then in ecstasy, unconscious of the outer world, dreading not discovery, wholly absorbed in the contemplation of the work of redemption.

## Sufferings on Account of Mixed Marriages

I SAW many churches of this country in a sad state, as if betokening their future decay, and young ecclesiastics hurrying through their duties negligently. Entire parishes seemed dying out. I saw the nuptial house of Münster. The old woman and her daughter were absent, but there was an old man in it—a diplomatist, a pettifogger, whom the devil seemed to have raised up, so smooth, so cunning was he. A sort of council was being held and I saw the stern superior and Overberg earnestly acting together on some question of marriage. It made me sad to see only five others, one a very aged person, standing up for the right with these two men; the rest were all against them. The gathering was numerous and, to my great alarm, they began to dispute and quarrel. The superior's party at once withdrew, leaving the others to side with the Lutherans. But the saddest part of it was that some secretly joined the wicked party again.

I went again to the nuptial house which I found crowded with people of two different parties. Downstairs were the good around Droste and Overberg and with them the youth in blue uniform who seemed about to be converted. But he no longer wore his uniform, and seemed to be in high favor with the above-named gentlemen; they trusted him, he was all in all to them.

Tables stood around with chalices on them. The young people were sent out, as if on messages, but affairs did not go well. To the upper story they had built an outside staircase up which people were crowding, men and women, ecclesiastics and seculars, Catholics and Protestants. All up there was motion, activity, but the people were entirely separated from the Church, quite antagonistic to her. And yet I saw among them several priests whom I knew siding with the Protestant party against those downstairs. They ran up and down the whole time betraying the good party. But what alarmed me most was to see that the young man who gave himself out for a convert, whom the Catholic party so implicitly trusted, was an infamous traitor who secretly revealed upstairs all that went on below. I wept, I wanted to press through the crowd and disclose his treachery, but my guide restrained me, saying: "It is not yet time. Wait, let him betray himself!"

This spectacle lasted a long while, when something happened upstairs and the Protestant party were all cast out together. All that had mounted by the outside staircase, that had not entered the sheepfold by the right door, were ignominiously expelled and took to flight. I saw in the garden a flower bed out of which arose a narrow ladder that reached to heaven. They who had been driven out were not allowed to mount it. I saw people ascending and descending to help up others. I saw some apparently very distinguished people turned away, while others mounted the ladder which hung down from heaven. It was guarded by a youth with a drawn sword who repulsed the unworthy.

*The preceding vision referred to mixed marriages, from which Anne Catherine endured lifelong torments. She used to lie for whole days a prey to violent cramps of the bowels, her arms extended in the form of a* cross. *She saw again in the nuptial house the Lutheran cook and her project of marrying her illegitimate daughter to the young schoolboy who was now of age. She beheld the clergy open to all sorts of attacks on the score of such marriages, now so numerous, and she exerted herself to enlist the prayers of others in behalf of their members vacillating between right and wrong—all this she saw in pictures back as far as the Mosaic period, since the Church has never countenanced such unions excepting in cases of absolute necessity. She saw how detrimental they are to the Church, how they weaken her influence:*

I saw Moses before reaching Mount Sinai, separating entirely from the people and sending away some of the degenerate Israelites who had married among the pagans. They had chosen wives from among the Madianites, I think, and so lost their nationality. Their descendants had mingled with the Samaritans and these again with the Assyrians, and finally had became heretics and idolators. I saw such marriages contracted out of necessity during the Babylonian captivity, but they teemed with fatal consequences. I saw such unions tolerated in the infancy of the Church on account of the state of the times and for the propagation of the faith. But never has the Church consented that the offspring should be reared out of her own fold, an event that happens only by violence. As soon as she was solidly established, the Church positively prohibited such marriages. I have seen whole countries from which the orthodox faith has entirely disappeared in consequence of them; still more, I have seen that, if the new system of marriage and education succeeds, in less than a century affairs will be in a bad state in our own land."

*In July, 1821, Brentano writes:* For the last week Anne Catherine has writhed on her bed from the intensity of her sufferings, groaning and finding relief in no position. She is however always in contemplation and spiritual action, occupied day and night with the ecclesiastical affairs of Germany, whose miseries she sees far and near. She says it is difficult to converse with those around her, as she is always absent in spirit. *She says:*

I have to go from place to place, to pastors and statesmen, sometimes individually, sometimes collectively, to suggest such or such things to them; the whole day is often spent in this manner. On entering their council halls I see, perhaps, one of the members advocating or subscribing to something useless or prejudicial and I urge him to desist, not to violate justice. I constantly have visions of schools. I see great boys oppressed by infants yet unborn (but whom I know), and grown girls ruled by little ones. They are pictures of the new systems that spring from the unlawful union of pride and false illumination. All this is purely symbolical, but I generally recognize the fathers of such children, or systems.

*One morning the pilgrim found her in a high fever and convulsed with pain, though in contemplation and utterly unconscious of all around her. While he stood regarding her compassionately, Gertrude (her sister) announced a beggar. The pilgrim sent her about half a franc in Anne Catherine's name and unseen by her. Scarcely had the woman received the alms than Anne Catherine began to smack her lips as if she had just tasted something, murmuring: "How sweet! How sweet! Whence came that morsel you gave me?" Then, although unable to move an instant before, she sat up in her bed and said with a smile, but still in ecstasy: "See how you have strengthened me with that sweet morsel! It was fruit plucked from a heavenly tree that you gave me!" The pilgrim, amazed at the incident, recorded the following words in his journal: "How close is the union of this soul with Christ, since the words of the gospel are so plainly verified in her: What you do to the least of my brethren, you do unto me!"*

## The Essence of Rationalism

I WAS at the nuptial house and I saw a large, boisterous wedding party arriving in coaches. The bride had around her a crowd of attendants. She was a tall, insolent, extravagantly dressed person, a crown on her head, jewels on her breast. Around her neck hung three tinsel chains and lockets with numberless trinkets shaped like crabs, toads, frogs, locusts, cornucopias, rings, whistles, etc. She was dressed in scarlet, and on her shoulders wriggled an owl whispering first into one ear, then into the other. It seemed her familiar spirit. The woman pompously entered the nuptial house with her suite and baggage, driving out all whom she had found therein. The old gentlemen and the ecclesiastics had scarcely time to gather their books and papers together, for all had to depart. Some went with disgust, others betraying a little interest in the courtesan. They either betook themselves to the church or scattered around in groups, sauntering here and there. The woman upset everything in the house, even the table with the goblets on it; only the bridal chamber and the apartment dedicated to the Mother of God remained undisturbed. Among her followers was that cunning hypocrite whom I had lately seen serving two masters; he was all-powerful with her. The learned boy was her son; he had now grown up and he boldly pushed himself in everywhere. One thing was very remarkable: the woman, her baggage, her books, all swarmed with shining worms, and she bore around her the fetid odor of those sparkling beetles that one recognizes by their smell. The women with her were mesmeric prophetesses who prophesied and supported her. It is well there are such people. They pursue their wickedness until they go too far, when they are discovered and the good are separated from the bad. After upsetting the whole house, she went out into the garden and trampled it under foot; wherever she passed, the flowers faded and died, all turned to worms and infection.

But this ignoble bride wanted to marry, and no one would suit her but a pious, intelligent young priest, one of the twelve, I think, whom I so often see doing great things under the guidance of the Holy Spirit. He was among those who had fled from the house on her entrance, but she enticed him back with the sweetest words. When he returned, she showed him everything and wanted to place him over all. He hesitated a little, when she threw off all reserve and used every imaginable artifice to induce him to marry her. The young priest became indignant, solemnly cursed her and her arts as those of an infamous courtesan, and quickly withdrew.

Then I saw all her attendants trying to escape, swooning, dying, turning black. The whole house grew dark and swarmed with worms that ate into everything, and the woman herself sank worm-eaten to the ground, all dried up like tinder. I crushed some of the worms lying there dead and shining and found that they too were all dried up, burned to ashes.

When everything had fallen to dust and silence reigned around, the young priest returned with two others, one an old man who looked like a Roman legate. He carried a cross which he set up in front of the charred nuptial house. After having drawn something from the cross he entered the house and threw open the doors and windows while his companions outside prayed, consecrated, and exorcised. Then a furious storm arose. The wind blew through the house, driving out before it a black vapor that floated toward a great city and hung over it in heavy clouds. The nuptial house, thus purified, was again occupied by people selected from among the former occupants, and some of the retinue of the unchaste bride, who were now converted, were installed in it. All began again to prosper and the garden once more flourished.

## The Body of the Church—Labors of the Harvest

I WAS in the church of the nuptial house (*in June, 1820*), where a ceremony was being performed, as if preparatory to the setting out of harvesters. I saw the Lord Jesus as a shepherd, the apostles and disciples with the saints and blessed in an upper choir, while in the nave of the church were crowds of priests and laymen still alive, many of whom I know. The ceremony seemed intended to invoke a blessing on the harvest, to bring laborers to it. Jesus seemed to be inviting them in these words: "The harvest is great, but the laborers are few; pray, therefore, the Lord of the harvest to send laborers into his harvest." Then he sent the apostles and disciples forth with blessings and prayers, just as he had done while on earth. I too went out to the harvest with some of the priests and laics still alive. Some excused themselves and would not go, when immediately their places were filled by the saints and blessed spirits.

Then I saw the harvest field near the nuptial house and in it a body rising up toward the sky. It was horribly mutilated, the hands and feet cut off, and large holes in many parts of it. Some of the wounds were fresh and bleeding, others covered with decayed flesh, and others were swollen and gristly. The whole of one side was black and worm-eaten. My guide explained to me that it represented the body of the Church, as also the body of all humankind. He showed me in what way each wound referred to some part of the world, and I saw at a glance far distant nations and individuals who had been cut from it. I felt the pain of the amputation of these members as acutely as if they had been cut from my own person.

"Should not one member sigh after another, suffer for another? Should not one strive that the other be healed and again united to the body? Should not one suffer for the welfare of another?" said my guide. "The nearest, the most painful amputations are those made from the breast around the heart." I thought, in my simplicity, that this must mean brothers and sisters, near relations, and Gertrude came to my mind. But then it was said to me: "Who are my brethren? They who keep my Father's commandments are my brethren. Blood relations are not the nearest to the heart. Christ's blood-relations are they who were once of the same mind, Catholics who have fallen away from the faith."

Then I saw how quickly the side of the body was healed. The proud flesh in the wounds are heretics, and dissenters form the gangrened part. I saw every member, every wound, and its signification. The body reached to heaven—it was the Body of Christ. The sight made me forget my pains, and I began to work with all my strength to cut, to bind, and carry the sheaves to the nuptial house. I saw the saints helping from on high and the twelve future apostles taking part successively in the labor.[1] I saw also some living laborers, but they were few and at great distances apart. I was almost worn out, my fingers ached from binding, and I was drenched with perspiration. I had just one sheaf more of good wheat, but the ears pricked me. I was quite overcome.

Suddenly a polished fop with very insinuating manners stepped up to me saying that I must cease working, it was too much for me, and that, after all, it did not concern me. At first I did not recognize him, but when he began his pretended loving insinuations and promised me a fine time, I discovered that it was the devil and I repulsed him indignantly. He instantly disappeared. I saw the harvest field surrounded by an immense vine, and the new apostles working vigorously at it and calling upon others to do the

---

[1] See "Apocalypse, Tribulation, Twelve New Apostles" in *Inner Life and Worlds of Soul & Spirit*.

same. They stood at first widely apart. When the harvest was over, the laborers all joined in celebrating a great feast of thanksgiving.

## Consoling Symbol of the Effect of Prayer

I AM still much fatigued from my work, every limb aching. From the harvest field I went into a large empty barn and found some poor people famishing in a corner. I began to think how I could assist them, when in came crowds of ecclesiastics and laics of all ages and callings, rich and poor, from far and near, known and unknown, all seeking help. My guide told me that I could supply the wants of all, if I worked hard. I expressed my readiness, when he took me over a heath to a large field of wheat and rye, where I set all the people to work at the harvest, binding the sheaves and carrying them away. I directed all. I set the most distinguished to oversee the others. But they were for the most part both lazy and awkward; their sheaves would not stand. I had to put one in the center and lean the others up against it. They carried the wheat to the barn where it was threshed and divided. In the upper story a quantity was stored for the pope, some for a very pious bishop whom I did not know, and some for the vicar-general and our own country. I saw the different parishes and priests receiving their share, some much, others little. The good received most, and the best, more wheat than rye; the bad got nothing at all. Very little came here: the pastor of H— got a very large share; the confessor, a very small portion, and what remained was distributed to any who wanted it. Sometimes a simple vicar received a portion while the pastor got nothing. My guide made the division of it. I am so worn out by this work that I cannot get rested.

## Labors and Sufferings from the Profanation of the Blessed Sacrament

DAILY *during the ecclesiastical year Anne Catherine traveled to the holy land under the care of her angel, who chose the route both going and returning. This he determined by the various tasks she had to fulfill for the sick, the dying, the needy, and the souls in purgatory—in accordance with the order laid down by God. No one was excluded from her charitable ministrations, but the head of the church received her chief attention when in need of aid to lighten the burden of his pastoral charge. Rome was as familiar to her as the holy land. The Vatican, the various churches of the Eternal City, were as well known to her as the Temple, the palace of David, the cenacle, and other holy places of Jerusalem. On these journeys she visited those places sanctified by the birth, labors, and death of the saints, who frequently appeared to her and gave an account of the various details of their life and sufferings.*

*Every day brought its own special tasks, its own particular visions on the mysteries connected with the work of redemption, so that we must not be surprised at her inability to relate all, weighed down as she was by corporal and mental sufferings. The connection between the Church's calendar and Anne Catherine's mission was close and real. Only the contemplative can understand the multiplicity and variety of action thereby entailed. Although the fragments contained in the following communications are short, they are nevertheless most striking, and sufficient to convince the reader of the marvelous ways by which this soul was led in the accomplishment of works whose surprising manifestation will redound to the greater glory of God on the Judgment Day.*

*In July, 1820, she related the following:*

I was commanded to travel over the world in order to see its misery. I went through St. Ludger's vineyard to that of St. Peter, viewing everywhere the sad state of humankind and the Church, represented by different degrees of cold, fog, and darkness—though here and there I beheld bright spots and people standing in prayer. I had visions of these individuals. Wherever I went, I was taken to the needy, the abandoned, the sick, the persecuted, the imprisoned, for whom I prayed, aiding and consoling them in many ways. Everywhere I saw the state of the Church, the saints of the countries, bishops, martyrs, religious, and anchorites—all upon whom the grace of God had descended. I saw especially those who had had visions and what their visions were. I saw them appearing in prayer to others and others to them. I saw all that they had done, and I understood that the Church has always had such servants, visions, and apparitions. They existed even in the time of Promise, constituting one of her richest graces and contributing largely to her welfare and union. I saw everywhere holy bodies lying in tombs. I saw their influence, their connection with the saints, and the blessing emanating from them through their union with their souls.

In this immense vision I had scarcely any other joy than that of seeing the Church founded upon a rock and of knowing that love follows her and imitates Jesus, from which spring eternal blessings. I was told that in the Old Testament God sent angels to humankind and warned them in dreams. But, after all, that was not so clear and perfect as the spiritual teaching of Christianity—and yet, how faithfully and simply the people of the Old Law followed such divine inspirations.

When I arrive in any country I generally see in the chief city, as in a central point, its spiritual state indicated by cold, fog, and darkness. I see the headquarters of corruption and pictures of its greatest perils. I understand all. From them I see streams and pools spreading through the land like poisoned veins, and in their midst pious souls in prayer, churches containing the blessed sacrament, countless holy bodies, good works being performed, sin expiated or prevented, assistance given to the needy, etc.

When I see the sins and abominations of a nation, their good and evil works—when I have discovered the source of the poison, the cause of their maladies—I see as a necessary result the suffering, chastisement, destruction they entail, and a total or partial cure effected in proportion as the good performed by its own people produces salutary effects, or the charitable efforts of others done for the love of Jesus bring forth streams of grace and salvation. Over some places sunk in darkness I see destruction floating in threatening pictures; over others are strife and bloodshed darkening the air—and from them frequently issues another striking picture with its own signification. These dangers and chastisements do not stand alone. They are connected with the crimes of other countries, and thus sin becomes the rod that strikes the guilty.

While all this appears in dark, earthly pictures over these lands, I see above them the good, luminous germs giving rise to other pictures like a world of light, representing what is done for it by its holy members through the treasures of grace they pour out upon it from the merits of Jesus Christ. I see above desecrated churches other churches floating in light—and I see the bishops, doctors, martyrs, intercessors, prophets, and all the privileged souls that once belonged to them. Pictures of their miracles, graces, visions, revelations, and apparitions pass before me. I see their influence far and near, the effects it produced even at the most remote distances. A blessing still lingers over the paths they have trodden, since they are still united with their country and flock through pious souls who keep alive their memory. I see that their bones— wherever they rest—are in mysterious communication with them and become the sources of their loving intercession. Unless supported by God's grace, one could not contemplate such misery and abomination side by side with so great mercy and love—one would die of grief.

If on the road there are some needy souls for whom the Lord deigns to receive the prayers of a poor creature, I am conducted to them and I behold the cause of their misfortunes. I draw near to their bed if they sleep, I approach them if awake, and I offer to God a fervent prayer for them that He may receive from me in their behalf what they cannot, or know not how to do for themselves. I often have to take upon myself a part of their sufferings. Sometimes they are people who have implored the prayers of others, or even my own, and this is the reason I have to take these journeys—they are all for my neighbor's relief. Then I see the poor creatures turning to God, from whom they receive consolation and all they need, rarely in a miraculous way but by ordinary though often unexpected means. This shows that corporal and spiritual distress comes most frequently from man himself, who instead of turning like a child to beg and receive help from the ever-open hand of God shuts himself up in himself, incredulous and defiant. My intervention—I who have the gift of seeing—is in itself the hand of God that sends to many a blind, closed heart one who sees, who is open to the light, who is as a channel for His plenteous mercy. On these journeys I am often directed to hinder sin by intervening to strike terror into, to disconcert, some evil-minded person. I have more than once aroused mothers whose infants were in need of them or in danger of being smothered either by themselves, or drowsy nurses, etc.

I went over Ludger's vineyard (in Münster) where I found things in a miserable state, as usual; through that of St. Liborius (Paderborn), in which I last labored, and which I found improved; and then by the place where lie Nepomecene, Wenceslas, Ludmilla, and other saints. This place is full of holy remains but there are few pious priests among the living, and I saw that the good, holy people generally live hidden. I went southward to a great city (Vienna) with a high tower, around which are many streets and avenues. A broad river flows by the city (the Danube). I turned to the left into a high mountainous district (the Tyrol) where dwell many pious souls, especially in the thinly settled parts. Still journeying toward the south I arrived at a city on the sea (Venice) in which I lately saw Ignatius and his companions, Mark, and other saints; but great corruption prevails there. I went into Ambrose's vineyard (Milan) and there I saw many visions and graces granted to him, and especially his influence over Augustine. I learned many things about him, his knowledge of a person who possessed in some degree the gift of recognizing relics. I had visions on this point and I think the saint has referred to it in a book. I learned also that no one ever had this faculty so fully as God has imparted it to me, and this because of the shameful neglect of relics and because the veneration of them must be renewed.

I saw as I went south an incredible number of churches and saints favored with various graces. I saw clearly the works, visions, and apparitions of Benedict and his companions; also the two Catherines of Sienna and Bologna, Clare of Montefalco, and their visions and apparitions. During my great vision, in the diocese of Ambrose it seemed to me that the saint spoke from heaven, for I saw the influence and ministry of women and virgins in the Church through the gift of contemplation, apparition, and prophecy, and he said something on the discernment of true and false visions—but I cannot repeat his words.

I ought to say that in the different countries I generally saw holy bishops in the first rank, then priests, monks, nuns, hermits, and laics. I saw the apparitions of saints to them in their lifetime and in time of pressing need, when they bore them counsel and consolation from God. I saw in this great country Magdalene di Pazzi and Rita of Cascia, and many of Catherine of Sienna's visions, missions, etc.

I came to the Church of Peter and Paul (Rome) and saw a dark world of distress, confusion, and corruption, through which shone countless graces from thousands of saints who there repose. Could I relate but a portion of what I saw in this central point of the Church it would furnish material for a lifelong meditation. Those popes whose relics I possess I saw most distinctly. I must have some of Callistus I, the seventeenth pope, which I have not yet found. This pope had many apparitions. I saw John the Evangelist's death and his appearing to Callistus—once with Mary and once with our Savior—to strengthen him in time of need. I saw several apparitions made to Xystus, of whom I have a relic, and numberless others of the apostles and disciples to one another and to their successors, giving them warning in times of distress. In these apparitions I saw a certain order of rank and dignity and their correspondence to the needs of him who received them. The messengers from the Church Triumphant are delegated with due regard to the importance of the occasion on which they are sent and not in accordance with the blind judgment of the world. With regard to the gift of recognizing relics, I must add that St. Praxedes possessed it to a certain degree.

I saw the pope surrounded by traitors and in great distress about the Church. He had visions and apparitions in his hour of greatest need. I saw many good pious bishops, but they were weak and wavering, their cowardice often got the upper hand. I saw the *dark fellow* plotting again, the destroyers attacking the Church of Peter, Mary standing with her mantle over it, and the enemies of God put to flight. I saw Peter and Paul laboring actively for the Church and their basilica greatly enlarged.

Then I saw darkness spreading around and people no longer seeking the True Church. They went to another, saying: "All is more beautiful, more natural here, better regulated"—but as yet I have seen no ecclesiastic among them. I saw the pope firm, but greatly perplexed. The treaty thought to be so advantageous to us will be of no use; things will go from bad to worse. The pope shows more energy now; he has been advised to hold out till death, and this he gained by his late act of firmness. But his last orders are of no account, he enforces them too feebly. I saw over the city terrible evils from the north.

Thence I went over water in the midst of which lie islands with their good and evil; the most insolated are the happiest, the brightest. I traveled westward into Xavier's country (Portugal), where I saw many saints and the whole land full of soldiers in red. This country was quite tranquil compared with that or Ignatius, which I now entered and found in frightful misery. Darkness lay over the whole land where reposes the treasure of the saint's graces and merits. I was at the central point and I recognized the place where long before I had had a vision of people cast into a fiery furnace around which their enemies were gathered—but they who had kindled the flames were themselves consumed by them.[1] I saw unheard-of abominations spreading over the land and my guide said to me: "This is Babel!"

I saw throughout the whole country a chain of secret societies with influences at work like those of Babel. They were connected with the building of the tower by a web fine as that of a spider, which extended up through all ages. Its highest blossom was the diabolical woman Semiramis.[2] I saw all going to ruin, sacred things destroyed, impiety and heresy flowing in. A civil war was brewing and a destructive internal crisis was at hand. I saw the former labors of innumerable saints, as well as the saints themselves, of whom I shall mention only Isidore, John of the Cross, Jane of Jesus, and chiefly Teresa, many of whose visions I saw. I was shown the labors of St. James, whose tomb is on a mountain. I saw what numbers of pilgrims here find salvation. My guide pointed out Montserrat. He showed me the old hermits who formerly dwelt there, and I had a touching vision of them. They never knew the day of the week. They counted time by dividing a

---

[1] The preceding March, Anne Catherine had seen, under the symbol of a burning furnace into which the innocent were cast, the condemnation of the good, the destruction of faith and morals in the country of St. Ignatius; and she understood that they who prepared the ruin of the innocent should share the fate of their victims.

[2] See "Semiramis" in *First Beginnings*.

loaf into seven parts of which they ate one part each day. Sometimes when in ecstasy they made a mistake of a whole day. The Mother of God used to appear and tell them what to announce to men.

I saw such misery in this country, so many graces trodden under foot, so many saints and their visions, that the thought arose in my mind: "Why must I, miserable sinner, see all this! The greater part of it I cannot understand, much less relate"—then spoke my guide: "'Repeat what you can! You know not how many souls will one day read it and be consoled, reanimated, and encouraged by it. There are numerous accounts of similar graces, but sometimes they are not related as they should be. Ancient things are distasteful to the people of this age, or they are often maliciously misrepresented. What you relate will be published in a better way, and will be productive of blessings far greater than you can imagine." This consoled me, as for a few days I had been discouraged and scrupulous.

From this unhappy land I was taken over the sea a little toward the north to an island in which St. Patrick had been (Ireland) and here I found faithful, sincere Catholics, but very much oppressed. They held relations with the pope, but very secretly, and there was still much good in the country because the people were united. I had an instruction at this point on the communion of the church's members. I saw St. Patrick and many of his works. I learned much of his history and I saw some pictures of the great vision of purgatory he once had in a cave, when he recognized many of the poor souls whom he afterward delivered. The Blessed Virgin used to appear and instruct him what to do.

From St. Patrick's island I crossed a narrow sea to another large island (England), dark, cold, and foggy, in which I saw here and there a band of pious sectarians; but, for the rest, all was great confusion, the whole nation divided into two parties and engaged in dark, disgusting intrigues. The more numerous part was the more wicked. The smaller one had the soldiers on their side, and, though better than the other, yet it was not of much account. I saw the two parties struggling together and the smaller one victorious. But there was abominable scheming going on, every one seemed a spy to watch and betray his neighbor. Above this land I saw a host of God's friends of former times, so many holy kings, bishops, and apostles of Christianity who left their homes to labor among us in Germany: St. Walburga, King Edward, Edgar, and St. Ursula, and I learned that the tradition which makes the 11,000 virgins an army of maidens is not true. They were a kind of confraternity like our own charitable associations and they did not go all together to Cologne, for some of them dwelt widely apart. I saw great misery in the cold, foggy country, wealth, crime, and ships.

I continued my journey eastward over the sea into a cold country in which I saw Sts. Bridget, Canute, and Eric (Sweden and Denmark). It was poorer, a more tranquil state than the last, but it also was dark and foggy. It is a land rich in iron, but not fertile. I do not remember what I did or saw here; the inhabitants were all staunch Protestants. Then I passed into an immense dark country subject to great tempests and full of wickedness. The inhabitants are excessively proud. They build great churches (Russia) and think themselves in the right way. I saw them everywhere arming and working; all was dark and menacing. I saw St. Basil and others. I saw the *fellow* lurking near the shining palace. I went now on to the south, etc.

*Anne Catherine went on then to China, as we may judge from her description of the country, where she beheld many early martyrs and apostles of Christianity and the good effected in her own day by the efforts of the Dominicans. She visited the scene of the labors and death of St. Thomas, as also that of St. Francis Xavier and his companions; and she traversed the isles in which the light of the gospel is now breaking. One large island she mentioned particularly, in which the faith is making rapid strides. The people, both Catholics and Protestants, are truly good and gladly receive instruction; the latter being well-inclined toward Catholicity, the church is crowded at all public functions. The city is so densely peopled that they are beginning to extend its limits. The native population are excellently well disposed. They are of a brown complexion, some of them quite black. They were accustomed to go almost naked but they now dress as their teachers prescribe. Anne Catherine saw their idols, which she described—the island seems to be the same for which she had prayed on Christmas night. In India she met the people whom on a former occasion she had seen drawing the sacred waters of the Ganges and kneeling before a cross. They were now in a better condition, receiving instruction, and about to form into a community—it was here she had a vision of St. Thomas and St. Xavier.*

*Thence she went into the neighborhood of the mountain of the prophets, traversed the dark country of Semiramis where she met Sts. Simon and Jude, saw the huge columns of the ruined city, passed through the land of St. John the Baptist and that in which the evangelist John wrote his gospel, and entered the promised land, to find ruin on all sides. The holy places are hardly recognizable, though grace still operates through them. Here her visions became general, portraying the malice of men by frustrating the abundant means of salvation offered them. On Mount Carmel she had a vision of St. Berthold and the discovery of the holy lance at Antioch. She saw many fervent religious, monks and nuns, still serving God there:*

I saw that my relic of the knight of Malta is one of St. Berthold, whom the hermit Peter of Provence took on the crusade. They were together at the siege of Antioch. When their need was most pressing, Berthold thought: "If we had the lance with which our Lord was wounded, we should surely conquer"—then he, Peter, and another, though unknown to one another, severally invoked God's assistance. The Blessed Virgin appeared to all three separately. She told them that the lance of Longinus was concealed in the wall behind the altar of the church, bidding them communicate this intelligence to one another. They obeyed; they sought and found the sacred lance walled up in a chest behind the altar. The iron point was rather short, and the shaft broken into several pieces. Victory followed the lance everywhere. Berthold had vowed to devote himself to the Blessed Virgin on Mount Carmel if the city were delivered; he became an anchorite, and later the founder and general of the Carmelite Order.

*Anne Catherine then spoke of other holy monks and hermits whom she had met on her spiritual journey through the holy land, and of many chosen souls who like herself had been taken there in ecstasy. She found all dark and dreary in the country in which the Israelites had sojourned, and she met there some ignorant but well-meaning monks belonging to a certain sect. She passed many half-ruined pyramids belonging to the earliest ages and saw St. Sabbas and other saints of the desert. Thence she turned to the land of St. Augustine and Perpetua, pushed on southward through frightful darkness, and visited Judith, whom she found pensively planning some way of escape, that she might receive instruction—for she was at heart a Christian. Anne Catherine begged God to help her.*[1]

*After this she crossed over to Brazil, where also she met saints, visited the islands, saw many new Christian settlements, passed through America, found a new impulse given to religion and met St. Rose and others. She returned over the sea to Sardinia and found Rosa Maria Serra, the stigmatizée of Ozieri, still alive, to the astonishment of all who knew her, though old and bedridden. She saw another similarly favored whom she had met some time previously at Cagliari, a maritime city of Sicily. The people of this country were in a tolerably good state. She went on to Rome, thence to Switzerland, visited Einsiedeln and the abodes of the ancient hermits, of Nicholas von der Flüe, and others. She saw in passing St. Francis de Sales, and St. Chantal's convent; crossed into Germany where she saw Sts. Walburga, Kilian, the emperor Henry, and Bonifacius; recognized Frankfort; saw the infant-martyr and the old merchant in his tomb; crossed the Rhine and met Sts. Boniface, Gear, and Hildegarde—of whom she had special visions. She was told that to the latter had been imparted through the grace of the Holy Spirit the power of committing her visions to writing, although she had never learned to read or write; of calling down chastisement upon prevaricators; and of prophesying concerning the wicked woman of Babylon. No one ever received so many graces as Hildegarde, whose revelations are fulfilled even in our own day.*

*Anne Catherine now met Elizabeth of Schoenau and, on visiting France, saw Sts. Genevieve, Denis, Martin, with a host of others; but frightful misery, corruption, and abomination reigned in the capital—it appeared to her to be in a sinking condition and that no stone would be left upon another. Thence she went to Liege, Belgium, and saw Sts. Juliana and Odilia; in Brabant, she had visions of St. Lidwina, who was wholly insensible to the corruption that consumed her body, her miserable state of poverty, or the tears that froze on her cheeks as they flowed— for Mary stood by her bed extending her mantle over her. Mary of Oignies she saw in a country still inhabited by pious Christians, and*

---

[1] See "Judith" in *Scenes from the Lives of the Saints*.

returning through Bockholt she found many of the same stamp on the frontiers of Holland. While passing through Saxony she had seen Sts. Gertrude and Mechtilde. She had visions of their gifts and graces, and of what they had done for the Church. In the country of the infant-martyr she struck terror into two men who were about murdering a poor courier in order to seize his papers.

This journey exhausted the poor invalid; its frightful pictures agitated her soul like the waves of an angry sea. Without the support received from on high she would, as she declared, have been unable to endure the sight of even a small part of the miseries that passed under her eyes. She saw upwards of a thousand saints, with the detailed life and visions of about one hundred. But she beheld none of the clairvoyants of the day among them; indeed, she had never seen one of the latter under favorable colors—they all appeared in a suspicious light and in the train of the abominable bride of the nuptial house. She saw the twelve future apostles of the Church, each in his own country and present position. The saints of whom she possessed relics appeared to her more distinctly than others. From this fact she inferred that there are among her treasures some of apostles and disciples which she would discover later.

This extended journey was accompanied by corporal sufferings in expiation of the outrages offered to her divine Spouse in the blessed sacrament of the altar. She was taken into the various churches she met on her way, there to atone by her fervent prayers for the affronts to which Jesus was exposed from the tepidity, indifference, and incredulity of the age. The first communication on this subject relates to the celebration of Corpus Christi in which she herself took part, 1819. It is given, as follows, by the pilgrim:

All night I went around among the unhappy and afflicted, some known to me, others unknown, and I begged God to let me bear the burden of all who could not approach the holy communion with a light and joyous heart. Then I took their sufferings on my own shoulders. I found them so great as to weigh me down almost to the earth. The poor people passed before me in pictures, and from each I took a part, or the whole, of his burden, according as I could get it. I drew it from his breast under the form of fine, flexible rolls, light as a tender switch, but so numerous as to make an enormous package when bound together. My

own torments were under the form of a long white leathern girdle, about a hand in breadth, streaked with red. I bound all the
rolls together, folded them in two, and fastened the great, heavy
package over my cross with the two ends of my girdle. The rolls
were variously colored according to the different sufferings they
symbolized—if I reflected a little, I should be able to name the
colors of many whom I knew. I took the huge bundle on my
shoulders and made a visit to the blessed sacrament to offer these
sufferings for the poor, blind creatures who know not that infinite
treasure of consolation.

First I went into a chapel, unfinished, unadorned, but in which,
notwithstanding, God was waiting on the altar. There I offered
my package and prayed to the blessed sacrament. It seemed as if
this chapel had sprung up merely to give me strength, for I was
almost sinking under the burden I carried on my right shoulder in
memory of the wound made on our Lord's shoulder by the cross.
I have often seen that wound, the most painful of all on his sacred
body.

At last I came to a place in which a procession was being made
and I saw at the same moment similar processions in distant
places. In the one in which I took part figured most of those
whose sufferings I bore, and I saw to my astonishment the same
colors issuing from their mouths as they sang, as were the rolls I
had drawn from them. The blessed sacrament had the appearance
of a little luminous, transparent infant in the center of a resplendent sun, surrounded by myriads of angels and saints in great
splendor and magnificence. It is inexpressible! If the others had
seen what I saw, they would have sunk to the ground, unable from
terror and amazement to bear the monstrance further. I prayed
and offered my pack.

Then the procession entered into a church that now appeared
in the air, surrounded by a garden and cemetery. The graves of
the latter were covered with lovely flowers: lilies, red and white
roses, and white asters. From the east side of the church advanced
in unspeakable splendor a priestly figure like unto our Lord. He
was soon encircled by twelve resplendent men, and these again
by numerous others. I had a good position and could see everything. There issued from the Lord's mouth a little luminous form

that gradually increased, took a more definite shape, and then again decreasing entered the mouth under the figure of a little shining child—first of the twelve, then of all the others around the Lord. This was not the historic scene I see on Holy Thursday, the Lord reclining at table with his apostles, but it reminded me of it—all was luminous and sparkling, a divine function, a church festival. The whole church was crowded, some sitting, some standing, some hovering in the air. There were seats raised in tiers, but perfectly transparent. I saw in the Lord's hands a figure into which entered the little luminous body that issued from his mouth and around which appeared a spiritual church highly ornamented—it was the blessed sacrament in the monstrance as it is when exposed for adoration or benediction. The Lord repeatedly uttered into it his loving Word, and the Body, ever one and the same, entered the mouth of all the assistants.

I laid down my burden awhile and received the heavenly manna. When I took it up again, I beheld a troop of people whose bundles were so filthy that I dreaded to touch them. I was informed that they were still to be severely judged and punished according to their works of penance, but I felt no pity for them.

The feast ended, and it seemed to me as if I had seen some men who would rekindle over all the world faith and fervor in the admirable mystery of the Real Presence of God. The chapel in which I had first rested with my burden was in a mountain as, when a child, I had seen the altars and tabernacles of the early Christians—it represented the blessed sacrament in time of persecution. The cemetery signified that the altars of the unbloody sacrifice should stand over the tombs and relics of martyrs, that the churches themselves should be erected over them. I saw the Church under the form of a spiritual, heavenly festival. A four-branched candlestick stood before the altar. I saw the feast of Corpus Christi, first directly through Jesus, then through the blessed sacrament itself, the treasure of the Church. I saw the feast celebrated by numbers of the early Christians, by those of our own times, and by many belonging to the future, and I received an assurance that its worship would flourish with new vigor in the Church.

On the feasts of the holy peasant Isidore many things were

shown me on the importance of celebrating and hearing mass, and I saw how great a blessing it is that so many are said though even by ignorant and unworthy priests, as it averts all sorts of dangers, chastisements, and calamities from humankind. It is well that many priests do not realize what they do, for if they did they would be so terrified as not to be able to celebrate the holy sacrifice.

I saw the marvelous blessings attached to hearing mass. It facilitates labor, promotes good, and prevents loss. One member of a family returning from mass carries home a blessing to the whole house and for the whole day. I saw how much greater is the advantage attached to hearing a mass than to having one said without assisting at it. I saw all defects in the celebration of mass supernaturally supplied.

*May 18th*: Her desire for the blessed sacrament becomes more violent. She languishes, laments the privation of her daily bread, and cries out in ecstasy: "'Why dost Thou leave me thus to languish for Thee? Without Thee I must die! Thou alone canst help me! If I must live, give me life!"—When she awoke, she exclaimed: "My Lord has told me that I now must see what I am without him. Things are changed—I must become his nourishment, my flesh must be consumed in ardent desires." Her visions at this holy season are sad; so much distress and misery, so many offences against God! She cannot relate them.

*On the feast of Pentecost (May 21st) the pilgrim, who had witnessed Anne Catherine's anguish and tears on the preceding evening, found her this morning radiant as a spouse of Christ, breathing but joy and holiness*:

I have been in the cenacle with the apostles, and I have been fed in a way that I cannot express. Nourishment under the form of a wave of light flowed into my mouth. It was exceedingly sweet but I know not whence it came. I saw no hand and I began to fear lest perhaps, having broken my fast, I should not be able to receive holy communion in the morning. I was not here, and yet I distinctly heard the clock strike twelve, stroke for stroke. I counted each one. I beheld the descent of the Holy Spirit on the disciples, and how the same Holy Spirit on every anniversary of this feast spreads all over the earth wherever he finds pure hearts desirous of receiving him. I can describe this only by saying that I saw here and there in the darkness a parish, a church, a city, or one or more individuals suddenly illumined. The whole earth lay in darkness below me, and I saw by a flash of heavenly light here a flower bed, there a tree, a bush, a fountain, an islet, not only lit up, but rendered quite luminous.

Through the mercy of God all that I saw last night was good; the works of darkness were not shown me. All over the world I saw numberless infusions of the Spirit; sometimes, like a lightning-stroke, falling on a congregation in church, and I could tell who among them had received the grace; or, again, I beheld individuals praying in their homes, suddenly endued with light and strength. The sight awoke in me great joy and confidence that the Church, amid her ever-increasing tribulations, will not succumb; for in all parts of the world I saw defenders raised up to her by the Holy Spirit. Yes, I felt that the oppression of the powers of this world serves but to increase her strength. I saw in St. Peter's at Rome a grand feast celebrated with myriads of lights, and I saw the pope and many others receiving the strength of the Holy Spirit.

I did not see the dark church last night (Protestant) which is always a horror to me. I saw in different places the twelve enlightened men whom I see so often as twelve new apostles or prophets of the Church. I feel as if I know one of them, that he is near me. I saw the Holy Spirit poured out on some of our own land. I knew them all in my vision, but it is seldom that I can name them afterward. I think I saw the stern superior. I felt certain that the persecution of the Church here in our own country will turn out well, but great troubles await us.

*On Whit-Monday a painful task of reparation to the blessed sacrament was announced to her:*

I knelt alone with my guide in a large church before the blessed sacrament, which was surrounded by indescribable glory. In it I saw the resplendent figure of the infant Jesus before whom since my childhood I have always opened my heart and poured out my prayers. As I presented my petitions, I received an answer to each one from the blessed sacrament in the form of a ray that pierced my soul and filled me with consolation. I was, also, gently reproved for my faults. I passed almost the whole night before the tabernacle, my angel at my side.

*Anne Catherine's humility would not allow her to give the details of this vision. It was immediately followed by apparitions of St. Augustine and two holy Augustinians, Rita of Cascia and Clare of Montefalco, who prepared her to undergo sufferings such as they themselves had formerly endured for the blessed sacrament. She fell into ecstasy and, to the amazement of her confessor and the pilgrim, who were conversing together in the antechamber, she suddenly stood up on her bed (a thing she had not done for four years), her countenance radiant with joy, her hands raised to heaven, and recited slowly and devoutly in a sweet, clear voice, the whole of the* Te Deum. *Her face was emaciated and slightly sallow, but her cheeks were flushed and a look of enthusiasm beamed from her dark eyes. She stood upright, firm and secure in her position. At certain parts she joined her hands and inclined her head suppliantly, her voice betraying a tender, caressing accent like a child reciting verses in its father's honor. Her ample robe fell below the ankles, giving her a most imposing appearance, and her prayer, repeated in a loud voice, excited in the hearer a feeling of mingled piety and awe. Next day she said:*

St. Augustine stood by me in his episcopal robes, and O he was so kind! I was rejoiced to see him and I accused myself of never especially honoring him. He replied: "Still I know thee. Thou art my child!"

When I asked him to relieve my pain, he presented me a nosegay in which was a blue flower, and a feeling of strength and relief instantly pervaded my whole person. The saint said to me: "Thou wilt never be entirely well, for thy way is that of suffering. But, when in need of help and consolation, think of me. I shall always give them thee. Now rise and say the *Te Deum* to thank the Most Holy Trinity for your cure." Then I arose and prayed. I was perfectly strong and my joy was very great. Afterward I saw St. Augustine in his glory.[1]

---

[1] A full telling of this remarkable vision of St. Augustine will be found in "Augustine" in *Scenes from the Lives of the Saints.*

The apparition of the living is something very special, the counterpart as it were of the apparition of saints upon earth. They appear in the garden of the saints like spirits under certain, indeterminate forms, and receive all kinds of fruits and flowers. I see some who seem to be raised into this sphere of grace by prayer, and others who seem to receive such favors without conscious effort on their part; they are vessels of election. The same difference exists between these two classes as between one who takes the trouble to gather fruit in a garden and another who sees it falling at his feet as he walks along, or to whom God deigns to send it by this or that saint.

After this my guide led me on my own road to the heavenly Jerusalem, and I saw that I was now far beyond the place where I had seen the little notes of warning. I climbed a mountain and reached a garden of which St. Clare of Montefalco had charge. In her hands I saw luminous wounds and around her brow a shining crown of thorns—for although she had not had the exterior marks of the wounds she had felt their pain. Clare told me that this was her garden and that, as I loved gardening, she would show me how it should be carried on. There was a wall around it, but it was only symbolical, for one could both see and pass through it; it was built of round, variegated, shining stones. The garden was laid out in eight beautiful beds all verging toward the center. There were some handsome large trees in full bloom, and a fountain that could be made to water the whole place. A vine was trained all around the wall.

I stayed almost all night in the garden with St. Clare. She taught me the virtue and signification of every plant and how to use. it. We passed from one flower bed to another but I do not now remember where she got the roots. It seemed to be supernaturally in the air, or from an apparition. I worked with her near a fig-tree, though I do not now recollect at what. I only remember that there were beds of bitter-cress and chervil. Clare told me that, if my taste were too sweet, I must take a mouthful of cress, and if too bitter, a mouthful of chervil. I have always been very fond of these herbs. I used to chew them when I was a child, indeed I could have lived on them. The hardest thing for me to understand was Clare's management of the vine: how she trained it, divided it, and pruned it. I could not succeed. It was the last thing she taught me in the garden. During our work the birds flocked round us, perched on my shoulders and were just as familiar with me as they had been in the convent cloister. Clare told me that she had the instruments of the passion engraven on her heart and that, after her death, three stones had been found in her gall. She spoke also of the graces she had received on the feast of the Holy Trinity, bidding me prepare for a new labor on the coming feast. She looked very thin, pale, and exhausted.

I saw, too, St. Rita of Cascia. As she prayed one day before a crucifix, she begged in her humility for one single thorn from the crown of her crucified Savior, when a ray of light shot from the crown and wounded her in the forehead. She suffered in that spot a lifelong, indescribable pain, matter continually oozing from it—which caused her to be shunned by all. I saw also her great devotion to the blessed sacrament. She told me many things.

*On the eve of the feast of the Most Holy Trinity, the task foretold by St. Clare began. Anne Catherine said:*

When I saw the bad preparation of so many persons who were going to confession, I renewed my petition to God to let me suffer something for their amendment; and then, indeed, my task began. It seemed as if I were being pierced incessantly by fine darts of pain shot at me like arrows, and in the night they became more intense than I had ever felt before. They began around my heart, which felt like a furnace of pain tightly bound in flames. Waves of fiery pains swept thence through all parts of my body, through the marrow of my bones, to the tips of my fingers, my nails, and my hair. It was like the regular flow of the tide from my heart to my hands, feet, and head and back again, my wounds being the principal centers.

My sufferings increased until midnight, when I awoke steeped in perspiration and unable to move. I had only one consolation—the indistinct idea of the cross formed by the principal centers of my pain, which seemed to be grinding me to powder. At midnight I could bear it no longer, for my stupor made me forget its cause; so I turned like a child to my father, St. Augustine. "Ah! dear father, St. Augustine, you did promise to help me whenever I invoked you! Ah! see my distress!"—my prayer was instantly heard. The saint stood before me, telling me most kindly why I was suffering so, but that he could not take away my pains since I was to endure them in union with the passion of Jesus Christ; he bade me be comforted although I was still to suffer three hours more.

I was greatly consoled, though in intense agony, knowing that it was for the love of Christ's passion and to satisfy divine Justice for sinners. I rejoiced to be of some use and I threw my whole heart into my pains. I accepted the grace of expiatory suffering with loving confidence in the mercy of the heavenly Father. St. Augustine reminded me moreover that three years ago, on the morning of All Saints, my Spouse had appeared to me as I lay at the point of death. He had given me my choice either to die and go to purgatory, or to live longer in suffering, and that I had replied: "Lord, in purgatory my sufferings will be of no avail. If then it be not contrary to thy will, let me live and endure all possible torments if thereby I can aid but a single soul!" Then, although I had at first asked for death, my Savior now granted my second request by prolonging my life of suffering. When my holy father recalled this circumstance I distinctly remembered it and, from that moment until the end of the three hours, I calmly and thankfully endured the most cruel tortures. Pain forced from me the bitterest tears and the sweat of death.

I had another vision of the Most Holy Trinity under the form of a resplendent old man seated on a throne. From his forehead streamed an indescribably clear, colorless light; from his mouth flowed a luminous stream slightly tinged with yellow, like fire; and from his breast near the heart, another stream of colored light. These streams formed in the air above the old man's breast a cross which sparkled like the rainbow, and it seemed to me that he laid his hands on its arms. Innumerable rays issued from it. They fell first on the heavenly choirs and then down upon the earth, filling and quickening all things.

A little below the Holy Trinity and to the right I saw Mary's throne. A ray darted to her from the old man and another from her to the cross. All this is quite inexpressible. But in vision, although dazzling and swimming in light, it was perfectly intelligible: one and three, vivifying all, enlightening all, and most wonderfully sufficing for all. Below the throne were the angels in a world of colorless light; above them the twenty-four ancients with silver hair, surrounding the Most Holy Trinity. All the rest of the boundless space was filled with saints who were themselves the luminous centers of shining choirs. At the right of the Trinity was St. Augustine surrounded by his choirs, but much lower than Mary, and all around lay gardens, shining palaces, and churches.

I felt as if I were wandering among the starry heavens. These vessels of God are of every variety of form and appearance, but all are filled with Jesus Christ. The same law governs all, the same substance pervades all though under a different form, and a straight line leads through each into the light of the Father through the cross of the Son. I saw a long line of royal females extending from the Mother of God, virgins with crowns and scepters, though not earthly queens, souls who had preceded or followed Mary in the order of time. They seemed to serve her as the twenty-four ancients serve the Most Holy Trinity. They were celebrating the feast by a marvelously solemn movement severally and all together. I can compare it only to beautiful music. The angels and saints advanced in one or many processions to the throne of the Most Holy Trinity like the stars in the sky revolving around the sun. And then I saw down on the earth innumerable processions corresponding to the celestial ones, also celebrating the feast—but how miserable! how dark! how full of breaks! To look upon it from above was like looking down into the mire— still there was much good here and there. I saw also our own procession here in Dülmen and I noticed a poor little ragged child. I know where it lives. I shall clothe it.[1]

---

[1] It is singularly touching to see the goodness and compassion of her heart. In the midst of the wonders presented to the eyes of her soul, she pauses to notice the wants of a poor little child, and even to find out its abode. As it passed before her house, she exclaimed: "Ah! show I should love to bring that poor ragged little creature up here and dress it. See how sadly it walks among the other children in their holiday clothes." If one still in the body can see and feel thus, how great must be the compassion of the angels and saints, our brethren in glory, of Mary, of Jesus, of God Himself, who all love us more than those on earth, and who see more clearly! How can one who prays with faith lose courage? CB

*On the evening of Holy Trinity Sunday a dance was held in the house in which Anne Catherine lodged. Next day she spoke of it as follows:*

I suffered intensely last night, on account of the indecent dances and games going on in the house. In the midst of the noisy assembly I beheld the devil, a conspicuous figure under a corporal form, urging on certain individuals and inspiring them with all kinds of evil desires. Their angel-guardian called to them from afar, but they turned a deaf ear and followed the evil one. No good came from it; not one went home unharmed. I saw all sorts of animals by their side; their interior was full of black stains. I frequently ran among them, inspiring fear, preventing sin.

To console me I had visions on the life of two saints, Francis de Sales and Frances de Chantals, chiefly upon their spiritual union; the former often received counsel and support from the latter. Once on the occasion of an odious calumny against him, I saw him consoled by Frances, who was distressed at seeing him so much afflicted by it. They showed me the foundation, propagation, and dispersion of the Visitation Order and spoke of the restoration of its different houses. Their words came to me as if from a distance. They said that the times are indeed sad, but that after many tribulations peace will be restored and religion and charity reign once more among men. Then convents will flourish in the true sense of the word. I saw a picture of this future time which I cannot describe, but in which I saw the whole earth arising from darkness and light and love awaking. I had also numerous pictures of the restoration of religious orders.[1] The time of antichrist is not so near as some imagine; he will still have many precursors—I saw in two cities some teachers from whose schools they will come.

*On May 30th, the feast of Corpus Christi, Anne Catherine's sufferings recommenced as on Holy Trinity:*

---

[1] St. Hildegarde, also, describing the actual state of the times, predicts a renewal of life in the Church. After prophesying the partition of the German Empire and the increasing hostility of the secular power toward the pope, she says: "The pope will retain under the sovereignty of the tiara only Rome and some unimportant parts of the adjoining territory. The spoliation will be effected partly by the invasion of armed soldiers and partly by conventions

Again I felt those pains like fine rays falling upon me, piercing me in all directions like threads of silver. Besides, I had to carry, to drag so many people along that I am all bruised; so that not a bone in my body is not, as it were, dislocated. When I awoke, the middle fingers of both hands were stiff, bent, and paralyzed, and my wounds have pained intensely all night long. I saw in numerous pictures the coldness and irreverence shown the blessed sacrament, by which I understood the guilt of those who receive it unworthily, negligently, and by routine; and I saw many going to confess in very bad dispositions.

At each view, I begged God to forgive and enlighten His creatures. My guide took me into all our own parish churches and showed me everywhere how the blessed sacrament is worshipped. I found things best at Überwasser, Münster. Around the churches I often saw immense morasses with people sunk in them. I had to draw them out, clean, and sometimes carry them on my back to the confessional. My guide constantly pointed out new miseries, saying: "Come, suffer for this one, etc." In the midst of my labor I often wept like a child, though I was not wholly destitute of consolation. I beheld the manifold and marvellous workings of grace by means of the blessed sacrament as a light shining over all its adorers. Yes, even they who think not of it receive a blessing in its presence. Lastly I went into our own church and saw the pilgrim crossing the cemetery and thinking of the dead. The sight pleased me, and I thought: "He is coming to me![1] St. Francis de Sales, St. de Chantal, St. Augustine, and other saints consoled me. I saw too that I am instrumental in relieving and healing souls, and that I suffer in union with the passion of Jesus.

---

and measures concerted among the people. . . . But after a while impiety will be vanquished for a time. It will indeed try to raise its head again, but justice will be so firmly administered that the people will sincerely return to the faithful practice of the simple manners and wise discipline of their forefathers—yes, even princes and lords, such as bishops and ecclesiastical superiors, may imitate the virtuous example of their inferiors, and every one will esteem in his neighbor only piety and justice." *Libor divinorum operum*, Para III, Visio X c 25, 26.

[1] About six o'clock AM, the time the pilgrim went to mass. Why should her other visions be less true than this fact? CB

# Institution of
## the Blessed Sacrament

IN *the midst of these sufferings that followed one another in quick succession, Anne Catherine had on Corpus Christi rich and detailed visions upon the institution of the blessed sacrament and its worship down to the present time. But her weakness was so great that she was scarcely able to communicate even what follows:*

I saw a vision of the institution of the blessed sacrament. The Lord sat at the center of the long side of the table. On his right was John, on his left a graceful, fine-looking apostle very like to John. Next to the latter sat Peter, who often leaned over him. The Lord sat and taught for awhile, then arose and all the rest with him. They looked on in silence, wondering what he was about to do. He took up the plate with the bread, raised his eyes, made incisions in the bread with a bone knife, and broke it into pieces. Then he moved his right hand over it as if blessing it, at which moment there flashed from him into the bread a bright ray of light. Jesus became all resplendent, drowned, so to say, in the splendor that spread over all present. The apostles now grew more recollected, more fervent. Judas was the only one that remained in darkness, repulsing the light. Jesus raised his eyes, elevated the chalice, and blessed it.

For what I saw passing in him during this ceremony, I have but one expression: I saw and felt that he was transforming himself. The bread and chalice shone with light. Jesus placed the morsels on a flat plate like a patena and, taking them one by one in his right hand, he communicated all present, commencing I think with his mother, who advanced to the table between the apostles opposite Jesus. I saw light issuing from the Lord's mouth, and the bread shining and entering into that of the apostles under a luminous human form. All were filled with light, Judas alone was dark and gloomy. The Lord then raised the chalice by the handle and gave them to drink—and here again I beheld a flood of light streaming over the apostles. After the ceremony, all stood for awhile filled with emotion, and then the picture vanished. The morsels that the Lord gave the apostles were like two little rolls joined in the middle, down which was a furrow.

*The above vision was followed by others relating to the changes that have been introduced in the form of the sacrament, its distribution and worship, of which Anne Catherine relates the following:*

I saw that in course of time whiter bread was used for the blessed sacrament, and the morsels were smaller. Even in the time of the apostles I saw Peter at Jerusalem giving only a morsel to communicants; at first it was square but at a later period it was round. When the apostles dispersed—the Christians having no churches as yet but only halls in which they assembled—the apostles kept the blessed sacrament at their homes. When they carried it to the place of assembly, the faithful followed reverently, whence originated processions and public veneration. Later on the Christians got possession of the great pagan temples, which they consecrated and in which was preserved the blessed sacrament.

When men communicated, they received the sacred host in their hand and then swallowed it; but the women made use of a small linen cloth. Up to a certain time they were allowed to take the sacred species to their homes. They hung it around their neck in a little box, or casket, with a gold drawer wherein it reposed folded in linen. When this custom ceased to be general, it was still permitted to certain very devout persons.

I had a vision also of the holy communion under two kinds. In the early ages, and afterward at certain periods, I saw the faithful very enlightened, full of faith and simplicity; but later I beheld them straying, misled, and persecuted. I saw the Church inspired by the Holy Spirit, introducing various changes in her discipline when devotion and veneration toward the blessed sacrament had grown weak. Among those that separated from the Church, I saw the sacrament itself cease. I saw the feast of Corpus Christi and public adoration instituted at a time of great coldness. Incalculable graces were thereby bestowed upon the whole Church.

Among many other pictures I saw a great celebration in a city known to me, I think Liege, and in a far-off, warm country whence come fruits like dates, I saw Christians assembled in church. The priest was at the altar, when a frightful tumult arose outside and a brutal tyrant appeared riding a white horse. He was surrounded by his followers. He led by a chain a raging wild beast that struck terror into all the beholders. The man's intention seemed to be to force the animal into the church by way of insult, and I thought I heard him say he would show the Christians whether their God of bread were really a God or not. The people looked on in horror while the priest, turning toward the entrance, gave benediction with the blessed sacrament.

Instantly the furious beast stood spellbound! The priest advanced, still holding the sacred host, when the animal meekly fell on its knees, and the tyrant and his followers were completely changed. They knelt to adore, and entered the church confused, humbled, and converted.

Last night I endured pain so violent that I often cried out. It passed through all my members, and I was shown pictures that explained to me its cause—that is, sins committed against the holy eucharist. I had also a picture I cannot describe. I learned from it that our Lord himself watches over the parishes of bad priests in most wonderful ways and animates the people to piety.

*On June 2nd, the pilgrim found Anne Catherine calm but suffering greatly, retaining but a slight remembrance of her visions of the preceding night. She had again seen St. Clare of Montefalco's garden. St. Clare explained to her that its eight divisions, of which three were already under cultivation, signified the eight days of the octave of Corpus Christi. She told her the mysterious signification of the plants, and what sufferings were indicated by them. In the garden near the fountain is a rose-bush surrounded by thorns.*

*The following day Anne Catherine lay quite unnerved by pain and scarcely able to speak. She begged the pilgrim's prayers for two very serious cases: one a family in the country in great dread of an impending misfortune, and another in the city, in misery brought on by sin. On Sunday in the octave she lay even more prostrate than she had been since the eve of the feast, and said:*

I passed the night awake and in unspeakable torment, my pains interrupted only by visions of people in distress who approached my bed as visitors do in the daytime, recommending themselves to my prayers and recounting to me their needs.

I found myself in a large church surrounded by many parishes. A long communion table was prepared in it. I saw both priests and laymen entering the houses around, to call the occupants to receive the blessed sacrament; but the latter gave a thousand different excuses. One house was full of young people trifling and amusing themselves, etc. Then I saw the servants sent out to invite the poor, the lame, and the blind whom they met on the streets—and I saw numbers of such entering, the blind led and the lame carried by those who prayed for them. I was almost exhausted. I saw many among the lame whom I know to be perfectly well. I asked a blind citizen how he had lost his sight, for until then I had not thought him blind—but he would not admit that he could not see. I met a woman whom I had known when she was a little girl and I asked her if it were not by marrying she had become a cripple. But she too thought there was nothing the matter with her. The church was far from being full.

*That afternoon Anne Catherine, in obedience to an inspiration, sent for a man who often abused his wife. She exhorted him in words so earnest to treat her kindly, that he was moved to tears. The wife also came to be consoled and encouraged by Anne Catherine's counsel, and the children whom she had clothed for the feast thanked her most gratefully. Then her pains recommenced. Every member was convulsed, the wounds in her hands grew red, the middle fingers contracted, and thus she lay in unmitigated suffering till the evening of June 7th. Once she said while in ecstasy that she was now enduring an excruciating trial, that she had reached the fig-tree in the southern end of the garden (St. Clare's) and that she had eaten one fig that contained all sorts of torments. Four beds still remained to be cultivated (four days of the octave).*

*Anne Catherine had no relic of St. Clare of Montefalco, but the saint came in virtue of her connection with the Augustinian Order, to which Anne Catherine belonged, and because their sufferings had been similar. "O that these four days were over!" sighed the pilgrim, "for her sufferings do but increase!" And yet it was not without regret that she saw morning dawn upon her nights of dreadful agony, for at night she could at least suffer in peace, whereas day added its burden of vexations and interruptions to her weighty cross:*

It was also shown me interiorly that, despite men's wickedness and the decadence of religion, the Church has had in every age living, acting members raised up by the Holy Spirit to pray and lovingly to suffer for her. While these living members remain unknown, so much the more efficacious is their action—and the present age is no exception. Then I saw, shining out through the darkness that envelopes the world, scenes of holy souls praying, teaching, suffering, and laboring for the Church. Of all the pictures that rejoiced and encouraged me in my sufferings, the following did me most good:

I saw in a great maritime city far away toward the south a sick nun in the house of a pious, industrious widow. The nun was shown me as a holy person chosen by God to suffer for the church and other intentions. She was tall, extremely emaciated, and marked with the stigmata, though this was not publicly known. She had come from a suppressed convent and had been received by the widow, who shared her means with her and some priests. The piety of the inhabitants of the city did not please me. They had many exterior devotions, but they gave themselves up not less ardently on that account to sin and debauchery.

Far away from the last-mentioned city, off toward the west, I saw in an ancient convent lately suppressed an infirm old lay-brother confined to his room. He too was shown me as an instrument of prayer and suffering for his neighbor and the Church. I saw the sick, the poor, and many in affliction receiving consolation and assistance from him. Again I was told that such instruments are never wanting, that they never shall be wanting to the Church of God. They are always placed by divine providence where they are most necessary, nearest the centers of corruption.

*On Wednesday, June 7th, nine o'clock PM, occurred the crisis of Anne Catherine's present suffering. The pains left her bones and the intolerable agony she had endured for the last days sensibly abated. She fell into a state of utter prostration, unable to move a limb, utter a sound, or give the least sign of life. Her confessor became uneasy. He put several questions to her, which she understood but to which she could answer only after the lapse of some hours. Then, weeping and stammering like a child, she begged him to pardon her silence and told him that her pains had ceased. Next morning, Thursday, she lay like a corpse, but without pain. As she herself remarked, she had fainted just as she reached the goal, and death seemed inevitable. The doctor spoke of quinine, but she made him understand that she was without fever and that in such paroxysms she generally experienced chilly sensations. "God alone can help me," she exclaimed,[1] and then went on to say that Jesus had sweetly relieved and consoled her; that Clare of Montefalco had appeared to tell her that the work in the garden was finished; the vine was the blood of Jesus Christ; the fountain, the blessed sacrament; that the wine and water had to be mingled together; and that the rosebush near the fountain signified the sufferings in store for her toward the end of her life. She was too weak to give further details, excepting that at break of day she had recited the Te Deum, the Seven Penitential Psalms, and the Litanies, and now she was to have four days of uninterrupted rest to commune with God alone. When she recalled her pains of the last eight days, as well as the mercy of God to her, she could not restrain her tears. Her friends were touched with compassion at her altered appearance. And yet not one of them—not even the pilgrim—dreamed of taking her words literally and granting the longed-for repose. He writes for June 9th:*

She is pale as a corpse but is allowed no rest since no one wards off annoyances from her. After her last martyrdom in union with Christ's passion she spoke of three days' repose, as the body of Jesus had lain that time in the tomb, but she knows not whether she will get it. The doctor wanted to rub her with liquor; but the confessor, who expected her death, would not allow it.

*Anne Catherine could with difficulty ward off the pilgrim's questioning, because, as he says, "From her interior state and continued visions he concluded that the end is not so near, even if the confessor thinks so." The latter stood at the bedside and sought to revive her by holding out to her his consecrated fingers. Hardly had he conceived the thought, when she suddenly raised her head and moved toward his hand. As she lay thus, pale and motionless, St. Clare of Montefalco, Juliana of Liege, St. Anthony of Padua, and St. Ignatius of Loyola severally assisted and consoled her.*

*The first-named appeared and said to her:* "You have cultivated the garden of the blessed sacrament well and your work is now over; but you are exhausted, I must bring you some refreshment."

---

[1] No remedy has ever been able to interpose an obstacle to the designs of God over her. We are blind, blind in everything. Science itself is but specific blindness. CB

And instantly [continues Anne Catherine] I beheld the saint descending toward me resplendent with light. She gave me a three-cornered morsel upon either side of which was an image, and then disappeared. I ate it with relish. I am sure that I have eaten the same before. It was very sweet and strengthened me greatly. New life has been given me through the mercy of God. I live still, I can still love my Savior, still suffer with him, still thank and praise him!

I saw the eight flower beds that I have been cultivating these last days in St. Clare's garden. Without the help of God it would have been impossible for me to do it. The fig-tree signified search after consolations, weak condescension, too great indulgence. Whenever I worked at the vine, I was bound to it in the form of a cross. I saw all that I had accomplished in these eight days, for what faults I had atoned, what chastisements warded off, etc. I saw all under the appearance of a procession in honor of the most blessed sacrament, a spiritual festival in which the Blessed celebrated the treasures of grace bestowed on the Church during the year by means of the blessed sacrament. These graces appeared as costly sacred vessels, precious stones, pearls, flowers, grapes, and fruits. The procession was headed by children in white, followed by nuns of all the different orders especially devoted to the blessed sacrament, all wearing a figure of the host embroidered on their habit. Juliana of Liege walked first. I saw St. Norbert with his monks, and numbers of the clergy—secular and regular. Unspeakable joy, sweetness, and union reigned over all.

*On June 5th, Anne Catherine had a vision of St. Boniface,[1] after which she spoke as follows:*

I beheld pictures referring to the defects in divine worship and how they are supernaturally repaired. It is hard for me to say how I saw it, how the different scenes blended and harmonized, one explaining another. One thing was especially remarkable—that the failings and omissions in divine worship on earth only increase the indebtedness of the guilty. God receives the honor due Him from a higher order. Among other things I saw that when priests

---

[1] See "Anthony of Padua" in *Scenes from the Lives of the Saints.*

have distractions during the sacred ceremonies, mass, for instance, they are in reality wherever their thoughts are—and during the interval a saint takes their place at the altar. These visions show frightfully the guilt of carelessly celebrating the holy mysteries. Sometimes I see a priest leaving the sacristy vested for mass; but he goes not to the altar. He leaves the church and goes to a tavern, a garden, a hunt, a maiden, a book, to some rendezvous, and I see him now here, now there, according to the bent of his thoughts, as if he were really and personally in those places. It is a most pitiful and shameful sight! But it is singularly affecting to behold at this time a holy priest going through the ceremonies of the altar in his stead. I often see the priest returning for a moment during the sacrifice and then suddenly running off again to some forbidden place. Such interruptions frequently last a long time. When the priest amends, I see it in his piety and recollectedness at the altar, etc. In many parish churches I saw the dust and dirt that had long defiled the sacred vessels cleared away, and all things put in order.

*On the night of June 12–13th, Anne Catherine was consoled by visions of the life of St. Anthony of Padua. Two days later, on June 15th, she returned to her visions of the blessed sacrament:*

I turned toward the blessed sacrament to pray, and I was ravished in spirit into the church in which the feast of Corpus Christi was celebrated for the first time upon earth. It was built in ancient style and adorned with ancient pictures, but it was not old itself, nor did it present any appearance of decay—on the contrary, all was bright and beautiful. I knelt before the high altar. The blessed sacrament was not in a monstrance but shut up in a tabernacle in a high round ciborium, surmounted by a cross. A vessel of three compartments could be drawn out of it: the upper one contained several little vessels that held the holy oils; the second, several consecrated hosts; the lowest one, a flagon made of shining mother-of-pearl in which there was, I think, some wine. Near the church was a cloister of pious virgins. On one side of the church stood a small house occupied by a very devout virgin named Eva. There was in her room a little window with a slide through which—day or night—she could see the blessed sacrament on the high altar. That she was very devout to it I could perceive by all her movements. She was dressed respectably, not exactly like a nun, but more like a pilgrim. She did not belong to the city. She was of good family and had moved there only through devotion, to be able to live near the church.

In the neighborhood of this city I saw a convent on a mountain, not built in the usual conventual style, but several small houses joined together. One of the religious was blessed Juliana, who had been instrumental in the institution of the feast of Corpus Christi. I saw her walking in the garden dressed in the gray habit of her order. She seemed to be full of sweet simplicity and often paused in contemplation before the flowers. On one occasion I saw her kneeling near a lily, meditating on the virtue of purity, and I also saw her in prayer when she received the command to introduce the feast of Corpus Christi. It gave her great anxiety, and I saw that another spiritual director was shown her to whom she was to make known the revelation, since the first one had paid no heed to her. While she was in prayer I saw in the distance a pope likewise engaged, and near him the number IV. Urged by a vision, and in consequence of a certain favor someone had received from the blessed sacrament, he resolved to establish the feast in the church. Between these two pictures, I found myself again in the church before the blessed sacrament. I saw come forth from it first a shining finger, then a hand, and lastly there stood before me a youth resplendent with light and covered with pearls. He said: "Behold these pearls! Not one is lost, and all may gather them." The whole world was illumined by the rays that shot from the glorious youth. Then I poured out my soul in thanksgiving for I knew by this picture that the blessed sacrament with all its graces has, at length, become an object of special devotion among the faithful.

Toward midday I beheld on the horizon over a lovely fertile plain, five broad, luminous bands—like the sun in color and brilliancy—that united to form a dome overhead. They came from five great, distant cities like the bands of a rainbow in the blue sky. On the dome, in indescribable splendor, was enthroned the most blessed sacrament in a richly adorned monstrance. Above and below the five arches hovered myriads of angels going to and fro between the cities and the blessed sacrament. The pomp attending this picture, the devotion and consolation it inspired, I cannot express.

On June 17th, as I was fainting with desire for the blessed sacrament, a dying religious was shown me (Juliana Falconieri). She could not always receive holy communion, on account of her frequent vomiting. But to console her, the priest used to lay the host upon her breast in a corporal, and this relieved her greatly. As her death drew near, they brought the most blessed sacrament to her and she begged to have it laid upon her breast in a little linen cloth, instead of the stiff corporal. The priest did as she requested, the nuns kneeling around her bed. I saw the dying sister smile sweetly; her countenance became lovely, rosy, and radiant—and she was dead! The priest stooped to remove the host, but the linen was empty—the sacred host had entered her breast, leaving the mark of a circle in which was a red cross with the Savior's figure. I saw crowds flocking to witness the miracle. I longed for a similar favor, but it will not be granted.

I saw a little chapel standing on a vine whose branches encircled and even entered it. In the center was a shoot on which stood Jesus, Mary, and Joseph, and around them in prayer were all the saints who had been marked with the stigmata. One among them was conspicuous, a tertiary of the Order of St. Dominic, named Osiana. She did not live in a convent, she lived at home.

I saw a little person whom I heard called Maria of Oignies. She lived not far from Liege, Juliana's city, which I could see at no great distance. At first I saw a man with her. I knew not before that she was married. She lay at night on the bare boards. Later on I saw her in another place, where the houses were crowded together, and here she served the sick. Then I saw her in another place kneeling all alone at night before the blessed sacrament in a church. Again, I saw her lying ill a long time. Those around her were unable to understand her singular malady with its frequent changes, and they scoffed at her abstinence from food. It was shown me how much she had suffered for others, how many poor souls she had helped; and then I saw for my own consolation a picture of her glory in heaven. The Church has always had such members.

*On June 18th, St. Ignatius consoled and assisted Anne Catherine, and on June 21st she beheld some scenes in the life of his companion St. Aloysius.*[1]

I had a painful labor to perform (*June 27th*) in a church in which, through fear of profanation, they had walled up the blessed sacrament in a pillar. Mass was said secretly in a cave below the sacristy. I cannot say where this was, but the church was very old and I was in dread of the blessed sacrament's being exposed to danger. Then my guide exhorted me to pray and to ask prayers of all my acquaintances for the conversion of sinners and, above all, for faith and perseverance for the clergy—"For terrible times are approaching, non-Catholics will use every artifice to oppress the Church and snatch from her her possessions. The troubles will ever increase."

*For several subsequent days Anne Catherine experienced intense pains in her stigmata. She exhibited all the symptoms of dropsy, the malady of a poor woman living in France and which Anne Catherine had taken upon herself. During it she was occupied in a labor of prayer that had been imposed upon her. The following is her account:*

I was taken by my guide up an immensely high staircase and I saw people in prayer coming from all directions, drawn, as it were, by threads. I was on the top of the staircase, but still about five feet below a great, dazzlingly bright city, or rather a world. An immense blue curtain was drawn aside to allow me to gaze into the magnificent scene. Rows of palaces and flower gardens ran toward the center, where all was so brilliant that one could not look upon it. Wherever I turned my eyes I beheld hierarchies of saints and angels whose intercession I implored. The virgins and martyrs were the first to present their petitions before the throne of God, and they were followed by the other choirs. The Most Holy Trinity appeared to draw near to them like the sun breaking through the clouds. The angelic choirs were composed of small, delicate forms swimming in light. The cherubim and seraphim were winged spirits, their wings formed of sparkling rays, and I saw the choirs of angels and guardian angels. Among the holy

---

[1] See "Ignatius (Xavier, Aloysius and Others of His Order" in *Scenes from the Lives of the Saints.*

virgins I saw souls who had lived in the married state, St. Anne and others of early times, St. Cunegundes and other chaste spouses, but not Magdalene. There were no birds or animals in the gardens. When I looked down from the steps on which I stood, all was gray to right and left—it was blue only behind the curtain. I saw islands, cities, fields, and gardens, earthly regions that appeared in proportion as my thoughts wandered toward them. I saw all sorts of people praying, their prayers mounting like pennants, like written scrolls to the hearts of the Blessed from whose countenance they shot in dazzling rays to the throne of God. I saw some of these scrolls turning black and falling down again to earth, and some unfinished ones taken up and offered by others. It was like an exchange between men and between the saints and angels. There was great movement among the latter as they bore aid to the needy and miserable: for instance, to ships in distress. Last night, though very sick, I was carried away by my guide. It was strange how curious I was to know what was behind the blue curtain!—I thought the mountain of the prophets lay to the left as I ascended.

*On July 1st, she added the following:*

I think my wounds of the crown must have bled during my great vision on the intercession of the saints, for I saw so much of the dolorous passion! While the saints in turn offered before the throne of God their share of compassion for sinners, I saw all Christ's sufferings and the sympathy they excited, all the thorns of the crown, and other things relating to the passion.

*Toward the close of August, 1820, Anne Catherine suffered inexpressibly from the continual sight of the tepidity and indifference of both priests and lay people toward the most blessed sacrament, and side by side with the latter she beheld honest pagans aspiring after salvation:*

I saw in all places priests surrounded by the graces of the Church, the treasure of Jesus Christ's merits as well as those of the saints; but they were tepid, they were dead. They taught, they preached, and offered the holy sacrifice most slothfully.

Then a pagan was shown me standing on a pillar and addressing a multitude below. He spoke so feelingly of the new God of all the gods, the God of a strange people, that his hearers were seized with the same enthusiasm as himself. I am assailed day and night by these visions, I cannot get rid of them. Present misery and decadence are always shown me side by side with past good, and I have to pray unceasingly.

Mass badly celebrated is an enormous evil. Ah! it is not a matter of indifference how it is said! I have had a great vision on the mystery of holy mass and I have seen that whatever good has existed since Creation is owing to it. I saw the *A* and the *O*, and how all is contained in the *O*.[1] I understood the signification of the circle in the spherical form of the earth and the heavenly bodies, the aureola of apparitions, and the sacred host. The connection between the mysteries of the Incarnation, the Redemption, and the holy sacrifice of the mass was also shown me, and I saw how Mary compassed what the heavens themselves could not contain.

These pictures extended through the whole of the Old Testament.[2] I saw the first sacrifice offered and the marvelous significance of holy relics when placed in the altar on which mass is said. I saw Adam's bones reposing in a cavern under Mount Golgotha deep down, almost to water level, and in a straight line beneath the spot on which Jesus Christ was crucified. I looked in and saw Adam's skeleton entire, with the exception of the right arm and foot and a part of the right side. Through the latter I could see the ribs of the left side. In the right side lay Eve's skull exactly in the spot whence the Lord had drawn it. I was told that Adam and Eve's resting-place has been a point of dispute, but they have always lain just where I saw them. There was no mountain on this spot before the deluge; only in consequence of that event did one appear. The tomb was untouched by the waters. Noah had in the ark a portion of their remains, which he laid on the altar when offering his first sacrifice. Abraham did the same at a later period, the bones of Adam having come down to him through Shem. The bloody sacrifice of Jesus upon Golgotha over the bones of Adam was a foreshadowing of the holy

---

[1] The Alpha and Omega.

[2] A remarkable short summary here follows; for a far more complete account, see relevant sections in *Mysteries of the Old Testament*.

sacrifice of the mass over relics placed under the altar stone. For it the sacrifices of the patriarchs were but a preparation. They too possessed sacred relics by which they reminded God of His Promises.

The five openings in the ark were emblematic of the Savior and his Church. At the time of the deluge fearful disorders reigned over the earth and humankind was steeped in vice. They plundered and carried off whatever they pleased, laying waste their neighbor's houses and lands, and dishonoring the matrons and maidens. This passage of scripture: "The sons of God saw that the daughters of men were fair," signifies that the pure stock, "born of God, not of the flesh, nor of blood, nor of the will of men,"[1] mingled with impure races, gave birth to a powerful people in an earthly human sense, and so sullied the line from which the messiah was to spring. Noah's own relations were corrupt—all save his wife, his sons, and their wives, who dwelt in his immediate vicinity. They used to build in those early times great stone buildings, and erect around them tents or huts of osier. The further Noah's family removed from him, the worse they became, the more corrupt in their morals—they even robbed him and revolted against him. It was not that they were rude or savage, for they lived quite commodiously in well-arranged households; but it was because they were given up to vice, to the most abominable idolatry. They made idols for themselves out of whatever pleased them best.[2]

I saw, also, Moses praying before an altar on which he had laid the bones of Jacob, which he generally carried around him in a box. As he poured out something on the altar there arose a flame into which he cast incense; he invoked God by the Promise made to those bones. He prayed until he sank down exhausted. In the morning he arose again to pray. Jacob's bones were afterwards placed in the Ark of the Covenant. Moses prayed with arms out-

---

[1] John 1:18.

[2] There follows here a long account of Noah and the ark which will be found integrated with much additional visionary material in "Noah and His Family" in *First Beginnings*.

stretched in the form of a cross. God resists not such a prayer, for it was thus that His own Son faithfully prayed until death. I saw, also, Joshua praying like Moses when the sun stood still at his command.

I saw the pool of Bethsaida, its five entrances betokening the five wounds, and I had many pictures of it at various times. I saw a hill some distance from the first Temple, where in time of danger a pit had been dug wherein to hide the sacred vessels, candlesticks, and censers. I saw several of the last named with two handles. In the center of the pit was placed the sacred fire of the altar, and over the top were laid all kinds of beams; the whole was then covered with earth so that the spot was not noticeable. The beam that formed the trunk of the holy cross was found here. It had formerly been a tree by the brook Kidron. Its lower branches shot out over the water and came, at last, to be used as a bridge. After the hill had been leveled, it was used for various purposes. I saw Nehemiah, when returned from captivity, making excavations around the pit in which the sacred fire had been buried. He found a mass of black mud formed by the swampy earth, from which he removed the vessels. When he smeared the sacrificial wood with it, it immediately burst into flame.

*Anne Catherine's visions now changed from the Mosaic to the Christian era, and she saw men clothed with the highest spiritual and worldly dignity vying with one another in honoring the most blessed sacrament:*

I saw the holy Pope Zephyrinus who, on account of his zeal for the dignity of the priesthood, suffered much both from Catholics and heretics. He was very strict in the admission of candidates, whom he closely examined and of whom he rejected many. Once out of an immense number he chose only five. I often saw him disputing with heretics who unrolled parchments, spoke angrily, and even snatched his writings from him.

Zephyrinus exacted obedience from priests, sending them here and there, and silencing them if they would not obey. I saw him send a man, not yet ordained, to Africa, I think, where he became a bishop and a great saint. He was a friend of Zephyrinus and a very celebrated man. I saw the pope exhorting the faithful to bring him their silver-plate, when he replaced the wooden chalices of the churches by silver ones. The cruets were of clear glass. Zephyrinus retained the wooden vessels for his own use, but as some were scandalized at it, he had them partly gilded, and all the rest he gave to the poor. I saw him contracting debts for the relief of a poor family, whereupon one of his female relatives reproached him for running into debt for strangers rather than for his own poor relations. He replied that he had done it for Jesus Christ, at which she indignantly withdrew. Now, God had allowed him to see that, if he did anything for this woman, she would be perverted.

I saw that he caused candidates for the priesthood to be examined and ordained in the presence of the faithful. He drew up strict rules for their observance when bishops celebrated, assigning to each his own rank. He also ordained that Christians of a certain age should receive the blessed sacrament at Easter in the Church. He no longer permitted them to carry it to their homes suspended from their necks in a box, since it was often taken into improper places where feasting and dancing were going on.

Zephyrinus bore deep veneration for the Mother of God, and he had many visions of her life and death. He arranged a bed for himself just like the couch on which she had died. He always kept it concealed by a curtain, and with fervent devotion he used to lie down to rest in the same position in which he had seen her die. He also wore secretly under his robe another of sky-blue in honor of Mary's sky-blue mantle. I saw him receiving again, after their canonical penance, sinners who had been separated from the faithful for adultery and impurity. He had disputes on this point with a learned priest (Tertullian) who was too rigid and who afterward fell into heresy.

It was shown me how St. Louis of France at the age of seven prepared by a rigorous fast for his first communion. He told this to his mother. She had accompanied him to the church to implore the Mother of God for light as to whether her son should receive holy communion or not. Mary appeared to her and said that her son must prepare for seven days and then communicate, that she should receive at the same time and offer her boy to her (Mary) and she would ever be his protectress. I saw that all took place as was directed, and I learned that religious instruction at that period was both given and received in a different and more earnest manner than in our day. In all his expeditions Louis had the blessed sacrament with him, and wherever he encamped the holy sacrifice was offered. I saw him also on the crusade. Once during a violent tempest the crew of his own vessel and those of the other ships cried to him for help, begging him to intercede with God for their delivery from danger. As the blessed sacrament was not on board, the saintly king took up a new-born, baptized infant, went on deck, and held it up in the storm, begging God to show pity for its sake. Then, turning slowly around, he gave benediction with the child and the storm instantly ceased. He afterward exhorted his grateful people to an increase of devotion toward the blessed sacrament, telling them that, if God had wrought so great a miracle for the sake of an innocent baptized child, what would He not do for the sake of His only Son?

*Side by side with such scenes as the above, Anne Catherine beheld others of a different nature intended to animate her to renewed zeal in her task of prayer and expiation:*

In a certain city I saw over a gay party of ecclesiastics and seculars, men and women who were feasting and jesting, a heavy black fog stretching off into a region of darkness. In it sat satan under a hideous form, and around him as many devils as there were guests in the assembly below, all busily engaged in inciting the latter to sin, whispering to them and inflaming their passions. They were in a dangerous state of excitement and freely conversed in a light and wanton strain. The ecclesiastics belonged to the number of those whose motto is: "Live and let live!"—who argue thus: "In our day one must not be singular, nor play the misanthrope, let us rather *rejoice with those that rejoice.*" And in such dispositions they daily celebrate holy mass.

I saw but one young girl in the party still perfectly innocent, and that was owing to her devotion to her patron, a saint whose name is well known and whom she was in the habit of invoking. I saw how they bantered with her and tried to lead her astray. But over her appeared a break in the darkness through which her patron shed light upon her and kept the evil spirits aloof. Then satan from his dark circle called out to the saint, asking what he wanted and how he dared encroach upon his rights—boasting with a contemptuous smile that all the priests below were his, since in their present state they said mass daily, thereby plunging deeper into his meshes. The saint bade him retire, telling him that, through the merits of Jesus Christ, he had no right over the girl, whom he could not even approach. Satan boastingly retorted that he would yet catch her, that he would make use of a stranger who had once made an impression upon her, and who would soon do the work.

Satan's figure was horrible: short arms with claws, long feet and knees turned outward so that he could not kneel even if he wished; his face was human, but cold, wicked, fearful, and he had certain appendages like wings. He was black and obscure, spreading darkness wherever he went. As I was surprised to hear him speaking of his *rights*, I was told that he really did acquire a positive right over every baptized person who, though endued with the power of Jesus Christ to resist him, yet freely and voluntarily delivers himself up to sin. This vision was most impressive and affecting. I knew the people as well as the girl protected by her patron.

I went to several dying persons, and one case touched me deeply. A worldly, dissipated woman lay on her death bed. She would not be converted; she had no faith, she disdained the sacraments. I made the stations for her with some souls. Then we prostrated before the crucifix of Coesfeld and prayed so perseveringly that the Savior detached his hands from the cross and descended. Instantly I found myself again by the dying one, before whom stood the Savior clothed in a mantle which he opened to show his wounds. The woman was seized with fright, entered into herself, made a contrite confession, and died.

I went with my guardian angel into seven churches to pray before the blessed sacrament, and to offer the passion of Jesus Christ in atonement for the injuries and affronts committed against it by bad priests. The patron of each of the churches was present, and joined in the devotion with my angel. The prayers we said were like litanies. Two of these churches were in distant lands over the great waters; I think the people were English.

*On Sunday, August 28th, the pilgrim found Anne Catherine toward noon still in ecstasy, praying with her arms extended. When returned to consciousness, she was unable at first to recall her surroundings or the hour of the day; but after some time she related the following:*

This morning I had to say prayers enjoined upon me last night. First, I heard a mass here in our own church, after which I saw the pilgrim communicate, and this was followed by several other masses. I saw all the faults and negligence of both priests and seculars, and endured all kinds of sufferings on their account. I offered up all for them, presenting to God in reparation His crucified Son at each elevation of the host. I did this not only here, but in all the churches, perhaps a thousand, to which I was transported most wonderfully and rapidly, for I went into all I had ever visited in Europe or elsewhere. What I saw could not be told in two large volumes.

At the close of this manifold labor of prayer, I had toward noon a picture of St. Peter's, which seemed to be floating above the earth in the air. Crowds, great and small, priests and lay people, women and children—yes, even old cripples—ran to support it. I was in an agony lest the church would crush them all, for the foundations and the lower part seemed to be crumbling away; but the people put their shoulders under it and held it up. In so doing, they all became of the same height and every one was in his right place, the priests under the altars, laymen under the pillars, and the women under the entrance. Still I feared that its weight would be too much for the supporters, when I saw the heavens open above it and the saints sustaining it by their prayers and helping those below. I was hovering and flying in the air between the two. Then I saw the church borne forward a short distance, and a whole row of houses and palaces in front of it sank into the earth like a wheat field trodden underfoot. The church was deposited in their place.

Then I had another picture. I saw the Blessed Virgin over the church surrounded by apostles and bishops, and below a grand procession and solemn ceremonies. I saw all the bad bishops who thought they were able to act by themselves—who received not for their labors the strength of Christ through the intercession of their saintly predecessors—driven out and replaced by others. I saw immense blessings descending from heaven, and many changes effected. The pope regulated everything. I saw numbers of poor, simple-hearted men arise, many of them quite young. I saw many aged church dignitaries who had entered the service of bad bishops and neglected the interests of the church, now on crutches as if lame and paralyzed, led by two persons to receive pardon.

*At the close of this labor undertaken that the unbloody sacrifice might be offered in a becoming manner, Anne Catherine had another very comprehensive vision. In it was shown her the holy mass as the line of demarcation between humankind both in time and in eternity; and she saw also its cessation at the time of Antichrist. She said:*

I had a great picture of the church, but I can no longer give the details in order. I saw St. Peter's surrounded by fields, gardens, countries, and forests; and I saw multitudes from all parts of the world, many of whom I knew naturally or by my visions. Some of them were entering the church and others passing it indifferently. A great ceremony was going on. Over the church floated a luminous cloud from which came out the apostles and holy bishops and formed into choirs above the altar. Among them were Augustine, Ambrose, and all who had labored for the exaltation of the Church. It was a grand solemnity and mass was being celebrated.

In the middle of the church on a desk lay a great open book with three seals hanging from one side and two from the other. I saw the evangelist John, and I was told that the book contained the revelations he had had at Patmos. Before it was opened something happened, which I have forgotten, and it is a pity there is a break here! The pope was not present, he was concealed somewhere. I think the people knew not where he was, and I do not remember now whether he was praying, or whether he was dead. All present, lay people as well as clergy, had to lay their hand on a certain passage of the gospels. Upon many of them descended as a sign a light from the holy apostles and bishops, but for many others the ceremony was only an empty form. Outside the church I saw numbers of Jews who wanted to enter, but could not as yet. At the close of the ceremony there came a great crowd, an innumerable multitude; but the great book was suddenly shut as if by an invisible power. It reminded me of the evening in the convent when the devil blew out my candle and shut my book. All around in the distance I saw a terrible, bloody combat, and off toward the north a great battle going on. The whole picture was grand and imposing. I am sorry I have forgotten the passage in the book on which they had to put their finger.[1]

## Dedication of the Church of St. Savior at Rome

I WAS in Rome. I saw a very beautiful church, lately finished, delivered into the pope's hands by the architect, a man clad in ancient style and wearing round his neck a golden chain and collar. The pope praised the work, but the architect replied boastingly that he could have built it much better had he wished. Now, they took him at his word and refused him his pay, since he had not made the church as beautiful and magnificent as he could have done. He had, as he himself acknowledged, neglected such and such a piece of sculpturing that would have greatly embellished it. The architect exclaimed: "O had I only been silent," and he laid his finger on his lips, "they would have accepted my work as perfect!" Then he was taken into custody and not released until he had improved his work and sculptured his own likeness on the wall, his finger on his lips.

The architect then wrote to the pope, saying that he would perfect his share in the material construction when the latter would have perfected his own part in its spiritual edification, denouncing

---

[1] In the original edition of Fr. Schmöger's biography of Anne Catherine there follows next extended accounts of visions relating to souls in purgatory, the angelic hierarchies, and the heavenly Jerusalem. They were inserted at this point in that biography for chronological reasons, as having been received primarily on the following occasions: feasts of All-Saints and All-Souls (1819), feast of the Guardian Angels (1820), feast of St. Michael the Archangel (1820), feasts of All-Saints and All Souls (1820). However, they are not primarily biographical, and so, owing to their inherent interest as offering extended insight into the topics mentioned, they are presented, along with hitherto untranslated material, in *Inner Life and Worlds of Soul & Spirit*, the companion to this present volume.

at the same time numerous points of ecclesiastical discipline and fraternal charity that greatly disfigured the Church. "The exterior," said he, "needs not to be more perfect than the interior." On the receipt of this letter the pope set him at liberty, in accordance with the precept: "Do not to others what you would not have others do to you."

Then the church was consecrated with magnificent ceremonies, and I saw an indescribably beautiful church full of saints and angels high up above it in the air. In it was reproduced—but with far more perfection and elegance—all that went on in the church below; for instance, its heavenly choirs responded to all that was chanted in the earthly procession. During this procession, I was suddenly called away to a person dying in a hospital. I had to go over a road covered with snow, and I was afraid that by my footprints it would be discovered that I was barefoot; but on my return I found all traces effaced.

I went again into the new church and stood high upon a wall where I could see the blessed sacrament borne processionally in a ciborium. Above it floated a banner of light, and over that again a resplendent host surrounded by dazzling glory. As it neared me, this supernatural host flew toward me; but I did not receive it, I only adored it. At the same moment I saw the consecration of the church going on and heard the responses sung by the celestial choirs above. I went up to it and assisted at the celebration of the feast of St. Martin. I saw many circumstances of his life as also of his death, and the wonderful propagation of his spiritual influence. This was represented by bands of light streaming from the church that he held in his hand. From their extremities sprang forth other churches that likewise propagated the faith and bore similar fruits.

Then my guide took me up to the top of the spiritual church, which appeared to increase in size until finally it became a tower full of luminous, transparent sculpturing. From it he showed me the earth spread out like a map. I saw and recognized all the countries in which I have so often been. I saw the Ganges and spots where lay piles of sparkling precious stones, and I thought of those stolen from the tomb of the three kings. Deep down in the sea I saw treasures of precious things, merchandise, chests, and even whole ships. And I saw also the different parts of the world. My guide pointed out Europe and, showing me a little sandy patch in it, uttered these remarkable words: "Behold hostile Prussia!"—then, pointing further north, he said: "See mischief-making Moscovy!"

# Sufferings For Others,
## Conversion of Sinners &
## the Dying, Feasts

### Pope Pius VII

THE *last five years of Pius VII's pontificate were a time of trial not less severe than that of former years—that is, his arrest by Napoleon's minions, his imprisonment, and the ill-treatment attending it. We may reasonably conclude that captivity was far less painful to the august and magnanimous sufferer than the network of deceit, treason, and artifice spread by his enemies around the holy see to prevent the discharge of his duties as supreme pastor toward the Church in Germany. During these two periods of his pontificate, fraught with anxiety and suffering, Anne Catherine was perhaps the most remarkable of the hidden instruments destined by almighty God to serve the pope against his adversaries. As at a later period Gregory XVI and Pius IX found their faithful auxiliary in Maria von Moerl, so did Anne Catherine during the whole reign of Pius VII faithfully typify the apostolic community at Jerusalem earnestly supplicating for Peter imprisoned by Herod.[1] The very small part she was able to communicate is quite sufficient to convince us both of the truth of her visions and the vast extent of her mission:*

I had to go to Rome (*November 15, 1819*), for the pope is too yielding to his enemies in weighty affairs. There is a *dark man* in Rome who knows how to attain his ends by flattery and promises. He hid behind some cardinals. The pope, in the hope of obtaining a certain advantage, has consented to something that will turn out to the prejudice of the Church. I saw it under the form of conferences and an exchange of writings. Then I saw the dark man

---

[1] Acts 22:5.

proudly boasting to his party: "Now, I have it! Now we'll soon see where the rock is upon which the Church is built!" But he was too quick with his boasting. I had to go to the pope, who was kneeling in prayer. I seemed to hover over him. It was very strange! I repeated earnestly the message entrusted to me for him, but there seemed to be something between us, and he spoke not. Suddenly he arose, touched a bell, and sent for a cardinal whom he commissioned to recall the concession that had been granted. The cardinal looked thunderstruck and asked whence came this change. The pope answered that he would give no explanation. "Let it suffice," said he, "that it must be so," and the cardinal went away stupefied. I saw many people in Rome deeply saddened by the intrigues of the dark man, who looks like a Jew.

I went afterward to Münster to the vicar-general. He was seated at a table, reading a book. I was charged to tell him that he spoils things by his severity, that he ought to attend more seriously to the particular needs of his flock and remain at home more for such as wished to see him. It seemed to him that he found in his book a passage suggestive of these thoughts, and he began to feel dissatisfied with himself. I went also to Dean Overberg, whom I found as usual calm and recollected, advising and consoling women and girls of all classes, and quietly praying in his heart all the time.

My guide told me (*January 12, 1820*) I must go to the pope and stir him up in prayer, and that I should be told all I had to do. I arrived in Rome and, singular thing!—I passed through the walls and stood on high in a corner looking down upon the people below. When I thought of this afterward during the day, it seemed to me very strange, though I am often thus placed with regard to others. I was told to say to the pope in prayer that he should be more attentive, as the affair then being so artfully negotiated was one of great moment, that he ought to use his pallium more frequently, for then he would be more abundantly endued with strength and grace from the Holy Spirit. There is some connection between this little mantle and the ornament worn by the high priest of the Old Law when he prophesied. It is thought that the pope ought to wear it only on certain days, but necessity knows no certain days. He must also solemnly convene the cardinals oftener. He manages his affairs too quietly, too privately; consequently he is often deceived, the enemy daily becomes more cunning. There is now some question of Protestants sharing in the government of the Catholic clergy. I had to tell the pope to invoke the Holy Spirit for three days and then he would act right. Many of those around him are good for nothing. He ought to convict them openly of their want of uprightness and then they would, perhaps, amend.

*January 13th*: I was still in Rome with the pope, who is now firmly resolved to sign nothing. But his adversaries are resorting to more artful measures, and once more I saw the movements of the cringing, cunning dark man. They often appear to resign what they are sure of gaining later.

*Anne Catherine's labor for the pope was accompanied by great sufferings of which the pilgrim speaks, as follows:*

Sister Emmerich is full of courage. She seems to be always in a state of expectancy, eagerly awaiting the moment to give assistance. Once she exclaimed that she saw the two deceased nuns approaching her, and immediately began those tortures she has now endured for a week. Her arms are suddenly jerked up as if by an invisible power, and present the appearance of being fastened to a cross by cords; her feet are closely crossed one over the other; and the tension of the whole body becomes so great that one watches nervously to see it snap asunder. Her feet quiver violently from the pain, her teeth are clenched, and stifled groans escape her. Every member trembles convulsively. Her bones are heard to creak; the upper part of her body is raised; her hands drawn back; her muscles distended. She is stiff as a wooden statue and light as a hollow paste-board figure. That her state is altogether involuntary, that she is acted upon by some external force, is perfectly evident. Her body makes all the movements of a person extended on a cross. This lasted for about ten minutes, when the arms suddenly fell; she swooned away, and passing into a state of contemplation she began to say that three unknown persons had bound her to a cross.

Then she saw mounting a ladder numbers of holy souls just released through her mediation and who thanked her as they passed. And now her torture recommenced: she was scourged, bound to a cross, and subjected to a repetition of the same cruel sufferings, which lasted, like the first, for about ten minutes, the perspiration streaming down her face. She begged the pilgrim to replace her hands and feet in their natural position, which he did, putting at the same time some relics in her hand. This struggle was endured for all that were then dying unprepared or without the sacraments, of whom she saw about fifty, most of them young persons and priests. They were all helped in various ways.

She never beheld children among those to whom she was called upon to render such services. According to her own prediction, one more such crisis was in store for her to be endured for the Church. It came, in fact, that same day with all the circumstances attendant on the preceding. The imposition of her confessor's hands afforded relief. But when she recovered consciousness, it was found that she could not speak, her tongue having fallen back paralyzed. The confessor's blessing in the name of Jesus restored her its use. She lay perfectly exhausted, though with the placid, satisfied expression of one who had finished a painful but meritorious task. With childlike simplicity she exclaimed: "I shall have another weary night all alone! I will be thankful if a soul comes to me; but, in either case, I must be satisfied."

*Next morning the pilgrim found her all bruised, her limbs still trembling from the terrible tension put upon them. Being now able to speak, she explained that the suffering of the preceding day had been announced to her for the morning, but that she had begged a respite until the evening instead of enduring it three hours after midday, the time specified by her guide. She had been a passive victim during it. Three unknown persons had bound her to a cross and scourged her with rods and whips, but the sight of the miseries for which she suffered rendered all things sweet and aroused in her a thirst for still greater pains. She had seen that night that the pope yielded not to the wicked and artful proposals made him. She saw almost all the bishops sunk in the sleep of indifference. Soon a new pope would arise (about 1840–1850), one who would be more energetic. She saw the future pontiff in a city to the south of Rome. He was not clothed like a monk, though he wore something like a religious badge. The state of the Church she described as extraordinarily distressing; her enemies subtle and active, her clergy timid and indolent. They neglected the power they held from God, they even aimed at the tiara, which however they were never to attain.*

*During her martyrdom, she seemed to be lying in a horizontal position, on a mountain, the mountain of the prophets far away in the distance:*

I still feel the sharp pressure of last night's cords. Once I fell, and the cords around my body cut deep into my waist. I felt as if my every vein and nerve had snapped. The first time I endured such sufferings for my neighbor was after my confirmation, for before that I had only such as were self-imposed. All my singular accidents and maladies were of the same nature, especially those that befell me in the convent.

I was in a city beyond Frankfurth (*February 22, 1820*), in a country of vineyards, and I saw in one of the churches great disorder occasioned by bad priests. I had to console one old priest who had been misrepresented to his bishop by his wicked assistants because he had with the aid of the two sacristans driven them from the confessional and the church, which they had presumed to enter after having spent the whole night in carousing. The affair caused great excitement. The old priest said mass himself, otherwise there would have been no divine service; but he still lies under the accusation. No one will help him but God.

## Two Churches

(St. Mary of the Rotunda and the
Chapel of the Protestant Embassy, at Rome)

LAST night (*May 13, 1820*), from eleven to three, I had a most wonderful vision of two churches and two popes and a variety of things, ancient and modern. I shall relate, as well as I can, all that I remember of it:

My guardian angel came and told me that I must go to Rome and take two things to the pope, but I cannot now recall what they were. Perhaps it is the will of God that I should forget them. I asked my angel how I could make so long a journey, sick as I was. But when I was told that I should make it without difficulty, I no longer objected.

An odd-looking vehicle appeared before me, flat and slight, with only two wheels, the flooring red with white edges. I saw no horses. I was gently lifted and laid on it and, at the same instant, a snow-white, luminous child flew toward me and seated himself at my feet. He reminded me of the patience-child in green—so sweet, so lovely, and perfectly transparent. He was to be my companion, to console and take care of me. The wagon was so light and smooth that at first I was afraid of slipping off; but it began to move very gently of itself without horses, and I saw a shining human figure going on ahead.

The journey did not seem long, although we crossed countries, mountains, and great waters. I knew Rome the instant we reached it, and I was soon in the presence of the pope. I know not now whether he was sleeping or praying, but I had to say two things to him, or give him two things, and I shall have to go to him once again to announce a third.

Then I had a wonderful vision. Rome suddenly appeared as in the early ages, and I saw a pope (Boniface IV) and an emperor whose name I knew not (Phocas). I could not find my way in the city, all was so different, even the sacred ceremonies; yet I recognized them as Catholic. I saw a great round building like a cupola —it was a pagan temple full of beautiful idols. It had no windows, but in the dome was an opening with a contrivance for keeping out the rain. It seemed as if all the idols that ever existed were gathered together there in every conceivable posture—many of them very beautiful, others exceedingly odd. There were even some of geese, which received divine honor. In the center stood a very high pyramid formed entirely of those images.[1]

I saw no idolatrous worship at the time of which I speak, although the idols were still carefully preserved. I saw messengers

---

[1] This probably refers to the story honoring Juno's geese on the Capitoline Hill, credited with saving Rome from the Gallic hordes. During the Gallic siege of Rome in around 390 BC, Marcus Manlius held out for months with a small garrison on the citadel, while the rest of Rome was abandoned. When Gauls under the command of Brennus were attempting to scale the Capitoline, Manlius was roused by the cackling of the sacred geese, rushed to the spot, and threw down the foremost assailants.

from Pope Boniface going to the emperor and petitioning for the temple to be changed into a Christian church. I heard the latter declaring distinctly that the pope should allow the ancient statues to remain, though he might erect therein the cross, to which the highest honors should be paid. This proposal, as it seemed to me, was made not wickedly, but in good faith.

I saw the messengers return with the answer and Boniface reflecting as to how he might in some measure conform to the emperor's will. While he was thus deliberating, I saw a good, pious priest in prayer before the crucifix. He wore a long white robe with a train, and an angel hovered by his side. Suddenly he arose, went straight to Boniface, and told him that he should by no means accede to the emperor's proposal. Messengers were then despatched to the emperor, who now consented to the temple's being entirely cleared. Then I saw his people come and take numbers of the statues to the imperial city; but still many remained in Rome.

There followed the consecration of the temple, at which the holy martyrs assisted, with Mary at their head. The altar was not in the center of the building, but against the wall. I saw more than thirty wagon-loads of sacred relics brought into the church. Many of them were enclosed in the walls and others could be seen through round openings covered with something like glass.

When I had witnessed this vision even in the smallest details, I saw again the present pope and the dark church of his time in Rome. It seemed to be a large, old house like a town-hall with columns in front. I saw no altar in it, but only benches, and in the middle of it something like a pulpit. They had preaching and singing, but nothing else, and only very few attended it.

And then, a most singular sight!—each member of the congregation drew an idol from his breast, set it up before him, and prayed to it. It was as if each man drew forth his secret thoughts or passions under the appearance of a dark cloud which, once outside, took some definite form. They were precisely such figures as I had seen around the neck of the illicit bride in the nuptial house—figures of men and animals. The god of one was short and broad with a crisp head and numerous, outstretched arms ready to seize and devour all in its reach; that of another was quite small, with miserable, shrunken limbs; another had merely a block of wood upon which he gazed with rolling eyes; this one had a horrible animal; that one, a long pole. The most singular part of it was that the idols filled the place. The church, although the worshippers were so few, was crowded with idols. When the service was over, everyone's god re-entered into his breast. The whole church was draped in black, and all that took place in it was shrouded in gloom.

Then I saw the connection between the two popes and the two temples. I am sorry that I have forgotten the numbers, but I was shown how weak the one had been in adherents and human support, but how strong in courage to overturn so many gods (I knew the number) and to unite so many different forms of worship into one; and on the contrary, how strong in numbers and yet how irresolute in action was the other since, in authorizing the erection of false temples, he had allowed the only true God, the only true Religion, to be lost among so many false gods and false teachings. It was also shown me that those pagans humbly adored gods other than themselves, and that they would have been willing to admit in all simplicity the only God, the Most Holy Trinity. Their worship was preferable to that of those who adore themselves in a thousand idols to the total exclusion of Our Lord. The picture was favorable to the early ages, for in them idolatry was on the decrease, while in our days it is just the contrary.

I saw the fatal consequences of this counterfeit church; I saw it increase; I saw heretics of all kinds flocking to the city.[1] I saw the

---

[1] "I saw something very laughable in the dark church. One of its mighty patrons wanted to do something extraordinarily grand, so he sent word to the preacher that he would give him a white surplice to wear in the pulpit. Then came the preacher, a tall, handsome man with a beautiful tie under his chin. The patron put the surplice on him and sent him into the pulpit. I thought: The patron is raising a great, great tree; it will fall into a great, great pool; and there will be a great, great splash!' But it turned out otherwise. The preacher sat in state, carefully showing off his surplice; the congregation waited and waited, but not a word did he utter. And lo! when they looked more closely, they found that their preacher had no head. The surplice covered only a great, great bundle of straw. Many broke out into a laugh, others mocked, but as for the patron—he was perfectly furious."

ever-increasing tepidity of the clergy, the circle of darkness ever widening.

And now the vision became more extended. I saw in all places Catholics oppressed, annoyed, restricted, and deprived of liberty, churches were closed, and great misery prevailed everywhere with war and bloodshed. I saw rude, ignorant people offering violent resistance, but this state of things lasted not long. Again I saw in vision St. Peter's undermined according to a plan devised by the secret sect, while at the same time it was damaged by storms—but then delivered at the moment of greatest distress. Again I saw the Blessed Virgin extending her mantle over it. In this last scene, I saw no longer the reigning pope, but one of his successors—a mild but very resolute man who knew how to attach his priests to himself and who drove far from him the bad.

I saw all things renewed and a Church that reached from earth to heaven. I saw one of the twelve new apostles in the person of the young priest whom the unchaste bride wanted to marry. It was a very comprehensive vision and portrayed anew all that had been previously shown me regarding the Church's destiny. I was told that I should have to go again to the pope; but when all this will take place I cannot say.

## A New Church Under the Influence of Planetary Spirits

I SAW (*September 12, 1820*) a fantastic, odd-looking church being built. The choir was in three parts, each raised some steps above the last; and under it was a deep vault full of fog. On the first platform of the choir was a seat; on the second, a basin of water; on the third, a table. I saw no angel helping in the construction, but numbers of the most violent planetary spirits[1] dragging all sorts of things into the vault, where persons in little ecclesiastical mantles received them and deposited them in their various places. Nothing was brought from above; all came from the earth and

---

[1] Regarding planetary spirits, see also "Between Purgatory and Heaven" in *Inner Life and Worlds of Soul & Spirit*.

the dark regions, all was built up by the planetary spirits. The water alone seemed to have something holy about it—the Holy Spirit was above it.

I saw an enormous number of implements brought into the church, and many persons, even children, had different tools, as if trying to make something; but all was obscure, absurd, dead! Division and destruction reigned everywhere.

Nearby I saw another church, shining and rich with graces from on high, angels ascending and descending. In it were life and increase, but also tepidity and dissipation. And yet it was like a tree full of sap compared with the other, which was like a chest of life-less institutions. The former was like a bird on the wing; the latter, like a paper dragon, which instead of flying as it should, dragged its tail, adorned with ribands and writings, over a stubble-field.

I saw that many of the implements in the new church, such as spears and darts, were meant to be used against the living church. Everyone dragged in something different: clubs, rods, pumps, cudgels, puppets, mirrors, trumpets, horns, bellows—all sorts of things. In the cave below (the sacristy) some people kneaded bread, but nothing came of it, for it would not rise. The men in the little mantles brought wood to the steps of the pulpit to make a fire. They puffed and blew and labored hard, but the fire would not burn; all they produced was smoke and fumes. Then they broke a hole in the roof and ran up a pipe—but the smoke would not rise, and the whole place became black and suffocating. Some blew the horns so violently that the tears streamed from their eyes. All in this church belonged to the earth, returned to the earth; all was dead, the work of human skill, a church of the latest style, a church of man's invention like the new heterodox church in Rome.

I passed over a dark, cold country to a large city, and I saw again the great, odd-looking church with nothing holy about it, and innumerable planetary spirits laboring at it. I saw it in the same way that I see a Catholic institution being erected—angels, saints, and Christians all laboring in common, only here the concurrence of the laborers was shown under forms more mechanical. The planetary spirits ascended and descended and shot down rays upon the workmen; but all was done in accordance with human reason. I saw a spirit on high drawing lines and tracing figures, and down below the design, the plan immediately carried out.

I saw the influence of the proud, planetary spirits in their relation with the building extending to even the most distant places. All the steps deemed necessary or useful to the construction and maintenance of the church were taken in the most remote countries, and men and things, doctrines and opinions, contributed thereto. The whole picture was colored with intense selfishness, presumption, and violence. I saw not a single angel or saint helping in the work. It was an immense vision.

Far away in the background I saw the throne of a savage nation, the people armed with boar-spears and a figure saying in mocking terms: "Build it as solidly as you please, we shall overturn it!"

I went also into a large hall in the city, in which a hideous ceremony—a horrible, deceitful comedy—was being enacted. The hall was draped in black, and a man wearing a star on his breast was put into a coffin and taken out again. It seemed to be a threat of what would happen to him. In the midst of it all I saw the devil under a thousand forms. All was dark as night. It was horrible!

## Prayers for Souls

I HAVE had some rough work to do (*September 24, 1820*) in the nuptial house, but I could not finish. With a stiff broom quite unfit for the work I had to sweep away a quantity of trash, but I could not succeed. Then my mother came and helped me, as also the soul of her to whom I gave the picture of St. Catherine that I had received in a supernatural manner. She wore a little picture on her breast and conversed with me a long time. They are not yet in heaven, but in a very pleasant place where Abraham and good Lazarus[1] were—a charming place, mild and sweet like dew and honey. Its light is like that of the moon, yet white, more like milk. The vision of poor Lazarus was there given me merely that I might know where I was [Abraham's bosom].

---

[1] That is, poor Lazarus of the parable told in Luke 16:19–31, not the Lazarus whom Christ Jesus raised from the dead.

Paradise, which I again saw, as well as the mountain of the prophets, is more joyous, more delightful than Abraham's bosom, and full of magnificent creatures. My mother took me to the abodes of the souls. I remember, in particular, a mountain out of which issued a spirit shining with a copper-colored light and bound by a chain. He stood before me. He had been confined here a long time destitute of all assistance, for no one thought of him, no one helped or prayed for him. He uttered but few words, and yet I learned his whole history, of which I still remember a part:

During the reign of an English king who waged war upon France, he had commanded an English army in the latter country, which he frightfully and cruelly laid waste. He had been badly reared through his mother's fault—as I saw—but he had always cherished a secret veneration for Mary. Among other acts of violence, he was accustomed to destroy all the pictures he came across. One day, passing a most beautiful statue of the Mother of God, he was about to treat it in like manner when he was seized by a certain emotion that restrained him. He was soon after attacked by a violent fever. He wanted to confess, but became unconscious and died. But his lively repentance obtained for him mercy at the judgment seat. He was in a state to receive assistance, but his friends completely forgot him. He told me that he wanted masses more than all else, and that for a long time past a very slight assistance would have freed him. He was not in purgatory, for in purgatory proper, souls are not tormented by devils. He was in another place of torment and surrounded by dogs barking at him and tearing him, because he had during life subjected others to the same cruelty. Sometimes he was bound to a block in different positions and drenched with seething blood that ran through all his veins. The hope of deliverance was his only consolation. When he had told me the above he disappeared in the mountain, leaving the grass around him scorched and burnt. This was the third time I had seen him.

I was afterward transported with several souls, whom the Lord had delivered at my petition, into a Franciscan convent in which a lay brother was struggling in fearful death agony. The convent was situated in a mountainous district; it had not a large community, and there were some seculars among them. The dying man had lived there three years. After a misspent life, he had entered the order to do penance. It was night when I arrived. I found a troop of evil spirits raising a horrible din around the house. It was swept by a tempest. The tiles were flying from the roof, the trees beating up against the windows, and demons—under the form of crows, other sinister birds, and frightful figures—were dashing around the place and even into the cell of the dying man. Among the assistants at his deathbed was a holy old monk around whom I saw many souls who had been delivered from purgatory by his prayers. The tumult increased and the monks fled in terror. But the good old man went to the window and adjured the evil spirits in the name of Jesus to say what they wanted. Then I heard a voice demanding why he wished to deprive them of a soul that had served them for thirty years. But the old monk, all the souls, and I myself resisted the enemy until we forced him to withdraw. He vowed that he would enter into a woman with whom the dying man had long sinned, and torment her till her death. I saw the evil one depart and the sick man die in peace.

Last night (*September 27, 1820*) I prayed much for the poor souls. I saw many wonderful things concerning their punishments and the incomprehensible mercy of God. Again I saw the unhappy English captain, and I prayed for him. I saw that the mercy and justice of God are boundless, and that nothing of the good still left in man is ever lost; for the virtues and vices of a man's ancestors contribute to his salvation or ruin according to his own will and cooperation. I saw souls receiving by wonderful ways assistance from the treasures of the Church and the charity of her members—all was a real reparation, a full compensation for sin. Mercy and justice, though infinite in God, do not neutralize each there. I saw many states of purification and especially the chastisement of those indolent, easy-going priests who are wont to say: "'I'll be satisfied with a low place in heaven. I pray, I say mass, I hear confessions, etc." They have to endure unspeakable torments and they sigh after works of zeal and charity. All the souls that once claimed their assistance now pass in review before them while they have to sit idle, though consumed by devouring desires to help those in need. Their sloth has become their spiritual torment, their repose is turned into impatience, their inactivity is now a chain that binds them fast. These chastisements are not imaginary—they spring clearly and wonderfully from past offences as disease from a germ.

I saw the soul of a woman deceased some twenty or thirty years. She was not in purgatory, but in a place of more rigorous punishment. She was not only imprisoned, but also punished in inexpressible pain and affliction. In her arms was a dark-skinned child that she incessantly killed, but which always came to life again. The mother was condemned to wash it white with her tears. Yes, souls can shed tears, otherwise they could not weep in the body.

The poor creature begged my prayers and related to me her fault—or rather, I saw it all in a succession of pictures. She belonged to a Polish city and was the wife of an honest man who kept an inn for the accommodation of ecclesiastics and others of retired life. The wife was thoroughly good and pious and had a very holy relative, a missionary in the Congregation of the Most Holy Redeemer. Her husband being obliged to absent himself from home for a short time, there came to lodge at the inn a stranger, a wicked wretch, who, using violence, forced her into sin. This drove her almost mad. She repulsed the miserable man, but he refused to leave the house even when her husband's return drew near. Her agony of mind became frightful. The fiend suggested to her to poison her seducer, which she actually did, when remorse well-nigh drove her to despair; and, yielding again to the evil one's whisper, she later on destroyed the fruit of her womb. In her misery, she sought a strange priest to whom she might confess. A vagabond disguised as a priest had presented himself at the inn. She made her confession to him with unspeakable grief and torrents of tears. Shortly after she died, but God in his mercy was mindful of her bitter repentance; and although unabsolved and without the sacraments, yet he condemned her to the place of punishment wherein I found her. She must by her own satisfaction complete the years God had destined for her child, before which it cannot attain to light. Such children have a growth in the other world. Five years after her death she appeared to her relative, the priest, during the holy mass. I knew the pious old man; he prayed in union with me.

On this occasion I saw many things concerning purgatory, and particularly the state of children put to death before or after their birth; but as I cannot relate it clearly, I will pass it over. Of one thing I have always been certain, however, and that is that all good in soul or body tends to light, just as sin if not expiated tends to darkness. Justice and mercy are perfections in God; the first is satisfied by the second, by the inexhaustible merits of Jesus Christ and the saints, and by the works of faith, hope, and love performed by the members of his spiritual Body. Nothing done in the Church in union with Jesus is lost. Every pious desire, every good thought, every charitable work inspired by the love of Jesus, contributes to the perfection of the whole body of the faithful. A person who does nothing more than lovingly pray to God for his brethren, participates in the great work of saving souls.

*April 12, 1820: A young peasant girl, having fallen into sin and dreading her parents' anger, had secretly given birth to a child that died shortly after in consequence of the mother's imprudence. She hid the body away, but it was soon discovered. The affair was deeply afflicting to Anne Catherine; she suffered and prayed incessantly for the guilty one's repentance. She said:*

I know the girl. She came to see me about a year ago, and since Christmas I have often seen her in vision covered up in a mantle. I always had a secret dread of its concealing something bad. I saw her last at the time for her confession, but she was not in good dispositions. I prayed for her and warned her confessor to pay particular attention to her—but she went not near him! Last night I was occupied with her and greatly distressed at her state. Although she is rather simple, she is not altogether innocent of the child's death. I saw the whole affair and prayed much for her. Then I remembered the two ex-Jesuits to whom I had gone to confession in my youth, and I thought, "How piously they lived! How much good they did! Nothing like this ever happened in their time"— but while these thoughts were passing through my mind the two holy men appeared to me, both in a very good state. One of them led me to his sister, with whom he had formerly lived and whom I knew. She was in a very singular place, walled up as it were in a narrow, dark, four-cornered hole in which she could only stand upright; but she was quite content and patient. She had many companions in the same position. Soon I saw her pass to a more roomy prison in front of the other. I could never have imagined that so pious a person would have anything to expiate! She begged me to come oftener to see her. I spoke for some time with the holy old priests and asked them something.

For a long while I have had interior lights on the state of children dying without baptism, and I have seen the unspeakable blessings, the treasures they lose when deprived of this sacrament. I cannot express what I feel on beholding their loss! I am so grieved to hear of such a death that I offer to God my prayers and sufferings in satisfaction for the neglect, that the want of charity in some may be compensated for by the body of the faithful, by myself as one of its members; therefore it was that I was so distressed about the child of the unhappy girl. I offered myself to God in satisfaction.

Last night (*April 10, 1820*) I had a painful vision, a difficult task. Suddenly there stood beside me the shining soul of a good wife of Coesfeld. She had been deeply devoted to her husband, who seemed to be a good and pious man. I had not thought of that couple for a long time. The wife died and the husband married again, but I knew not the second wife. The soul said to me: "At last I have been permitted by God to come to you. My state is a happy one, but my husband's gives me pain. During my last sickness he had with his present wife very sinful intercourse, and now in marriage he does not live with her in a Christian manner. I fear for his soul and that of his wife." On hearing this I wondered, for I had always thought him so good. She told me much more and begged me to warn her husband, who was coming to see me. I went with her to Coesfeld. I could see distinctly over the whole road, for she shone like a sun. This greatly rejoiced me. I recognized every turn of the road and found many places changed. She led me into her husband's house, in which I had often been before; in it, also, I found changes. We approached the bed of the married pair, who lay asleep. The wife seemed to perceive us, for she sat up. I spoke to her a long time, bidding her reflect on her state and lead her husband to do the same. She promised everything. I think the husband will come to see me and, since the soul has so earnestly begged me to pray for him and give him advice, I feel a little anxious as to how I shall introduce the subject if he does not begin it himself.

I have had a picture (*October 6, 1820*) of a pious Franciscan of the Tyrol who foresaw great danger menacing the Church in consequence of a political convention about to be held. He had been commanded to pray unceasingly for her, and I saw him doing so in a little convent on the outskirts of a town. He knelt at night before a miraculous picture of Mary. I saw the demons trying to distract him by raising a great din in the Church and dashing violently against the window panes under the form of crows. But the good monk was not disturbed; he went on praying with extended arms. As a consequence of his prayer, I beheld three figures drawing near to my bed: the first was a being like my guide; the others were souls seeking prayers—one a Catholic prince of Brandenburg, the other a pious Austrian emperor. They had been sent by the Franciscan's prayer to ask my help, for he had seen the same dangers as I. They petitioned to be raised to a higher state in which they would be better able to influence their present successors on earth. I learned that such souls have more influence over their descendants than others. Something very remarkable now happened to me. Their conductor took my hands himself and held them up. I felt his hand, smooth and soft and airy like down. As often as I allowed my hands to sink, he raised them up again with the words: "You must pray longer!" This is all I can remember."

Returning from Rome (*October 8*) with my guide, I went again to the Tyrol to see the pious Franciscan to whose prayer I was indebted for the visit from the sovereigns whom I had seen before in the mill.[1] He is the same old religious that lately chased the demons from the death bed of his dying confrere. When I arrived he was praying as usual, his arms extended, to ward off danger from the Church. He held his rosary in one hand. When he retired to rest, he used to hang it around his neck. I went from here with my guide and a beautiful, resplendent lady (I think Mary), to a charming high mountain on which were all sort of fruits and

---

[1] Regarding this mill, see "Return to Purgatory" in *Inner Life and Worlds of Soul & Spirit*.

lovely white animals gamboling among the bushes. Higher up we came to a garden full of magnificent roses and other kinds of flowers. In it were figures walking around. Here I saw the two sovereigns who had been promoted. They approached the gate (for I could not go to them) and again begged prayers that they might mount still higher, where they could better influence their descendants for the welfare of the Church. How I longed for some of those roses! I wanted a whole apronful! I thought if Abbé Lambert's foot were bound up in them, it would surely do him good. But my guide gave me only a few which were of no use.

*We see by the above that Anne Catherine asked for expiatory sufferings sufficient to obtain the Abbé's cure; but she received no definite assurance of obtaining them.*

## Emperor Henry at St. Mary Major

I HAVE had a vision (*July 12, 1820*) of Emperor Henry. I saw him last night in a beautiful church kneeling alone before the main altar. I know the church; there is a beautiful chapel of the holy crib in it. I saw it once before on the feast of Our Lady of the Snow. As he knelt and prayed, a light shone above the altar and the Blessed Virgin appeared alone. She wore a robe of bluish-white that shot forth rays, and she carried something in her hand. She covered the altar with a red cloth over which she spread a white one, and deposited upon it a magnificent luminous book set with precious stones. Then she lighted the candles from the sanctuary lamp. Many other lights in the form of a pyramid burned at the same time. Then she took her stand at the right of the altar.

Now came the Savior himself in sacerdotal vestments, bearing the chalice and veil. Two angels served him as acolytes, and two others accompanied him. Our Lord's head was uncovered. The chasuble was a large, heavy, red and white mantle shining with light and precious stones. The ministering angels were white. There was no little bell, but there were cruets. The wine was as red as blood and there was also some water. The mass was shorter than with us and there was no Gospel of St. John at the end. I saw the offertory and elevation; the host was like ours. The angel read the gospel and carried the book to Mary to kiss, and then, on a sign from Jesus, to Henry that he might do the same. At first he dared not obey, but at length gained courage to do so. At the end of the mass, Mary went to Henry and gave him her right hand, saying that she honored thus his chastity and exhorted him not to grow remiss. Then I saw an angel approach and grasp him by the right side as had been done to Jacob. Henry showed signs of intense pain, and afterward limped a little. During the whole of this ceremony there were numerous angels in adoration, their eyes fixed upon the altar.

## Feast of the Scapular

I WAS on Mount Carmel (*July 15, 1820*), where I saw two hermits who dwelt far apart. One was very aged and never left his cell; the other, a Frenchman named Peter, visited the old man occasionally and brought him something—but long intervals sometimes elapsed between his visits. I saw him taking journeys to Jerusalem, Rome, and to our own country, whence he returned with bands of warriors wearing crosses on their clothing. I saw Berthold with him. He was at that time a soldier. Later on, I saw the younger hermit take Berthold to the old man on Mount Carmel. Berthold had then become a hermit. He was afterward the superior of the hermits, whom he formed into communities, and for whom he erected convents.

Then I had another vision. I saw, after the hermits began to live in community, a monk on his knees in his cell. The Mother of God appeared to him with the infant Jesus on her arm. She looked just like the statue I had seen by the spring on the mountain. She gave him an article of dress in which was a square opening for the head to pass through. It fell in front over the breast. It was shining with light, the colors red and white intermingling, as in the vestment of the high priest that Zechariah showed to Joseph. On the straps that went over the shoulders were letters inscribed.

Mary spoke long to the monk. When she vanished and he returned to himself, he was filled with emotion on seeing himself clothed with the scapular. I saw him assemble his brethren and show it to them.

Then I had a vision of a church festival on Mount Carmel. I saw in the choirs of the Church Triumphant, as the first of the ancient hermits, and yet separated from them—Elijah. Under his feet were the words "Elijah, prophet." I did not see these pictures one after another, and I felt that a great number of years lay between them, especially between the vision of the reception of the scapular and the feast, for the latter seemed to belong to our own day.

Over the spring where once stood Mary's statue, now arose a convent and its church. The spring was in the middle of the latter, and above the altar was the Mother of God with the infant Jesus just as she had appeared to the hermit, living and moving in dazzling splendor. Innumerable little silken pictures hung at her sides, attached in pairs by two cords and glancing like the leaves of a tree in the sunshine, in the splendor that radiated from Mary. The Holy Virgin was surrounded by the angelic choirs, and at her feet—above the tabernacle wherein reposed the blessed sacrament—hung the large scapular she had given the hermit in vision. On all sides were ranged choirs of holy Carmelites, men and women, the most ancient in white and brown striped habits; the others in such as are now worn. I saw too the Carmelite Order—monks and nuns of the present day celebrating the feast in their several convents, either in choir or elsewhere, but all upon earth.

## Vision of the Feast
### of the Indulgence of Portiuncula

I HAD a vision of a feast (*August 1, 1820*), but I know not clearly what it signified; however, this is what I can recall: I saw a great aureola of saints looking like an immense wreath in which they sat, each distinguished by different emblems, such as palms, churches, etc. Below them floated innumerable relics and sacred objects in precious vases; they seemed to belong to the saints above. In the middle of the wreath floated a little church and over it the lamb of God with his standard. Throned above the altar were the Lord Jesus and his mother surrounded by myriads of angels. An angel flew into the circle and led St. Francis to Jesus and Mary in the little church, and it seemed as if the saint petitioned for some favor by virtue of the treasure of Christ's merits and those of his holy martyrs—that is, an indulgence for the little church. Then I saw Francis go to the pope, but not in Rome, petitioning for something, an indulgence, the same that I had seen in the vision. I saw that the pope would not grant it at first; but suddenly a light shone upon him, a writing floated before him, and he was inspired to grant what the saint demanded. I saw the saint returned from the pope, praying that night on his knees. The devil approached him under the form of a very beautiful youth, and reproved him for his penances. The saint recognized the temptation, fled from his cell, cast off his garments, and rolled in the thorns until he was all covered with blood, when an angel appeared and healed his wounds. This is all I can remember.

## Our Lady of the Snow

I SAW a noble couple in a grand mansion praying at night in their room before a picture of Mary on the wall. It was coarsely embroidered or woven, the robe in some places striped with red and blue and tapering off round the feet. Mary was crowned. She held the infant Jesus in her arms, his little hands clasping the orb of the world. Two lamps burned on either side of the little picture. The narrow kneeling-bench on which the spouses knelt side by side, could be turned up before the picture; it then looked like a wardrobe, and above it hung a curtain that could be lowered to hide the picture. I have seen in olden times many such woven pictures of Mary. They could be rolled up to take on journeys and hung wherever the owner wished to pray.

As the couple knelt there, I saw the Blessed Virgin as represented in the picture, but shining with light. She hovered before the picture—between it and the couple—and enjoined upon them to erect a church in her honor at Rome upon a hill that they would find covered with snow. The next morning they related the affair to the pope, and went with several ecclesiastics to the hill upon whose summit—the site of the future edifice—lay snow of extraordinary brilliancy. I saw them driving stakes as landmarks, when the snow at once disappeared.

Then I had another vision. I saw the church built and mass being celebrated in it by a pope named Martin. Just at the moment of communication a certain great personage was to be assassinated by a man stationed near for that purpose. The assassin had been chosen and instructed for the crime by the nobleman about to receive holy communion, and all in obedience to the orders of Emperor Constantius. I saw the murderer enter the crowded church, but he was instantly struck blind. He ran here and there, stumbling against the pillars and uttering cries. A great tumult was raised. Again, I saw Pope Gregory celebrating high mass in the church. The Mother of God appeared surrounded by angels, answered *Et cum spiritu tuo,* and served him at the altar. Lastly, I saw in the same church a feast celebrated in our own days. The Mother of God appeared under the same form as she had done to its founders. This is the church in which I lately saw the holy Emperor Henry praying while Christ himself said the mass. There is a chapel of the holy crib in it.

## Spiritual Warfare • St. Michael

BETWEEN *August and the end of October, 1820, Anne Catherine's labors were constantly directed to the welfare of the Church, which as usual she beheld typified by St. Peter's at Rome. The secret society— with its worldwide ramifications engaged in ceaseless war against the Bride of Christ—was shown her as the empire of Antichrist symbolized by the beast in the Apocalypse rising out of the sea and fomenting attacks upon the flock of Christ.*

*In relating this vision, the pilgrim makes the following remarks:*

It is indeed full of breaks, for Anne Catherine saw it under allegorical representations difficult for her to describe. What is most astonishing is that it touches upon many points of the *Apocalypse* of St. John, of which humanly speaking she must have been wholly ignorant, as she has very little knowledge of the holy scriptures or of any other book. If at times she seems to read, it is with a mind deeply absorbed in contemplation, and she sees very different things from those discussed in the volume before her. The vision is a follows:

I see new martyrs, not of the present but of the future—though even now they are oppressed. I saw a secret society undermining the Great Church (St. Peter's) and near them a horrible Beast that arose out of the sea. It had a tail like a fish, claws like a lion, and numberless heads that lay like a crown around one large head. Its jaws were large and red, its body spotted like a tiger. It was very familiar with the demolishers, lying near them while they worked, and, again, concealing itself in a cave.

Here and there throughout the whole world I saw many good, pious people, especially ecclesiastics, harassed, imprisoned, and oppressed, and I felt that at some future day they would be martyred.

When the Church was well-nigh overturned—the choir and altar alone remaining untouched—I saw the demolishers thronging into it, accompanied by the beast. But they encountered a tall, majestic woman who seemed to be with child, for she walked very slowly. The wretches were filled with fear on seeing her, and the beast lay paralyzed, furiously darting its head toward her as if to devour her. But she turned and fell prostrate on her face.

Then I saw the beast fleeing to the sea, the enemy hurrying off in disorder, and immense circles of combatants surrounding the Church—some on the earth, others high in the air. The first circle of combatants was composed of youths and maidens; the second, of married persons of all classes from royalty down; the third, of religious; the fourth, of warriors, led by a rider on a white horse; and the fifth and last was made up of citizens and peasants, many of whom were marked on the forehead with a red cross.

As this army drew near, the captives and oppressed were delivered and swelled the ranks, while the demolishers and conspirators were put to flight on all sides. They were, without knowing how, gathered together into one confused mass in the midst of a dense fog. They knew neither what they did nor what they ought to do, and ran pell-mell against one another, as I so often see them do.

Then I saw the Church speedily rebuilt and more magnificent than before, for its defenders brought stones from all parts of the earth. When the most distant circles drew near, the nearest withdrew to make way for them. The former appeared to represent the various labors of prayer; the latter, the soldiers, the deeds of war. I saw among these last, friends and enemies of all nations, simply soldiers like our own and dressed like them. They did not form a perfect circle, but a crescent opening toward the north into an immense dark abyss like a chasm, a precipice—like a descent into darkness, like that to which Adam was driven from paradise. I felt that a region of darkness lay beyond.

I saw that some out of these circles remained behind. They would not advance, but stood gloomily huddled together. I saw some also who would one day be martyred for Jesus. But there were many wicked people among them, and another separation was to take place.

The Church was completely restored. Above it on a mountain, was the lamb of God surrounded by a troop of virgins with palm branches, and five circles of celestial cohorts corresponding to the five circles below. They all arrived together, and all acted in concert. Around the lamb stood the four mysterious beasts of the Apocalypse.

*On the feast of the Purification, 1822, Anne Catherine related the following:*

I saw during the last days marvelous things connected with the Church. St. Peter's was almost entirely destroyed by the sect; but their labors were in turn rendered fruitless, and all that belonged to them—their aprons and tools—burned by the executioners on the public place of infamy. They were made of horse leather, and the stench from them was so offensive that it made me quite sick. In this vision I saw the Mother of God laboring so earnestly for the Church that my devotion to her greatly increased.

I see the pope in great distress *(August 10, 1822)*. He lives in another palace and receives only a few to his presence. If the wicked party knew their own great strength, they would even now have made an attack. I fear the pope will suffer many tribulations before his death, for I see the dark counterfeit church gaining ground; I see its fatal influence on the public. The distress of the pope and of the Church is really so great that one ought to pray to God day and night. I have been told to pray much for the Church and the pope.

Last night I was taken to Rome, where the pope—plunged in affliction—is still concealed in order to elude dangerous exigencies. He is very feeble, quite worn out by distress, anxiety, and prayer. His chief reason for lying concealed is because he can now trust so few. But he has by him a very simple-hearted, pious old priest, his true friend, whom his enemies—on account of his simplicity—think it not worthwhile to remove. Now, this good old priest is full of God's grace. He sees, he remarks, many things, which he faithfully communicates to the pope. More than once I have had to point out to him in prayer traitors and evil-minded men among the pope's high, confidential officers, that he might give him notice of them. In this way he has been warned against one who was all-influential up to the present; but who will be so no more. The pope is so feeble that he can no longer walk alone.

I know not how I went to Rome last night (*August 25th*), but I found myself near the Church of St. Mary Major. Around it I saw crowds of poor, pious souls, in great distress and anxiety on account of the pope's disappearance and the agitation and alarming reports throughout the city. Led by one common impulse, they had come to invoke the Mother of God. They did not expect to find the church open, but intended only to pray outside. I was inside, opened the door, and they entered, astounded at the door's opening of itself. I was standing aloof where they could not see me.

There was no service, only the chancel lamps were burning, and the people knelt in quiet prayer. Then the Mother of God appeared. She said that great tribulations were at hand; that the people must pray earnestly with extended arms, if only for the length of three *Our Fathers*—for it was thus that her Son had prayed for them upon the cross. She said that they should rise at midnight to pray thus, that they should continue to come to her Church, which they would always find open, and that they should above all pray for the extirpation of the *dark church*. She said also that the soldiers who were approaching the city would be of no assistance, that they would bring only misery and devastation in their train, since the war had been undertaken without prayer or the ministry of priests.

She added many other things. She said—which is most painful to me to repeat—that if only one priest offered the unbloody sacrifice as worthily and with the same sentiments as the apostles, he could ward off all calamities from the Church.

I know not whether the people saw the apparition or not, but they must have been impressed by something supernatural, for when the Blessed Virgin said they should pray to God with extended arms, all lifted up their arms. They were good and pious, but they knew not where to turn for counsel and assistance. There was no traitor, no enemy among them, and yet they were anxious and distrustful of one another. By this we may judge of their situation. It seemed to be an association of prayer.

*From this time, Anne Catherine assisted nightly at the pious exercises in St. Mary Major's. On August 31st, she remarked:*

Prayer is now general and continual, pious souls are everywhere kneeling at the tombs of the saints and imploring their aid. I have seen the saints whom they especially revere, and I have again seen the pope—he is in much trouble. I have had great anxiety on his account and I have redoubled my prayers.

On September 10th I saw St. Peter's utterly demolished, all excepting the choir and main altar. The Archangel Michael, girt and armed, descended into the church, and with his sword repulsed several bad pastors who were trying to enter. He drove them into a corner, where they sat looking at one another. The part of the church that had been demolished in a few instants was surrounded by light wickerwork so that divine service could be perfectly celebrated. Then from all parts of the world came priests and laics who built up the walls of stone, for the enemy had not been able to shake the firm foundation.

*Anne Catherine at this time passed whole nights praying with her arms in the form of a cross and frequently subjected to the assaults of the devil. The first night he rushed upon her three times to strangle her. She said:*

He reproached me with the faults of my youth, but I turned a deaf ear, gathered up my relics, and opposed him with them. And when at last I sat up in bed and made the sign of the cross all around with my relic of the true cross, he left me in peace.

*The following night she struggled with the enemy so victoriously that she sang the* Te Deum *several times. She had constant visions on the state of different dioceses, as we glean from the following entry in the pilgrim's journal for September 27th:*

Today at noon Anne Catherine entered the state of contemplation in a singularly touching and animated manner. Her eyes were open, she gesticulated and described what she saw, as if in conversation:

What are they doing in that great, beautiful church? It is the cathedral (of Münster), and everything has been carried back into the chapel where the silver ship once stood, where Bernard von Galen is interred! All goes there, all the graces, all, all! O how beautiful, how wonderful it is! There stands an empty chalice, and from it issues a ray that rises up to heaven in a great cross of light. On the left of the chalice is a beautiful bride with a church in her hand, and on the right of it, a wonderfully handsome youth who is to be her bridegroom; they are betrothed. But see! Outside the church, up in the air, is the Mother of God with the Infant Jesus, from whose hands issues a magnificent vine that spreads over all the chapel. Its grapes hang down and discharge their juice into the chalice. Right and left shoot out beautiful flowers of light, and magnificent ears of golden, luminous wheat fill the whole place with splendor. And all the bushes are covered with flowers and marvelous little shining fruits. All is light and beauty! All is gathered in and preserved there.

And behold! There stands, high, high up, a holy bishop of olden times—it is Ludger! He guards, he takes care of all! And now, what is that? O see, from the whole church, excepting the chapel, shoot forth wild, fiery flames, and in several parts of the city whole rows of houses are destroyed! There in the castle things go badly! But this must be understood only in a spiritual sense. The great church stands intact. Exterior things go on as usual, but the graces are all stowed away in the chapel.

*As Anne Catherine recounted the above, she pointed now here, now there, as if her hearers saw what was being unfolded before her own mental gaze. Next day she related what follows:*

I have seen yesterday's vision of Galen's chapel all over again. An entirely new church floated in the air above the old one and drew into itself all the beautiful things from Galen's chapel. The church below seemed to grow black and sink into the earth. I thought how nice it would be if the church in the air would only descend just as the other disappeared. This vision was very detailed, but I have forgotten some of it.

I followed a path running back of the cathedral and found in a field, half-meadow, half-heath, a homeless wandering boy, his feet torn and bleeding from the furze. I wanted to take him to the flower meadow. I told him there were beautiful flowers in it from which he could suck the honey, for I knew not what to do to relieve him. But he told me that it was his destiny, he must suffer and bleed until he had found an asylum. I thought of the youth who espoused the church yesterday in the Galen chapel.

*Anne Catherine saw also at this time a distant diocese falling to decay. It was shown her under the symbol of a desecrated church:*

I saw heart-rending misery, playing, drinking, gossiping—even courting—going on in the church. All sorts of abominations were committed in it; they had even set up a ninepin alley in the middle of it. The priests let things go their way and said mass very irreverently. Only a few of them were still a little intelligent and pious. I saw Jews standing around the doorways. All this grieved me deeply. Then my Lord bound me as he himself had been bound to the pillar, and he said: "So will the church yet be bound. She will be tightly bound before she shall again arise."

*On September 30, 1822, after a night spent in praying with ex-tended arms for the Church, Anne Catherine vomited blood and endured great pains in the breast. "St. Michael has prescribed for me a seven days' devotion with alms," she said. "I shall now be sick for seven days," and indeed, the following night verified the prediction. She was attacked by sharp pains, her whole body consumed, as it were, by an internal fire, to allay which she placed her relic of St. Cosmas on her breast and invoked his name aloud. Scarcely had she done so when she fell into a sweet sleep. On awaking, she beheld the saint before her, clothed in a long, white mantle resplendent with light. In his hand was a green branch covered with white flowers, and playing around him was a brilliant red aureola that dissolved into a beautiful blue. His younger brother Leontius stood at a little distance, and further back was Damian, the shortest of the three, Cosmas being the tallest. All Anne Catherine's pains had disappeared. She lay calm and serene, unable to express the marvelous character of her cure, which was as sudden and as marked as those previously bestowed through the intervention of Ignatius and Augustine.*

*On the following evening, the pilgrim found her exhausted and bathed in perspiration from her heavy spiritual labors. She repeated that*

*St. Michael, besides the seven days' task, had prescribed certain alms, pointing out what children were to be assisted and what each one was to receive. She groaned:*

The Church is in great danger. I must ask every one who comes to see me to say an *Our Father* for that intention. We must pray that the pope may not leave Rome, for unheard-of evils would result from such a step. We must pray the Holy Spirit to enlighten him, for they are even now trying to exact something of him.

Two men live at this time who long to ruin the Church, but they have lost one who used to help them with his pen. He was killed by a young man about a year ago, and one of the two men of whom I speak left Germany at the same time. They have their employees everywhere. The little dark man in Rome, whom I see so often, has many working for him, without their clearly knowing for what end. He has his agents in the new dark church also. If the pope leaves Rome, the enemies of the Church will get the upper hand.

I see the little dark man in his own country committing many thefts and falsifying things generally. Religion is there so skillfully undermined and stifled that there are scarcely one hundred faithful priests.

I cannot say how it is, but I see fog and darkness increasing. There are however three churches that they cannot seize: St. Peter's, St. Mary Major's, and St. Michael's. Although they are constantly trying to undermine them, they will not succeed. All must be rebuilt soon—for everyone, even ecclesiastics, are laboring to destroy. Ruin is at hand. The two enemies of the Church who have lost their accomplice are firmly resolved to destroy the pious and learned men that stand in their way.

*When the pilgrim visited Anne Catherine on October 4th, he found her perfectly worn out by the exertions of the preceding night. That the Archangel Michael's commands were being fulfilled was very evident. She said:*

I have had combats more terrible than any I have ever endured, and I am almost dead. I cannot say how fearfully I have suffered. This struggle was shown me long ago under the symbol of a person buffeted by demons, and now I know it was myself. I fought against a whole legion of devils who excite minds against me and do all they can to harass me.

Last night I had a vision of the pope. I saw St. Francis carrying the Church, and the Basilica of St. Peter borne on the shoulders of a little man with a somewhat Jewish-looking countenance. It looked very perilous. Mary stood on the north side of the Church with her mantle extended over it. The little man was almost bent double. He is, as yet, a laic. I know who he is. The twelve men whom I always see as the twelve new apostles ought to have helped him, but they arrived too late. However, just as he was about to fall, they all ran up with myriads of angels to his assistance. It was only the pavement and the back part of the Church, for all the rest had been demolished by the secret society, helped by the servants of the Church themselves. They bore it to another place, and it seemed as if rows of palaces fell before it like fields of wheat in harvest time.

When I saw St. Peter's in this ruinous state and so many ecclesiastics laboring—though secretly—at its destruction, I was so overcome that I cried earnestly to Jesus for mercy. Then I saw my Lord before me under the form of a youth. He spoke to me for a long time. He told me that this translation of St. Peter's signified that the Church would apparently fall to total ruin—but that, resting on these supports, she would be raised up again. Even if there should remain but one true Christian, the Church would again triumph, since its foundations were not cast in the intellect or councils of men. She had never yet been without members praying and suffering for her.

The Lord showed me all that he himself had endured for her, what efficacy he had bestowed upon the merits and labors of the martyrs, and he ended by saying that he would endure it all over again if it were possible for him again to suffer. He showed me also, in numberless pictures, the miserable aims of Christians and ecclesiastics throughout the whole world.

The vision grew wider, more extended, until it embraced my own country. And then Jesus exhorted me to perseverance in prayer and expiatory suffering. It was an unspeakably great and sorrowful picture. I cannot describe it! I was also told that very few Christians—in the true sense of the term—are to be found nowadays, and also that the Jews of our day are mostly pure Pharisees, though still more obstinate. Only Judith's people in Africa belong to the ancient Jews. I am greatly afflicted at what I saw!

I have been on a mission (*October 7, 1822*) among the Roman catacombs, and I saw the life of a martyr who with many others lived there concealed. He had made numerous conversions. He lived not long after Thekla's time,[1] but I have forgotten his name. Even when a boy he used to go with holy women to the catacombs and prisons to console the poor Christians. He lay concealed a long time in a hermitage, but afterward endured cruel torments, and ended his life with many others by decapitation. He carried his own head from the place of execution, but I do not remember his history very distinctly.

I went with the martyr and St. Frances of Rome into one of the catacombs, the ground of which was covered with shining flowers, the blossoms of his own and his companions' sufferings; for here it was that they had been executed. Conspicuous among them were beautiful white roses, one of which I found all at once sticking in my bosom (the saint's relic). In several other places I saw flowers—the sufferings of those martyrs whose intercession I had implored for the Church in her present tribulations. As I went through Rome with Frances and the saint, we saw a great palace enveloped in flames (the Vatican). I was in dread lest those within would be consumed, for no one tried to extinguish the fire; but when we drew near, it suddenly ceased and left the building black and scorched. After passing through numerous magnificent apartments, we reached that of the pope. We found him sitting in the dark, asleep in a large armchair. He was very sick and weak, no longer able to walk, and people were going to and fro before his door. The ecclesiastics most nearly connected with him pleased me not. They appeared to be false and lukewarm, and the simple-minded pious men whom I once saw by him were now removed to a distant part of the palace.

I spoke long with the pope, and I cannot express how very real my presence there seemed to be; for I too was extremely weak,

---

[1] See "Thekla" in *Scenes from the Lives of the Saints*.

and the people around were constantly obliged to support me. I spoke with the bishops soon to be appointed, and I again told the pope that he must not leave Rome, for if he did, all would go to ruin. He thought the evil inevitable and that his personal safety, as well as other considerations, would oblige him to go—a measure to which he felt himself strongly inclined and to which also he was advised by his counselors. Then Frances spoke to him a long time, while I stood by weak and fainting, supported by my companions. Before I left, the pope gave me a little saucer of sugared strawberries which, however, I did not eat, as I wanted them for a sick person.

*Later, Anne Catherine exclaimed, still in ecstasy*: Those strawberries have no very good signification. They show that many ties still bind the pope to earth. I saw Rome in such a state that the least spark would inflame it, and Sicily dark, frightful, abandoned by all that could leave it.

*One day while in ecstasy, she groaned*:

I see the Church alone, forsaken by all, and around her strife, misery, hatred, treason, resentment, total blindness. I see messengers sent on all sides from a dark central point with messages that issue from their mouths like black vapor, enkindling in the breast of their hearers rage and hatred. I pray earnestly for the oppressed! On those places in which some souls still pray I see light descending; but on others, pitchy darkness. The situation is terrible! May God have mercy! How much I have prayed! O city! O city (Rome), with what art thou threatened! The storm approaches, be on thy guard! I trust thou wilt stand firm!

Last night (*October 16th*) I made the way of the cross at Coesfeld with a crowd of souls who showed me the distress of the Church and the necessity of prayer. Then I had a vision of many gardens lying around me in a circle, and the pope's situation with respect to his bishops. He sat enthroned in one of these gardens. In the others were the rights and privileges of his bishops and their sees symbolized by various plants, flowers, and fruits. Their mutual connection, their communication and influence, I saw under the forms of threads, of rays extending from them to the see of Rome.

In these earthly gardens I saw the temporal, spiritual authority, and above them in the air I saw their future bishops; for instance, I saw above the garden of the stern superior a new bishop with the cross, mitre, and other episcopal insignia, and standing around him Protestants who wished him to enter the garden below, but not on the conditions established by the pope. They tried to insinuate themselves by all sorts of covert means; they destroyed a part of the garden, or sowed bad seed in it. I saw them sometimes here, sometimes there, cultivating the land or letting it lie untilled, tearing up and not clearing away, etc.—all was full of pitfalls and rubbish. I saw them intercepting or turning away the roads that led to the pope. When they did succeed in getting a bishop according to their liking, I saw that he had been intruded contrary to the will of the pope; consequently, he possessed no legitimate spiritual authority. Many such scenes were shown me, and it is for me to pray and suffer! It is very distressing! I see one who has few claims to holiness about to be installed in the see of a holy deceased bishop.

*Anne Catherine's sufferings during these contemplations were simply frightful. She felt as if her breast were girded tightly with cords; she had frequent vomitings, and so lively an impression of a huge, thorny crown that she dared not rest her head on a pillow. The wounds of her forehead and side bled several times. While in this state, she related the following fragments of a vision of the sacred passion:*

The crown of Jesus was very large and heavy, and stood far out from his head. When the executioners dragged his woven tunic over his head, the crown came off with it. I have an indistinct remembrance of their plaiting a smaller one (I know from what thorns) and putting it on him by the cross. The three holes in the latter were too far apart, and when they had nailed down one hand they had to stretch the other with cords to reach the second hole. The feet also were found to be too high up and had to be stretched in like manner. One of the executioners knelt upon the Savior's limbs while the others drove the nails. The sacred body was dislocated in every joint. One could, as it were, see through it, and below the breast it was quite sunken and hollow. It was a horrible moment when they raised the cross and let it fall into the hole prepared for it. The shock was so violent that the sacred body quivered.

161

I did not see Jesus go into purgatory; but when he was in limbo the souls came from purgatory to him and all were delivered by him. I saw the angel gathering and restoring to his sacred body, before the resurrection, the blood and flesh lost during the passion. And then I saw him issuing from the tomb in indescribable glory, his shining wounds so many holy, ineffable ornaments to his sacred body. He did not appear to the disciples in this radiant glory, for their eyes could not have endured the sight.

The Blessed Virgin had some linen stained with the blood of Jesus's circumcision and his other wounds. She gave the apostles, when they dispersed, crosses of about an arm's length, made of flexible reeds, which they carried under their mantles. They had also metal boxes for the holy eucharist and relics, which were, I think, pieces of the linen that Mary had. I think, too, that the Blessed Virgin wove them robes like that of her Son, for she made many such, sometimes on two needles, or again with a hooked needle.

*At the close of this painful task of prayer, Anne Catherine had a very consoling vision of which she communicated the following:*

I lay on a plank in the midst of thorns that wounded me whenever I moved. In the hedge were numbers of red and white roses and other white flowers. Jesus appeared to me as my Bridegroom and showed me his familiar communications with his brides Theresa, Catherine of Sienna, and Clare of Montefalco, whom I saw one after another in positions similar to my own: one seated in the midst of thorns, another rolling in them, and the third entirely surrounded by them. I saw how familiarly and confidently they addressed our Lord.

Clare of Montefalco was dragging a cross upon which many of her fellow-religious laid heaps of trifles, little nothings, until it became so heavy that she sank under its weight. Then Jesus reminded her that he too had fallen under his cross. Clare exclaimed: "Ah! then, stretch out to me thy hand as thy heavenly Father did to thee!"

Jesus showed me also how all who approached my bed pressed upon me, though without intending it, the pricking thorns. I saw too the infirmities, the sufferings, the sorrows—often very grievous—of all these brides. Then Jesus placed before me a shining table and covered it with a snowy cloth. Upon it was immolated by a priest of the Old Law a patient, spotless lamb. I received touching instructions on the purity of the table, the cover, and the lamb, the blood of which did not stain the cover. Then a red cover was placed on the table and over it a white, transparent one, upon which stood bread and a chalice from which the Lord gave me to eat and drink. It was he himself whom I received. After this he disappeared, leaving me consoled. Then I saw in a series of pictures an abridgment of his whole passion, how his friends misunderstood and abandoned him, and how they would and how they really do treat him at the present day. I saw him more truly present in the blessed sacrament than he was present on earth during his mortal life, and I saw that his passion still continues in the patient endurance and offering of their sufferings by his true followers. I saw too how many graces are trodden under foot in the mire. I came out of these visions calm and strengthened.

# Suffering-Works for the Church

## (May–June 1821)

### The Church Militant

ANNE *Catherine's assistance was about this time requested for an Ursuline nun, suffering from acute rheumatism. "I was by her,"* she said. *"I saw her illness, and I suggested to her not to ask for a cure, but for what would be most pleasing to God. She will be relieved, but she will not entirely recover." Anne Catherine's prayer for this invalid was, as usual, a real physical participation in her sufferings, as may be inferred from the pilgrim's notes of May 29th:*

Anne Catherine's malady is greatly aggravated. She looks like one in death agony. She can with extreme difficulty and only at long intervals pronounce a few words; but her soul is in peace. She is constantly in vision, laboring in a poor, neglected church. About noon she appeared to be dying. She lay stiff and cold, unable to ask assistance. Fortunately, her sister happened to approach her bed and, seeing her condition, raised her up, otherwise she would have strangled from the vomiting that came on suddenly. After this she again lay for awhile like one dead, when she sat up suddenly without effort or support, joined her hands, and so remained for about six minutes in an attitude of earnest prayer. "Ah! I have rested and thanked God for my difficult task!" she exclaimed: "O that broom I used was a very heavy one!" Her words came slowly, but her breathing was easier, though at intervals her pains were still very intense. They lasted for about five minutes at a time, her feet trembling so violently as to shake the chair on which they rested. Her labor was not yet finished, as she said. When her confessor exhorted her to patience, she replied: "Patience hovers yonder in a globe!" and fell again into her former suffering state.

*On June 1st the pilgrim found her in the morning serene and singu-
larly joyous, the pain in her head abated, though she could scarcely hear.
She said:*

I have had indescribable visions on the state of the church both
in general and particular. I saw the Church Militant under the
symbol of a city like the heavenly Jerusalem, though it was still on
earth. In it were streets, palaces, and gardens through which I
wandered and saw processions composed entirely of bishops. I
recognized the interior state of each. I saw their thoughts issuing
from their mouths under the form of pictures. Their religious
transgressions were represented by external deformity: for
instance there were some whose head seemed to be only a misty
cloud; others had a head, but a heart like a body of dark vapor;
others were lame or paralytic; others sleeping or reeling. Once I
saw a mitre floating in the air and a hand out of a dark cloud trying repeatedly, but vainly, to seize it. Under the mitre I beheld
many persons not unknown to me, bearing on their shoulders
amid tears and lamentations crosses of all kinds—and among
them walked myself. I think I saw almost all the bishops in the
world, but only a very few were perfectly sound.

I saw the pope very prayerful and God-fearing, his figure perfect, though worn out by old age and manifold sufferings, his
head sunk on his breast as if in sleep. He often fainted away and
seemed to be dying. I often saw him supported by apparitions
during his prayer, and then his head was upright. When it sank
upon his breast, then were the minds of many turned quickly
here and there—that is, viewing things in a worldly light. When
the hand out of the cloud tried to seize the mitre, I saw the
Church of our country in a miserable state, to which the learned
young schoolmaster had especially contributed. Protestantism
was in the ascendancy and religion was falling to utter decay. I
saw the majority of the clergy, dazzled by the false show of the
young fellow, furthering the work of destruction, and one in particular taking part in it through vanity and ignorance. He will see
his error only when it will be too late to retrieve it. The misery
under him will be great. Many simple-minded, enlightened men,
and especially the schoolmaster, are praying for the removal of
this pastor. I saw, at the most, only four ecclesiastics in the whole

country steadfast and faithful. These visions were so frightful that I came near crying out. I see in the future religion falling so low that it will be practised only here and there in farmhouses and in families protected by God during the horrors of war.

## Sufferings for Five Bishoprics of the Upper Rhine

I PASSED through Frankfurt and saw in a large house not far from a great church a society assembled for deliberation on evil projects; among them were ecclesiastics, and devils were crouching under the chairs.[1] I went again to the large house at whose entrance lay sleeping—under the form of a black dog with red eyes—satan himself. I roused him with my foot, saying: "Up, satan! Why do you sleep here?" "I can sleep quietly here," he replied, "for the people inside are attending to my work."

*Anne Catherine saw also in a symbolical picture the results following from this new way of establishing churches:*

I found myself lying in the only sound spot of a ship that was all punctured. The crew kicked and ill-treated me in many ways while I prayed earnestly for them that they might not fall into the deep from the sides of the vessel on which they were sitting. I saw the ship going to pieces, and I was sick unto death. At last they put me ashore where my friends were in waiting to convey me to some other place. I kept on praying that the unhappy people might also disembark, but scarcely had I reached the shore before the ship capsized and to my great grief all were lost. There was an abundance of fruit where I was.

*On Wednesday after Passion Sunday, March 22, 1820, the Frankfurt Convention held its first formal sitting to deliberate upon the means to be adopted to seize Jesus by stealth and deliver him to death. Its members said: "Let it not be in daylight, lest the pope perceive it and*

[1] Precisely at this moment the ecclesiastic and the lay delegates of the petty German States were convened for the second time to deliberate on the means to be adopted for the gradual extinction of Catholicity in the five dioceses.

*make opposition!" While this was going on, Anne Catherine's attention was attracted to them and she entered the lists against them:*

I am bearing an enormous weight on my right shoulder, for I am atoning by my many afflictions for the sins of others. I am almost sinking, and my visions on the state of humankind—particularly of the clergy—are so sad that I cannot help taking still heavier burdens upon myself.[1] I prayed God to touch the hard hearts of his enemies, that during these Paschal feasts they may return to better dispositions. I begged to suffer for the most hardened, or for those for whom He knows it to be most necessary.

Then I felt myself suddenly raised and suspended in the air in a shining vessel. There passed through me a shower of keen, indefinable pains, which have not yet ceased, and the oppression in my left side increased. When I looked below me I saw distinctly through a dark veil the manifold errors, wanderings, and sins of humankind—their stupidity and wickedness in acting against truth and reason. I saw pictures of all kinds. Again I saw the miserable old ship full of popular, self-sufficient men sail by me on the stormy waves, and I waited to see it go down at any moment. I recognized some priests among the crew, and with all my heart I offered my sufferings to bring them to repentance. Below I saw crowds of gray figures moving sadly to and fro in certain places, in old cemeteries long since forgotten. Again I saw souls wandering alone in solitary places, either where they themselves had perished or where they had taken the life of others—I do not now remember which, but I think their detention there had something to do with the expiation of the crime. I begged for fresh sufferings that thus I might obtain relief and pardon for them.

When I cast my eyes upward I saw, in contrast to the abominations below, a heavenly sight so beautiful as almost to dazzle me:

---

[1] Once she said: "I see so many ecclesiastics under the ban of excommunication! But they seem quite at their ease, almost unconscious of their state; and yet all who join associations, take part in enterprises, or adhere to opinions condemned by the Church, are really excommunicated by that fact itself. I see such men hemmed in as it were by a wall of fog. By this we may clearly see what account God makes of the decrees, orders, and prohibitions of the Head of the Church and how rigorously He exacts their observance while men coolly mock and scoff at them."

the saints, the angels, and the throne of the Most Holy Trinity. I beheld our Savior offering all his sufferings in detail to his heavenly Father for us, Mary renewing the offering of her sorrows through Jesus, and all the saints offering their merits and prayers in like manner. It was a vision in which variety and unity, action and repose, supreme magnificence, love, and peace were inexpressibly blended. As I continued to gaze upon it, I perceived all at once that I was lying in one side of a pair of scales, for I saw the needle and beam above me. In the other scale, hanging in darkness, lay God's most hardened enemies, around them many others seated on the rim—as if they had been on the sides of the ship. As at the sight I redoubled my patience and my prayers, as my pains also increased, the scale rose a very little; but it was too heavy and most of the men fell off. All, however, for whom I had given my sufferings as a counterbalance were saved. Above me I saw heaven and the efficacious merits of Jesus, and I rejoiced that with God's grace I had been able to gain something by my pains. These men are hard as rocks; they fall from sin to sin, each more grievous than the last.

*The cunning with which these plotters sought to hide their intrigues was shown to Anne Catherine under the form of the tempter:*

After my examen,[1] I was saluting the wounds of Jesus, when I suddenly fell into the greatest mental agony. An ecclesiastic appeared before me saying he had just returned from Rome with all sorts of sacred objects for me; but I felt intense repugnance both for him and his gifts. He showed me all sorts of little crosses and stars, but not one of them was perfect—all were crooked and deformed. He told me in many words that he had spoken of me to the pope, that I had not a suitable confessor, etc. His words were so plausible that, although I still felt aversion for him, I thought, "Perhaps I judge him too severely!" and again examined his singular-looking sacred objects, remarking, with the hope that he would not be offended, that I too had recently received holy

---

[1] The daily examen is a technique of prayerful reflection on the events of the day in order to detect God's presence and discern His direction for us. It is an ancient practice of the Church and emphasized especially in Ignatian spiritual practice.

things from Rome and Jerusalem, though not indeed artistically made; but that his articles seemed to have been picked up from some abominable old pit or tomb—whereupon he asked how I could have so bad an opinion of an innocent man. I wanted no further parley with him, and so I said: "I have God and the relics of the saints; I have no need of thee!" and I turned away from him, when he instantly disappeared. I was bathed in perspiration, I trembled in every limb, and I begged God not to subject me again to such agony.

Some days later satan again approached me, under the form of a priest. He cunningly tried to excite all sorts of scruples in my mind, saying principally that I meddled too much in outside affairs—but I soon discovered him when he said that he met me everywhere, that I gave him no peace.

*The evil plottings, which kept the episcopal sees so long vacant, were shown Anne Catherine in a touching vision of which, however, her terrible sufferings permitted her to communicate only a part:*

In a journey to the nuptial house I came to a cabin by a field where a bridegroom awaited the coming of his bride. The field belonged to the apostates. Nearby stood a large house in which I found a very good bride. She accompanied me, apparently right well pleased. Her brother also came with us, but there was something singular about him[1] and he turned back when we had gone only halfway. I took the bride to the bridegroom in the cabin. He received her lovingly and joyfully, presenting her tempting refreshments apparently of a spiritual nature. The bride gave him her hand and appeared truly good, but she still put off the marriage and made some excuse to withdraw. The bridegroom, greatly distressed, looked after her tenderly, resolving to wait for her, to take no other in her place. I felt so sorry for him. I gave him some money I happened to have about me, which he accepted. Now, I felt that he was the heavenly Bridegroom, that the Bride was his flock, and that the money I gave him was the prayer and labor I offered as security for her. Ah! If the Bride had seen the Bridegroom! Had she seen how he gazed and sighed after her,

---

[1] The secular power.

how he waited for her, she could not have left him with such indifference! What has he not done for her! How easy has he not made things for her! And yet she abandons him!

*The foregoing vision was repeated under various forms every time Anne Catherine was commanded to pray for the appointment of bishops to the vacant sees. In November, beginning with the feast of St. Martin, she performed an eight days' labor for this end during which the spiritual nuptials were constantly before her:*

I saw, a most beautiful and holy bride. I with four others was her bridesmaid. The bridegroom was a dark, gloomy man. He had five groomsmen, and they drank all day long. In the evening, however, there appeared another bridegroom who put the dark one out-of-doors, saying: "This bride is far too noble and holy for thee!" I spent these days in continual contemplation. I saw the bridal house as a church, and the bride so beautiful and holy that one could not approach her without fear and respect.

# A False Aspirant to
# the Hand of the Bride is Put
# Out of the Vineyard of the Church

ONE *day Anne Catherine was in a pitiable state. Her right arm and shoulder were paralyzed; profuse perspiration flowed so copiously from her head and breast as to soak the bed on which she lay; and she was tormented by incessant attacks of whooping cough which, she said, were to last for six hours. At intervals she swooned away from the violence of her sufferings. She afterward related the following:*

I found lately at the nuptial house hedges of walnut trees outside the choir of the church, where there used to be beautiful vines, and just behind the main altar was a high nut-hedge full of ripe nuts. I saw a distinguished ecclesiastic wearing a cross, (something like a vicar-general) who went to the hedge with a nutcracker in his hand. I saw it distinctly. He cracked and ate numbers of nuts, after which he hid the shells and went into the church. I felt the great impropriety of his entering the church after eating the nuts, for the act of cracking nuts is a symbol of treachery and discord. He was from the unhappy house connected by an outer staircase with the nuptial house. In it were assembled all who entered not by the true gate; but he was driven from the church. He was the cause of my profuse perspiration, the sharp pain in my shoulder, and the paralysis of my right side.

Seeing him, after he had been chased away, standing before a wall unable to advance or to go back, I grasped him by the shoulders and drew him with incredible difficulty to the top of the wall. I was told just to let him drop down on the other side. But I saw that he would be dashed to pieces, and so with great fatigue I carried him down and dragged him into a region quite new to me. Here I met first a great river, then a lake on whose banks stands a city (Constance). Around lay towns and villages. As I carried my heavy load across the lake, invisible hands placed under my feet two narrow planks, one after the other, which as I stepped on them rose and sank alternately. It was a difficult passage, but I accomplished it. Before me arose high mountains.

I have more than once seen this ecclesiastic (Wessenberg)[1] in the nuptial house. He is a worldly man to whom the Protestants are as well inclined as he is to them. He will help them as far as he can. He intruded himself into his high position by all sorts of artful means, signified by the nutcracker; he is strongly opposed to the pope and he has many adherents. I prayed very much for the Church and the pope, and then I was commissioned to perform this task. It would be well if this man could without scandal come to some terms with his partisans. The Protestants would thereby receive a severe blow, for they are continually exciting and defending him. They are getting the upper hand; but they will lose much if this unworthy priest does not succeed.

*Anne Catherine was at this time continually engaged in repelling the attacks of the enemies of the Church; consequently, her state was most distressing. The pilgrim writes:*

---

[1] Ignaz Heinrich von Wessenberg (1774–1860) was a German writer and scholar, and liberal Catholic churchman as well as vicar-general and administrator of the Diocese of Constance. He advocated a German National Church, somewhat loosely connected with Rome, supported by the State and protected by it against papal interference.

She is sick, very sick, but quite supernaturally so! Her state is one of constant change: sometimes drenched with icy death-sweats; again radiant as if in full health; and shortly after, falling from one swoon to another. But she rejoices in having already accomplished a great part of the task undertaken. When her sufferings become quite intolerable, she is so consoled and rejoiced by some beautiful vision that she often laughs with joy. For example, when sinking under her pains, St. Benedict appeared and said pleasantly to her: "Ah! you are always stumbling al-though so old!"—and St. Joseph took her to a beautiful meadow full of flowers, telling her to walk on them without bruising them. This feat, possible only to the child Jesus, she could not accomplish, whereupon St. Joseph said: "Now you see that you do not belong here!"

There was shown her then a rich treasure of pearls—that is, lost graces—which she by her sufferings was to gather up and pay off the debt of those who had squandered them. Her weakening, death-like sweats she offers for the poor souls whom she beholds hourly becoming brighter, and who thank her for the relief her charity affords them.

Again she saw the fatal intrigues of the false suitor in the nuptial house. "I met few ecclesiastics there according to my liking," she said. "I had to cook for them, that is, prepare spiritual nourishment for them. Many sat at table, and I saw him whom I had to drag so far enter and boldly seat himself with his five followers. I had prepared three dishes; but when I set them on the table, the insolent fellow cried out scornfully, 'The pope has given us a fine cook indeed! now we'll get nothing but gray peas!'"

*In Easter week, 1820, Anne Catherine had another vision in which was shown her the immense evil this man and his supporters would do the Church, as also the fatal consequences of the Frankfurt Convention:*

I saw a field[1] full of people, and hard by a circular building with a gray cupola, like a new church. In it were some learned men,

---

[1] The green field, or meadow, signifies the festivals of the Church, the ecclesiastical year, the communion of the faithful, from which the friends and abettors of the "new lights" wished not to separate, despite their incredulity, their revolt against legitimate authority. Like the Jansenists, they directed

and such crowds were flocking into it that I wondered how it could contain them all; it looked like the influx of a whole nation! Then the air all around grew darker and darker. A black vapor filled the church and poured out of its windows, spreading over meadows, fields, and parishes, till the whole country, far and wide, was changed to a bleak, wild moor. Then I saw numbers of well-meaning persons pressing toward one side of the field, where light and verdure were still to be found.

I cannot describe the dark, the frightful, the deadly influence of this scene: fields withered, trees blasted, gardens blighted, darkness spreading everywhere as far as the eye could see, and encircling the country as if with a black chain. I know not what became of the people in the church. They seemed to be consumed with it[1] as it grew blacker and blacker like a mountain of coal, and peeled off frightfully.

I went afterward with three angels into a green enclosure about as large as the cemetery outside Dülmen, and it appeared to me that I was laid on a high bench. I know not whether I was dead or alive, but I was habited in a long white robe. The greatest of the three angels said to me: "Thank God! it will now be fresh and light here!" and then there fell between the black church and me a glittering shower of pearls and precious stones like a rain from heaven. One of my three companions ordered me to gather them up[2] and then left me. I know not whether all went or not. I only remember that in my anxiety about the black church I had not the courage to gather up the precious stones. When the angel returned, he asked me if I had gathered them, and on my answering no, he bade me do so at once. I dragged around, and picked up three little stones like crystals with ground edges that lay all in a

their destructive darts against the Church from her very bosom; therefore it was that—though in the meadow—they stood apart. They erected a church in the Church, spreading therein the night of unbelief, the horrors of spiritual death.

[1] Depriving them of the life of grace by the destruction of faith and the Christian life springing from it.

[2] The merits of her prayers and sufferings which arrest the progress of decay.

row—one blue, another light red, and the third white—glittering and transparent. I took them to my little companions who ran to and fro, rubbing them against one another until the loveliest colors and rays of light flashed around, renewing the vegetation and bringing forth light and life. Then on the other side I saw the dark church crumbling to pieces. Suddenly a great multitude streamed out of it into the bright green fields and wended their way to a luminous city. Behind the black church all remained dark as night.

## Further Works in the Vineyard of the Church

DURING *the whole octave of Corpus Christi, 1821, Anne Catherine had visions upon the state of devotion to the blessed sacrament throughout Germany, the sight of which drew from her tears and sighs of bitter grief. If, as she said, there were some portions of the country in a less lamentable condition than others, it was where that most august sacrament was not altogether forgotten, where it was sometimes exposed for public veneration, sometimes borne in procession. Those districts that had fallen more or less under the influence of the new regime,* liberty, love, *and* toleration, *appeared under the form of a vineyard, withering and dying before the progress of* the lights. *In them she had to labor diligently, clearing and weeding until her hands were torn and bleeding. In December, though weighed down by all kinds of sufferings, she could not forbear asking almighty God to send her still fresh ones; for the mental anguish she endured at the sight of the coldness, neglect, and irreverence offered the blessed sacrament was greater than any physical pain could be. Her prayer was heard, but only on condition of her confessor's permission, that the merit of obedience might be added to that of suffering and supply the strength necessary for its patient endurance.*

*The pilgrim writes, December 12, 1821, in the octave of the immaculate conception of Mary:*

For several days Anne Catherine has had continual cramps, convulsive cough, spitting of blood. She swoons, she is perfectly prostrate, but her visions on the dangers threatening the faith are never interrupted. "I must suffer it!'" she exclaims in ecstasy, "I have taken it upon myself, but I hope to be able to bear it!" Once she seemed about to spring from her bed: "I must find my confessor, I must ask his permission, I must open another fountain in the heart of Jesus! It has already five sources, but they have been wholly obstructed by the sins of men. Alas! they permit not those fountains to flow upon them! I am to do it. I am to begin a new task, although my present one is not yet finished! I must get my confessor's permission!" The confessor was absent, and Anne Catherine several times repeated her petition to be allowed to open the obstructed sources.[1]

Anne Catherine lies today (*December 13th*) in a state altogether different from that of the last few days—painful paralysis of her members accompanied with acute rheumatism. A touch brings forth a groan, and still she had to be raised to a sitting posture several times during the night, on account of sharp pains of retention. She is too weak to explain the connection between her sufferings and her spiritual labors.

That afternoon, as the pilgrim and confessor sat in the adjoining room, they were not a little startled on seeing Anne Catherine suddenly leave her bed, approach them with a firm step, and kneel before the latter, her hands joined, saying: "Give me a blessing! I need it for a certain person." Father Limberg blessed her and, though looking like a skeleton, she returned to her bed as briskly as one in perfect health. At such moments her slightest motions are singularly striking and impressive; she seems wholly unconscious of her movements. Like the turning of a flower to the light, they appear to be involuntary and they excite surprise in the beholder. After a short silence, she exclaimed: "They are strewing the road with rose leaves—someone must be coming!" and then she was shown how the sources of grace in the sacred heart were cut off from many souls of goodwill by the suppression of devotional exercises, by the closing and profanation of churches. In reparation for the same, she was directed to make special exercises in honor of the divine heart. "Great periods of suffering," she

---

[1] The pilgrim at first thought her delirious, but he soon reported the following: "Her condition becomes more and more critical and inexplicable—torture, weakness, vomiting, bloody sweats, cramps, burning thirst, inability to drink, temptations to impatience and struggles against it."

said, "begin with visions of roses and flowers scattered over me; they signify my different pains. When I was seized with rheumatism, I saw a pyramid of sharp thorns covered with roses. I groaned with fright at the thought of climbing it." Once she uttered these prophetic words: "I see the enemies of the blessed sacrament—who close the churches and prevent its adoration—rushing to their own destruction! They fall sick, they die without priest or sacrament!"

*From Quasimodo*[1] *until the third Sunday after Easter, 1820, Anne Catherine's state became so aggravated in consequence of the attacks made by Wessenberg and his party on the celibacy of the clergy and the scandals arising from the same, that her friends, though long accustomed to such scenes, could scarcely bear the sight of it. Still, however, her physical pains were perhaps even more endurable to Anne Catherine than were the ill-advised efforts to relieve her and the disturbance occasioned her little household. The pilgrim's brother, Christian Brentano, was in Dülmen at the time and, finding a noisy game of ninepins going on just beneath Anne Catherine's window one day, he resolved to have her removed to a more retired neighborhood. For this end he sought to gain Father Limberg and Dr. Wesener's approval, hoping to win through the latter the consent of the old Abbé Lambert, then sick and confined to his bed. But the old priest, weighed down by infirmity and desirous of ending his days in peace, would by no means consent to the change. "Full of sadness," as the pilgrim says, he dragged himself to the invalid's bedside and protested against a removal. Anne Catherine, anxious and annoyed by the repetition of such scenes, fell into a most deplorable state. Then it was that all concerned urged the use of various ineffectual remedies. They forgot the supernatural character of her sufferings which, had they been other than they were, must have ended in death. In view of this irritating commotion, we may readily understand*

---

[1] Quasimodo Sunday is the second Sunday after Easter (now celebrated as Divine Mercy Sunday). *Quasi modo* is Latin for "just like." They are the first two words for the entrance antiphon of Quasimodo Sunday. The full antiphon is *Quasi modo geniti infantes, rationabile, sine dolo lac concupiscite, ut in eo crescatis in salutem, alleluia* ("Like newborn infants, you must long for the pure, spiritual milk, that in him you may grow to salvation, alleluia").

*the effort it cost her to preserve her patience unruffled, and the earnestness with which she longed for Dean Overberg's presence to lull the storm. The pilgrim gives us the following details:*

*April 15th:* I found Anne Catherine quite unable to speak from excessive pain. She had lain all night unable to stir on account of the violent suffering in her left side. She could neither stretch out her hand to the tumbler at her side nor move her feet from the bottle of hot water that had been placed in her bed, and thus she spent the night abandoning herself to the mercy of God. When her confessor visited her next morning, he ordered the dreaded brandy lotions, which only served to aggravate her misery."

*April 16th:* The pains in the wound of her side are excruciating. They began by a vision on St. Thomas's incredulity. Today, Sunday, as she was contemplating a scene from the gospel, the wound bled and she felt that with every breath she drew the air blew through it. To prevent this she laid her hand over the wound. The retention from which she suffers is very severe. To crown all, there is a game of ninepins going on under her window. A friend is endeavoring to persuade her to change her lodgings.

*April 17th:* Her pains increase; she is all swollen, and the retention is so sharp as sometimes to deprive her of consciousness. She lies like a corpse, like one who had died from starvation. Sometimes her hunger for the blessed sacrament becomes intolerable; her heart burns with desire, while her hands are icy cold.

*April 18th:* Her condition is truly pitiable! Father Limberg begged the parish priest of Haltern to come and give her his benediction, which he did, apparently to her relief. This evening a brandy lotion was again prescribed, to which the poor invalid submitted with a groan. "I have brought it upon myself!" she said, "I have prayed for expiatory sufferings, and now the fire must burn out. I abandon all to God!"

*April 19th:* The whole night she lay consumed by fever and not allowed to drink for fear of retention. The parish priest of Haltern again prayed over and relieved her. When the pilgrim visited her in the afternoon, he found her lying on the foot of the bed, her limbs gathered up; she was groaning with agony and her fever was high. The pain seems now to be centered in the left side of the vertebral column. Although in this pitiable state, she thanked

God for all and, thinking herself in purgatory, rejoiced in the thought of never being able to offend him again.

*April 20th*: Her pains continue; her bed is steeped with perspiration and even Gertrude (not easily moved) shed tears at her sister's sufferings. Anne Catherine declares that, unless relieved, she must surely die; she cannot longer support her pains. She is quite deformed. She sent in haste for the curé, who came immediately. He prayed and imposed hands upon her, when she instantly fell into a gentle slumber. Afterward she said in allusion to this crisis:

I begged God earnestly to forgive me if I had asked for sufferings beyond my strength, to pity me for the sake of his Son's precious blood, and to help me to do his holy will, if I can still be of any service on this earth. I felt sure that, had I died this time, I should in some measure have been guilty of my own death and that I should have had to do penance in purgatory. As I received no other answer than: "The fire thou thyself hast lighted must burn to the end!"—I became discouraged, for I saw myself in a very precarious state. I recommended my affairs to God, since I should have to leave them behind me in disorder. When the curé prayed and imposed hands upon me, it seemed as if a gentle stream of light passed through me. I fell asleep feeling that I was again a little child being rocked to rest. A luminous ray rested upon me, which vanished when he withdrew his hand; but I was relieved; I was again full of courage!

*Toward noon Anne Catherine had another attack, which the old Abbé Lambert relieved by the imposition of hands and the recital of the rosary. The pilgrim put into her hand the crusts that had fallen from her stigmata. She smiled with a surprised air and said: "There is a poor sick person in a most pitiable condition! The curé of Haltern must know her! There she lies over there! She is much worse off than I, but she is patient! Ah! she is in great danger, but the curé has helped her. I cannot bear to see her suffering so; it makes me worse! I shall pray for her. She must have been shown me for my humiliation, for she is far better, far more patient than I, though much more suffering!"—and here the pilgrim removed the crusts.*

*April 21st*: She appears better today. St. Walburga and Madeline von Hadamar have appeared and consoled her. She is in continual contemplation.

*April 22nd*: Her pains are not so severe, but she is so weak as to be hardly able to speak. Her confessor told her today: "You are averse to brandy lotions, yet I know they are good for the stomach and back."

*April 23rd, Second Sunday after Easter*: At the Abbé Lambert and Gertrude's request, the mistress of the house made Anne Catherine a small cup of chicken broth without seasoning; for, as they said, she would never get strong without nourishment. The poor invalid patiently yielded to their united solicitations, but no sooner had she done so than her stomach revolted and she lay until evening in a state calculated to draw tears from the beholders. Fever, chills, cramps, and total insensibility succeeded one another in rapid succession. At last, the doctor pronounced mortification as having set in, and her death was momentarily expected. But after some time she suddenly opened her eyes and said smilingly: "I am no longer ill, I have no pain!" The confessor ordered her to go to sleep, which however her burning fever prevented, and she replied in a deprecating tone: "I want to, but I cannot," and she began in a low voice to make tender acts of love to God. "What do you want with the saints?" asked Father Limberg. "Go to sleep! Fine obedience!" Again she replied: "Ah! I want to, but I cannot!" At last she fell into ecstasy, her whole body becoming rigid, with no sign of pulsation excepting under the touch of the priest's fingers.[1] The fever also left her.

*April 24th*: The doctor and the confessor are anxious about Anne Catherine. They fear mortification. She herself asks for Extreme Unction and begs them to send for Dean Overberg. They delay, however, giving her holy communion, as they expect the vicar-general this evening and desire him to perform that office for her.

*The vicar-general came not, and Anne Catherine lay for hours without assistance; but God took compassion on His faithful servant. The pilgrim reports under date of April 26th:*

---

[1] "This pulsation," says Brentano, "is a witness of the highest importance rendered by nature to the Church; but it is incomprehensible! Unfortunately, we do not attach to it its proper value."

The invalid, who seemed to be in agony, suddenly arose to a sitting posture, her hands joined, her countenance radiant with youth and health and wearing an expression of the tenderest piety; thus she remained for a few minutes, made a motion as if swallowing, and then sank back on her pillows entirely changed. Gaily and with childlike simplicity she exclaimed:

O! I have obtained something! I have been so long begging at that magnificent table, and at last I received a crumb that has entirely restored my strength. I am entirely changed! All is well. All is in the hands of God. I have abandoned all to Him, I am perfectly relieved! Something like a dark vapor went out from me and floated upward. It may stay away; I don't want it!

Next day she said: Although in contemplation I saw what was going on around me, what was being done to assist me, to arrange things as is customary in this lower world, it struck me as being so very ridiculous that I had to laugh, though I was in such pain.

*April 27th*: Anne Catherine was very weak this morning. When she received through the pilgrim the announcement of Dean Overberg's inability to come just then she wept, but soon regained her composure and related a vision she had had the night before: "I was a child again. I was home, sick unto death, and all alone, father and mother absent. But ever so many of the neighbors' children, those of the mayor and others, came in and waited on me, and were so sweet and kind! They got green branches (it was in May), stuck them in the ground, and made a little hut. They carried leaves to it and made a bed for me. Then they brought me the most wonderful playthings, more beautiful than I could ever have dreamed of: dolls, cribs, animals, cooking utensils, little angels—and I played with them until morning. At times I feel as if some of them were still lying around. I wept much this afternoon, and once I pressed the Mother of God right to my heart, saying over and over again: 'Thou art my mother, my only mother!' and that did me good."

*How often the poor sufferer had to struggle against the frightful evil that attacked the celibacy of the clergy may be seen by the following vision of August 16, 1821:*

I was taken to a flock (a diocese) at one end of the field by the

181

nuptial house (that is, a diocese surrounded by Protestant sects). Among the sheep were many good-for-nothing goats that injured them with their horns. I was ordered to drive them out, a task that proved both troublesome and difficult, as I knew not how to tell the good from the bad. Then appeared St. Stanislaus Kostka, who helped me. First I went to the banks of a swift, broad stream and called all the goats together. The saint told me that the worthless ones were those with long, stiff hairs behind their ears and on the nape of the neck. I seized seven such animals and cast them into the cold waters, which swept them off.

*August 19th*: I have had a frightful night! I was nailed, crucified by the world, the flesh, and the devil, and I had to struggle with an enormous ram; but I conquered him! I bent his horns over his neck, broke them, and laid them crosswise on his back. "Thou, also, shalt bear the cross!" I said.

*In a subsequent vision the fruit of her sufferings was shown her*:

I saw a number of young ecclesiastics in a seminary assembled for a repast and, as I came from a higher sphere, I had many things to provide for them. I collected all in various places, though not without great fatigue. All sorts of cripples and beggars helped me and also the souls of many deceased persons. My companions in religion were to assist me, but I had first to light them out of a dark cave.[1] Reverend Mother remarked to them how wonderful it was that I should have been commissioned to lead them to such a task. I had to distribute a dozen sugar-loaves made by myself. I had to drag the sugar-cane from a great distance and put it through the necessary processes. I distributed eleven; the twelfth I laid aside for the poor. But Sister Eswig made such a fuss about it, saying that I had put it away for myself, that I replied: "Very well! I shall divide it. But let everyone give me back a part of hers for my trouble!" and so, I got more than I had at first. This vision was very extended. I saw the revival of the priesthood and religious orders after a period of great decadence. I saw too by what prayers, labors, and holy souls this will be brought about after my death. It seemed as if a band of pious workmen arose from whom

[1] Purgatory.

these good results were to emanate. The gifts bestowed upon the clergy were very varied; each received what he most needed There appeared to be very peculiar plants and flowers among them. From the ecclesiastics the best were chosen.

*Again we find Anne Catherine's labors directed to the good of ecclesiastical seminaries, as the following vision shows:*

*May, 1821:* I was in a long hall, on either side of which at their desks were young men in long robes like seminarists; passing up and down among them was a tall man. I was in one corner. All at once the young men turned into horses and the tall man into an immense cud-chewing ox. The horses showed their teeth behind him and made all sorts of mocking grimaces. I was wishing the ox would show them his horns and make them behave, but all he did was butt the wall every time he came to the end of the hall. There was a hole in it already, and I thought the building would soon come down on top of us. I knew not how to get out when, all at once, one of the horses left his place to go to another. I perceived a door behind the seat he had vacated, and by it I made my escape.

*On the evening of January 15, 1822, Anne Catherine vomited blood freely, and then suddenly exclaimed:*

A pious, parish-priest has just died in Rome of old age! I received the general absolution with him! His soul went straight to purgatory, but he will very soon be released. We must pray for him. He was greatly attached to the pope, during whose captivity he did much good in secret. The pope himself has not long to live. [And again she said]: That good old priest was one of the twelve unknown apostles whom I always see supporting the Church and of whom I have often spoken. He is the second that has died. There are now only ten; but I see others growing up. He was a friend and counselor of the pope, but he would never give up his parish for a higher position.

## Coronation of a Pope

ON *January 27, 1822, the feast of St. Paul's Conversion (Münster), Anne Catherine suddenly fell into ecstasy, during which she prayed fervently. That evening she said to the pilgrim:*

There has been a thanksgiving feast in the spiritual church. It was filled with glory, and a magnificent throne stood in the middle of it. Paul, Augustine, and other *converted* saints figured conspicuously. It was a feast in the Church Triumphant, a thanksgiving for a great, though still future, grace—something like a future consecration. It referred to the conversion of a man whom I saw, of slight figure and tolerably young, who was one day to be pope. I saw him below in the church among other pious men; he had been connected with the good old priest whose death I saw the other day in Rome.

I saw many Christians returning to the bosom of the Church, entering through the walls. That pope will be strict; he will remove from him lukewarm, tepid bishops—but it will be a long time before this happens. All whose prayers have been instrumental in obtaining this grace were present in the church. I saw also those men eminent in prayer whom I so often see. The young man was already in orders and it seemed as if he were receiving some new dignity. He is not Roman, though an Italian from a place not far from Rome. I think he is of a pious noble family. He travels sometimes. But before his time there will be many struggles. It was an indescribably beautiful and joyous festival, and I was so happy! The church is still there—I want to go back to it!

*And at these words she relapsed into ecstasy, during which she rose in her bed to pray until ordered by her confessor to lie down.*

*Anne Catherine spent the fall of 1822 in continual labors for the Church in Germany. She made nightly journeys to Rome; averted dangers from couriers, whose dispatches robbers and assassins were lying in wait to seize; assisted the sick and leprous whom she found on the road, and took charge of their disgusting packages; protected brides from false bridegrooms (that is, opposed the illegitimate occupation of certain episcopal sees); and all this she did with so much fatigue, with corporal sufferings so intense, as to be able to give very little account of them. The following vision, however, distinctly points to the object of these journeys—that is, the ecclesiastical affairs of the Upper Rhine province. Just at this epoch strenuous efforts were being made to gain the Holy See to renounce all right to certain bishoprics and to recognize as lawful incumbents men who had formally ratified an engagement with their patrons to betray the Catholic faith and to ignore for the future the laws* and jurisdiction of the Church. Anne Catherine was the instrument employed by God to oppose these iniquitous projects.

I was on my way to Rome (*October 22, 1822*) when I found a singular-looking child on a heath by the roadside. It seemed to be only one day old. It lay in the center of a dark globe that looked like fog, but that in reality was formed of thousands of twisted threads proceeding from the most distant regions. I had to pierce this web to get at the child, which I found closely enveloped in a beautiful little cloak with a large scalloped cape. I felt something under the cloak fastened to the child's back, which I tried, though in vain, to remove, for I suspected it was nothing good—when this child of a day began to laugh! I shrank from it unable to account for its mirth. But I now know what it meant. The authors of the trick doubted not of its success. They had wrapped it (a book) up with the gentle child in order to have it secretly conveyed to Rome. I do not now remember to whom I confided the child, but I think it was to a secular. I saw many whom I knew exulting over my taking the child, for there are in Rome even among the prelates many whose sentiments are not Catholic and who had connived at the success of the scheme. I saw in Germany among worldly-wise ecclesiastics, and "enlightened" Protestants, plans formed for the blending of religious creeds, the suppression of papal authority, the appointment of more superiors, the diminishing of expenses and the number of ecclesiastics, etc., which projects found abettors in many of the Roman prelates.

*The child in the globe of fog typifies the plan conceived for the suppression of Catholicity enveloped, as in a cloak, by beautiful figures of rhetoric; the fog signifies imposture, which works in the dark; the laughing of the child, the premature triumph of the plotters (men devoted to the pleasures of the table) at having outwitted the sovereign pontiff despite his protests and briefs! The book under the mantle represents the writings forwarded to Rome in favor of the projects. They were on their way, indeed, but they were incapable of preventing the discovery and defeat of the plot.*

*Anne Catherine saw the same wicked designers hunting up the decisions of the early councils—on which occasion Pope Gelasius was shown her as opposing the Manicheans, prototypes of the modern Illu-*

minati. *The intention of annihilating the pope and his authority really existed, as the church-councilor Werkmeister—the most active and influential of the sect—openly and cynically boasted. This man, once a monk at Neresheim, then a church-councilor at Stuttgart, boldly arrogated to himself the glory of having incontestably demonstrated that "The papacy could and ought to be rooted out," setting forth, for the benefit of the secular powers, the surest means of attaining that end, a means that was afterward literally adopted by the Frankfurt Assembly of which we have made mention.*[1]

While these agents of the evil one seemed to grow stronger day by day in numbers and influence, while flattering themselves that they had even smoothed the way in Rome for the success of their plans, the prayers and sufferings of the poor stigmatisee of Dülmen arrested their work of destruction. She so courageously resisted the enemies of God, besieging Him with prayers so ardent that, in a short time, she was able to say:

God ordained that the pope should be ill at this moment, whereby he escaped the snare laid for him. The enemy has long been maturing his plans; but they will not succeed, they have been discovered. I had many visions on this head, but I only recall the following: I beheld the only daughter of the king of kings attacked and persecuted. She wept bitterly over the quantity of blood shed,[2] and cast her eyes on a race of valiant virgins[3] who were to do combat at her side. I had much to do with her. I begged her to remember my country, as well as certain others that I named, and I petitioned for some of her treasures for the clergy. She responded: "Yes, it is true that I have great treasures, but they tread them under foot." She wore a sky-blue robe. Then my guide exhorted me anew to pray and, as far as I could, to incite others to pray for sinners and especially for erring priests. "Very evil times are coming," he said. "The non-Catholics will mislead many. They will use every possible means to entice them from the Church, and great disturbances will follow."

[1] "Plan for the Reorganization of the Catholic Church in the Germanic Confederation," published in German, 1816.

[2] The numberless souls lost.

[3] Chaste priests, defenders of her rights.

I had then another vision in which I saw the king's daughter armed for the struggle. Multitudes contributed to this with prayers, good works, all sorts of labors and self-victories that passed from hand to hand up to heaven, where each was wrought—according to its kind—into a piece of armor for the Virgin-Warrior. The perfect adjustment of the various pieces was most remarkable, as also their wonderful signification. She was armed from head to foot. I knew many of those who contributed the armor, and I saw with surprise that whole institutions and great and learned people furnished nothing. The contribution was made chiefly by the poor and lowly.

And now I saw the battle. The enemies' ranks were by far the more numerous; but the little body of the faithful cut down whole rows of them. The armed Virgin stood off on a hill. I ran to her, pleading for my country and those other places for which I had to pray. She was armed singularly, but significantly, with helmet, shield, and coat of mail, and the soldiers were like those of our own day. The battle was terrible; only a handful of victorious champions survived!

# A Diocese
## Separated from the Rock of Peter

THEN I saw a church sailing on the waters and in great danger of sinking, for it had no foundation; it rolled on these like a ship. With mighty efforts I had to help restore its balance, and we sent many people into it—chiefly children, stationing them around on the beams and planks.[1] In the three aisles of the church lay twelve men prostrate and motionless in fervent prayer, and there were crowds of children at the entrance prostrate before an altar. I saw no pope, but a bishop prostrate before the high altar. In this vision I saw the church bombarded by other vessels, but we hung wet cloths before it and it received no damage. It was threatened

---

[1] A symbol of the future. This church, tossed to and fro and about to be engulfed by the waves, was to find by degrees a more solid foundation on the rock of Peter.

on all sides; it seemed as if its enemies wanted to hinder its land-ing. When by the help of extra weight it was again righted, it sank a little in the sand. Then we laid down planks to the shore. Instantly all sorts of bad ecclesiastics ran in with others—who had given no assistance in time of need[1]—and began to mock the twelve men whom they found in prayer, and to box their ears; but the latter were silent and went on praying. Then we brought great stones that we stuck all around for a foundation, which began to increase as if it were growing of itself. The stones came together, and it seemed as if a rock sprang up and all became solid. Crowds of people, among them some strangers, entered by the door, and the church was again on land.

*This vision lasted several nights and was accompanied by hard labor. Once Anne Catherine, still in ecstasy, uttered the following words: "They want to take from the shepherd his own pasture grounds! They want to fill his place with one who will hand all over to the enemy!" Then she shook her hand indignantly, crying out:*

O ye German cheats![2] Wait awhile! You will not succeed! The shepherd stands upon a rock! O you priests! You stir not, you sleep, and the sheepfold is everywhere on fire! You do nothing! O how you will bewail this some day! If you had said only one *Our Father*! The whole night have I seen the enemies of the Lord Jesus drag him around and maltreat him upon Golgotha! I see so many traitors! They cannot bear to hear said: "Things are going badly!" All is well with them if only they can shine before the world!

*In April, 1823*: I almost killed myself working last night. I am full of pains! First I had to drag a great man into the church. He had tried to prevent my adoring the blessed sacrament in a spiritual church and had seized me by the shoulders. When I caught him, he resisted; but I held him firmly by the hands and, not being able to free himself, he dragged me backwards on my knees. At last, after much struggling, I succeeded in bringing him before the

---

[1] The old liberal party who, when they could do so without danger or fatigue, sought to possess themselves of the rights of others.

[2] The so-called German *patriots*, who were opposed to the Latin tongue as the language of the Church. They sought to establish a national German Church, without God, without the sacraments, without the pope.

altar. The house from which he had come (the nuptial house) was on fire, which it seems he himself had kindled. With infinite trouble I had to save everything, to carry all to the sheepfold. The fire had already mounted to the roof and there was no human being to help me, although I saw many priests, whom I knew, walking leisurely around. At last an ecclesiastic approached with one who looked like a lawyer, and they helped me. We rescued from all corners of the house chests, boxes, mantles, candlesticks, and church chandeliers, and took them to the sheepfold. I worked myself to death! As the flames darted out through the roof, the priest rushed in and snatched up from one of the rooms a *son,*[1] a *child,* that he whom I had dragged into the church had tried to kill, but which was still alive. The servants slept over that room; but fortunately they were saved. The smoke and fumes soon cleared away. We three saved all.

*About this period, Anne Catherine was also engaged in the conversion of N—, whom she saw surrounded by a fog, cut off by a wall of separation as if under the ban of excommunication. She begged God to cure him corporally and spiritually:*

His condition is somewhat improved; his long illness has been a grace from God, and his sentiments on many points are quite changed. It is as if he died and came to life again an altered man. He confessed many things to the pope, accused himself of many things, gave up all, died to all, and then lived again. I saw him lying on his bed surrounded by high church dignitaries, and once too the pope was by him. Around lay writings, many of which he gave up. They spoke, they questioned, and I often saw him raising his hand as if affirming something; perhaps he could no longer speak distinctly, but I know not for certain. He seemed to be declaring that he disengaged himself from everything, that he gave up everything.

The pope was with him alone for some time, perhaps hearing his confession. I know not, but he used his hand as before, and I think he put his arm around the pope's neck. I know not whether

---

[1] The *son*, the *child*—that is, the plot to establish certain relations with the Greek schism. Anne Catherine saw this son go to Russia.

he was merely embracing him, or bidding him adieu, or whether the pope was forgiving him something. Then the latter went out. Among the papers that N— gave to the pope was one in particular relating to our church. It was not perfectly conformable to the pope's sentiments; indeed he even seemed not to have had any previous knowledge of it. It is well that events fell out thus! Affairs will now take a turn quite different from that which the enemy expected. N— wept, as did also the pope and all the assistants. It looked as if they were taking leave of him.

I have had much to do for the Church of this country, and I am now undergoing a frightful martyrdom! I am passing through horrible states! I have to work for the whole Church. I am quite bewildered by the disorder and distress I see all around, and by my own pains and labors. I have had a vision on the fatal condition of students of the present day. I saw them going through the streets of Münster and Bonn with bundles of serpents in their hands. They drew them through their mouth, and sucked their heads, and I heard these words: *These are philosophical serpents!*[1]

I have often seen that the simple, pious old schoolmasters—who are generally ignored as ignorant—form children to piety, while the skilful masters and mistresses put nothing into their heads because, by their pride and self-sufficiency, they deprive their labor of its fruit and, so to speak, consume it themselves. It is the same as with the blessing attached to good works which, when done in public or through motives of policy, have little efficacy. Where charity and simplicity are wanting, there is no secret success. I saw many pastors cherishing dangerous ideas against the Church. Full of sadness, I turned my eyes away and prayed for bishops; for if they become better, their priests will soon follow their example. I saw among other things that the house whence I had dragged that man, was the church under N—. In all the rooms lay his children, that is, *his plans*—a full collection of his views. My dragging him to the altar signified his conversion, his confession. He had set fire to the house, and I with others had to save the goods and convey them to the sheepfold.

[1] See "Dame Philosophy and Philosophical Snakes" in *Inner Life and Worlds of Soul & Spirit*.

They built a large, singular, extravagant church that was to embrace all creeds with equal rights: Evangelicals, Catholics, and all denominations—a true communion of the unholy with one shepherd and one flock. There was to be a pope, a salaried pope, without possessions. All was made ready, many things finished; but in place of an altar were only abomination and desolation. Such was the new church to be, and it was for it that he had set fire to the Old One; but God designed otherwise. He died with confession and satisfaction—and he lived again!

*Here the pilgrim remarks*: Her state makes me shudder! Her communications have ceased. She has been told that for the next fourteen days—that is, until Pentecost—she will continue to suffer for the Church.

*In the fall of 1823, Anne Catherine related what follows*:

I saw the pope when he fell.[1] Some persons had just left him. He had risen from his chair to reach something when he fell. I could not believe he was really dead. I felt he was still governing, that all went on by his orders. I saw him lying dead, and yet I thought him still acting. Pius was constantly in prayer, always communing with God, and he often had divine illuminations; he was very sweet and condescending. Leo XII cannot yet pray like Pius VII, but he has a resolute will.

On the feast of the Assumption I saw many things concerning N—. The pope and some cardinals seemed to be exhorting him to keep his promise and to devote himself in earnest to the good of the Church. N— had in childhood learned from his mother a short invocation in honor of Mary. He frequently repeated it morning and evening, and so obtained Mary's intercession with Jesus. I saw her warning him and sending him grace to amend.

November: These last days I had to urge a man employed in St. Peter's, at Rome, to make known to the pope that he is a Freemason. He did so, with the excuse however that he was only a treasurer, that he saw no harm in it, and that he did not want to lose his place. But the pope gravely represented to him that he must either resign the office immediately or give up his employment in the Church. I heard the whole interview.

---

[1] Pius VII died Aug. 20, 1823, of a fracture of the hip occasioned by a fall.

*With the month of January, 1823, began the spiritual task of collecting and distributing materials for sacerdotal ornaments, while at the same time Anne Catherine commenced to prepare her Christmas gifts for poor children. Her work was repeatedly delayed by the want of some indispensable article, by the awkwardness of an unskillful assistant, or by violent pains in her eyes. She had a thousand temptations to impatience; but she overcame all, she triumphed by prayer and perseverance. She says:*

I made a journey to Cyprus (and here she accompanied Jesus in his travels).[1] As I left the continent, I saw Marseilles on my right, and only once did I pass over a point of land. My guide and I moved along by the shore. I had various tasks to perform on the way: things to arrange, secret packages and letters that I carried under my arm, to deliver, often with great risk; obstacles to surmount; people to admonish in prayer; sleepers to awaken, the wounded to bandage; robbers and other evil-doers to disturb; prisoners to console; those in danger to warn; and for several days I had to urge a man who was the bearer of a letter which, like that of Uriah, contained instructions to those to whom it was addressed to make away with him. It was on this side of Rome. I whispered to him: "Where are you going? You are on the wrong road!" "No," said he. "'Here is the address on my letter." "Open it," I said, "there you will see." He did so, read the plot laid for him, and fled.

Then I had an immense labor on all kinds of ecclesiastical vestments in the house I had seen on fire last spring. I had to make an alb for a bishop whom I saw in the distance; but I had not wherewith to finish it, and so I asked alms from everybody. Dean Overberg said he could give only a groschen, and that mortified me. I had to make that alb because I must soon die… Again, in Switzerland, I had to beg materials for surplices. I rolled them into a large bundle and dragged it to Rome, where they were to be made up.

I was in Rome, in the midst of an assembly of ecclesiastics pre-

---

[1] A full account of Anne Catherine's visions regarding Jesus's journey to Cyprus may be found in Book II of *The Visions of Anne Catherine Emmerich*; details of the individuals who figured in that journey may be found in "The Cypriotes" in *People of the New Testament IV*.

sided over by the pope. There was question of re-establishing or organizing something, but the resources for it had been squandered. The ecclesiastics were for letting the affair drop, saying: "Nothing can be made of nothing"; but the pope was for going on with it. Then I interposed: "A good undertaking ought not to be abandoned. If there is nothing, God will supply." The pope told me that I had a good deal of courage for a nun, but that I was right.

Again I went to Rome, and I was very much vexed to find a quantity of church linen that had been washed in the time of the last pope and had been hanging there ever since. I myself had made and brought many pieces. Much of it had never been used but had lain neglected: laces, ribands, borders torn off, even great holes in them. The ivory crucifixes I had taken there were now minus the figures, only the crosses and marble stands remaining. On one they had even hung a little brass figure.

In the midst of this wash walked all sorts of distinguished ecclesiastics taking great notice of the school-examination and first communion dresses, and other unimportant articles, but paying no heed to the church linen that hung in such disorder. I was indignant at seeing five disgraceful chemises of costly and extravagant style conspicuous among the church linen. I was indignant, for they looked to me indecent and less proper for a bride and bridegroom than for adulterers. The upper part was miserably made, the shoulder straps of coarse pack-cloth; but the rest was of the finest, most transparent material, trimmed elaborately with lace and open-work embroidery. These chemises were provided with a hood to blindfold the eyes, as if shame and nakedness could be hidden under this infamous veil!

I was deeply afflicted at such a scandal; and grieving over my mutilated crucifixes, packed the things I had brought in a basket to take them back with me. One of the ecclesiastics wanted to hinder my packing, but another whom I knew took my part.

I saw also the deceased Abbé Lambert in the distance. (It was the eve of his feast, St. Martin's.) I asked him to help me and also why he had not yet come for me. He laughed, shook his finger, and said: "Did I not tell you, you were still to suffer much?" and then he turned away.

I insisted on having what belonged to me, succeeded in getting the marble stands of the naked crosses, and packed up everything. I asked how those vile chemises came there. I would have loved to tear them to pieces, and I found that, in compliment to some Protestant gentlemen, they had been received and tolerated. I took one down, and then only did I discover the hood; for at first I thought it a collar. I was so angry that I thought: "Wait! I'll sew your fine trimmings with cobbler's thread, that people may see what is wanting to you!" The pope too was very indignant at the sight of those shameful chemises. He tore one to shreds, and I saw that several cardinals and secular princes were quite displeased at his act.[1]

*Anne Catherine was so much the more affected by this vision as she knew how important, how decisive for afterlife, is the child's first communion. One day the pilgrim found her consoling and instructing her little niece, who was in a flood of tears because the teacher had demanded from each pupil a sketch of the Sunday sermon. The little thing had caught nothing of it, excepting a few words relating to the justification of the Pharisees in their own eyes. Her aunt told her that that would be quite sufficient. She remarked at the same time that the task imposed upon children was already the fruit of the impetus given by the mischievous young schoolmaster of the nuptial house; for the sermons and instructions were given in High German, while the poor little ones understood only the Low German patois.*

---

[1] "The five vile chemises signify the occupation of the five vacant sees by men who, instead of forming a chaste and lawful union with their Bride, the Church, founded on faith and fidelity, rested their adulterous claims upon treason and perjury under the patronage of the secular powers; men whose intrinsic vileness had to be veiled by high sounding expressions, *peace, gratitude, toleration,* etc. The picture could hardly be more striking, both upon this point and upon those that refer to school exhibitions and to the theatrical costumes worn at first communion. Such dresses banish from the souls of many hundreds of children that piety and recollection, that reverence and devotion, so necessary for the worthy reception of their eucharistic God." CB

# Journeys Undertaken
# for Her Neighbor

LAST night I performed a wonderful task. I was thinking yesterday evening of the misery of those who, living in a state of impurity, make insincere confessions, and I prayed earnestly for all such sinners. Then came the soul of a noble lady to my bedside, begging me to pray God for the conversion of her daughter, to pray for her with extended arms because his Son had so prayed. Her daughter lay dying after having concealed her sins in eighteen confessions. Then my guide took me a long journey, first to the east, afterward toward the west. I met on my road various cases requiring assistance. There were at least ten; but I only remember three:

In a beautiful city, more Lutheran than Catholic, I was taken by my guide to the house of a widow who was ill. Just as we entered, her confessor was leaving. The lady lay surrounded by friends and acquaintances, and I stood in the background, forgetting that I was there only as a spirit, as a messenger. I looked around and felt as an insignificant person would naturally do when treated with indifference by the great ones of the world.

I soon saw the lady's state. She was a Catholic, apparently pious, for she gave large alms. But she had fallen into manifold secret disorders, which she had concealed eighteen times in the confessional, thinking she could repair all by alms; her disease also she kept secret. I was quite confused and abashed before all these grand people. I heard the sick lady say laughingly to her friends, as they raised her in the bed: "I did not tell him (the priest) such or such a thing"—and then they all laughed. They withdrew as if to let her rest.

My guide now bade me remember that I had come as God's messenger, and to step forward. I drew near the bed with him and spoke to her—my words passing before her as luminous writing, one line after another. I know not whether she beheld

195

my guide or myself, but she turned pale and swooned from fright, in which state I saw that she read even more distinctly the words that appeared before her bodily eyes. My words were these: "You laugh, and yet you have eighteen times abused the sacraments to your own condemnation! You have... (and here I rehearsed her hidden sins). Eighteen times have you concealed all these in false confessions! In a few hours will you stand before the judgment seat of God! Have pity on your own soul! Confess and repent!"

She was perfectly overcome, the cold sweat ran down her forehead! I stepped back, and she cried out to her attendants that she wanted her confessor. They expressed great surprise, as he had just left the house; but she made no reply, she was in frightful anguish. The priest was called. She confessed all with plentiful tears, received the last sacraments, and died. I know her name, but I cannot tell it; some members of her family are still living. It is with a joyful, and yet a heart-rending feeling, that I perform such tasks.

I entered a country of vast swamps and bogs over which my guide and I floated. We came to a village and went into a peasant's house, the mistress of which lay very ill. There was no priest in the neighborhood. The woman was a hypocritical adulteress who lived apart from her husband, the more readily to sin with another. I brought up her wickedness before her eyes and told her that she must confess it to her husband and crave his pardon. This she did with many tears. Her accomplice also was forced to appear. The husband opened the door for him, and the wife declared to him earnestly that their relations with each other must cease. She did not die; she recovered.

I went to a large city and into a house with a beautiful garden full of groves, ponds, and pavilions. The parents were living; the mother a pious, good woman. They had a daughter, a very discreet maiden apparently, but who was in the habit of meeting her lovers secretly and by appointment in the garden. There I found her last night awaiting one of them. I stood by, begging God to come to her aid. Suddenly I saw a figure trying, but in vain, to approach her. I recognized satan. The girl grew agitated and withdrew into a summer house. I followed and found another figure enveloped in a mantle whom she took for her expected sweetheart. She went up to him, drew aside the cloak that concealed him, and there she saw (and I saw also) the figure of the Savior covered with blood and wounds, his hands bound, the crown of thorns upon his head! The piteous figure spoke: "Behold to what thou hast reduced me!" and the girl fell to the ground as if dead.

I took her in my arms, told her in what crime she was living, and urged her to confess and do penance. She recovered consciousness, and thinking no doubt that I was a servant or perhaps some stranger who had come across her, moaned plaintively: "O if I were only in the house! My father would kill me if he found me here!" Then I told her that if she would promise to confess and do penance I would help her to regain her room; otherwise, she would have to lie there until morning and steal in as best she could. She promised everything, her strength returned, and she slipped into the house as she was accustomed to do; but when safe in her room she again fell ill. The priest for whom she sent next morning was found by God's mercy ready to attend her. She confessed, repented sincerely, and died fortified by the sacraments. Her parents had no suspicion of her sins.

I saw ten such cases last night; but I am not successful in all, some will not give up their evil ways. It is horrible! I still must weep; the devil holds them so fast! I have found it particularly difficult to convert ecclesiastics given to such sins. I met some last night for whom prayer is the only hope.

In November, 1820, I took a great journey on which I had much to do, but I only remember the following cases distinctly:

Near Paderborn, my guide took me to a house, saying: "There is in this house a young girl immersed in frivolity. You must warn her. She will soon return from a dance. I shall give you the voice and language of a pious young neighbor and, while she prepares to retire, you will reproach her with her levity." Then I saw a picture of the girl's whole life—she was vain, giddy, fond of dress and dancing; in short, a practiced flirt.

And now I beheld her returning from the dance. She went to her room without a light and laid off her ornaments to go to bed. I drew near and said: "It is time for you to think seriously of your life. In laying aside this toilette, abandon also your evil courses.

Serve no longer the devil rather than your God who gave you body and soul, who redeemed you with his blood!" At these words, she grew angry, told me I had better go off home, what did I want there with my prattling. She needed no monitoress; she knew very well what she was about, etc. She jumped into bed without a prayer. When she had fallen asleep, my guide said: "Rouse her! I shall show her some pictures of her life!" I did not see the pictures, but I knew that she saw satan, herself, and her lovers. My guide called satan by another name, I think "the prince of this world." I shook her. She arose tremblingly upon her bed and in great terror hastily recited all the prayers she knew. I saw her run to her mother and tell her how frightened she had been and that she would never again go to a dance. Her mother in vain tried to dissuade her from her resolution. Next morning she did as I had directed and made a good confession of her whole life. I know for a certainty that she amended.

I went last night (*March 8, 1820*) on a journey through the snow and saw two poor travelers set upon and beaten by others with clubs. One fell dead and, as I ran to his assistance, the assassins seemed to be frightened and fled. The second was still alive. Some of his kinsmen came up and carried him to a physician's in the neighborhood. This I obtained by my prayers. I knew well that I ought not to add anything to my burden, and yet I was so anxious to suffer a part of his pains. I obtained my wish.

Then I made another long journey, and returning I again met snow. As I neared my home I saw a poor famished man who, while trying to get bread for his children, had met with a serious fall. He could not extricate himself from the snow. I helped him to get free, as also to obtain food. I think we shall hear of him soon.

*And, in effect, that very afternoon the pilgrim found Anne Catherine sick and drenched in perspiration, which state she said was to last till five o'clock. The profuse perspiration, a mixture of blood and water, had been imposed upon her for the relief of the wounded man. She said:*

People may think as they please, but I know that it is God's will for me so to do, so to suffer. I have done so from my youth; I am called by Him to such works of mercy. When only four years old I heard my mother groaning with pain at the birth of my sister. I slept with an old woman, and I began to pray to God, saying over and over: "I will take my mother's pains! Give me my mother's pains!"

## Journey to Palermo

ALL yesterday afternoon (*in August, 1820*) I felt that I should have to set out somewhere. Someone called for prayers and help, and last night I had a vision. In the island south of Italy, during a period of frightful murders and robberies that happened there lately, I saw one of the ringleaders earnestly beseeching God and the Blessed Virgin to help him. He had resolved to change a life that for too many years had been a godless one. He had a wife and children, but the former was among the most furious of the gang. During all his reckless life this man had worn a little picture of the Blessed Virgin, painted on parchment or something similar, concealed in his coat between the button holes. He never went without it, and he often thought of it. The picture was variegated blue and gold and quite neatly executed.

The man was a sort of subaltern over the armed insurgents. The latter wore no uniform. It seemed as if an attack was to be made before morning, for they were lying in the open air before a town. There was great misery throughout the whole country. Many good people had been murdered and many more are yet to perish in the same way, that they may not see the deluge of coming woes. The distress, rebellion, and disorder are truly frightful, and the people are very poor and superstitious. I saw that poor man in great agony of conscience unceasingly calling upon God and Mary: "Ah! if what religion teaches be true, then let the Blessed Virgin intercede for me, that I may not die in my sins and be damned forever! Send me help, for I know not how to free myself!"[1]

Hardly had I seen and *felt* the poor fellow's distress and anguish than I earnestly begged God to pity him, to save him; and instantly, without being conscious of having made a journey, I stood before him in the midst of his sleeping comrades. I cannot remember all I said to him, but only that he should rise and

---

[1] "I had also a vision of St. Rosalia, after whose feast these horrors began."

depart, for his place was not among them. I do not think he saw me; he had only an interior perception of my presence. He left the rebels, fled to the sea, and embarked in a little sailboat. I went with him. We sailed rapidly and securely by the still moonlight, and in an extraordinarily short time reached the capital of the island in which are the two little nuns who have the stigmata (Cagliari, in Sardinia). There I left him in safety. He wanted to reform, and lead a pious life unknown to the world.

I visited then the nun of Cagliari, who lives with a pious lady. I found her still tolerably well, praying for the cessation of those fearful calamities. I went also to see Rosa Serra in the Capuchin convent of Ozieri. She is very old, sick, and emaciated, and there is no mention made of her extraordinary graces. The nuns are good and very poor, their country at peace. On my return, I stopped at Rome and found the pope in deep affliction. He had been directed in prayer to admit no one to his presence for the time being. The dark church is gaining ground. There are numbers of unfortunate people ready to join it on the first sign of an outbreak. I saw the secret society from which all these plots emanate, working very actively.

## Rescue of a French Family in Palermo

FOR several days I have had repeated visions of an affair that came to an end last night. A family was shown me in that unhappy place in which there has just been a massacre. It is a noble household, husband and wife, several grown children, and one especially attractive male servant (formerly a slave) with brown complexion and crispy hair. I was first shown how this family came to settle there. They are French. I saw them before the Revolution living piously and happily in France. They were truly good, and especially devout to the Mother of God, before whose picture they burned a lamp every Saturday and said prayers in common. The slave was not then a Christian, though a good-natured, extremely active, and intelligent man. He was very slight, well-proportioned, and so nimble and handy that it was a pleasure to see him serving the family. I cannot endure slow, stiff, immovable people! I often think that the souls of the active are more easily influenced by grace. I saw how fond the master and the whole family were of this slave and how all, by a special inspiration from God, longed for his conversion to Christianity.

The gentleman and lady begged this favor of the Blessed Virgin. The slave fell sick. On the eve of the assumption, his master took a picture of Mary to him, saying that, since he could do nothing else, he might make as lovely a garland for it as possible; that she whom it represented would sympathize with his sufferings and obtain mercy for him from God; and that he should make the garland with all the love of his heart. The servant joyfully undertook to fulfill his master's request and skillfully twined an exquisite wreath around the picture.

As he worked, his heart was touched. The Mother of God appeared to him that night, cured him, told him that his garland was most pleasing to her, and that he must go to his master and ask for instructions and baptism. The slave obeyed next morning; and his master, who had earnestly prayed for this result, was radiant with joy at the success of his pious scheme. The slave became a Christian, and his devotion to the Mother of God was very great. He twined a garland for all her festivals, and if he had no flowers he used colored paper; he burned a light every Saturday before her picture; he was very pious.

The Mother of God failed not to reward the piety of this family. They were in great danger during the Revolution. They embarked and arrived safe in Sicily, where the gentleman became very rich, the owner of magnificently furnished houses, lovely gardens and villas supported in grand style. But he was no longer as pious as he used to be. He was mixed up with all sorts of wicked undertakings, and his public office brought him into connection with the revolutionary faction. His position was such as to force him either to take part in the rebellion, or expose himself to the greatest risks; he could not draw back.

Now, some of the old pious customs were still kept up in his family, and the light was burned on Saturdays in honor of the Mother of God. The good servant was now much better than his masters, and he wove his garlands as before. More than once I had to go to exhort the gentleman to amend his life and make his escape from the island. The first time (eve of the assumption) I went by night to his bedside and reminded him and his wife of their pious, innocent days when, before this same feast, they had converted the sick slave through the garland in Mary's honor. This was now the anniversary of that happy day. I contrasted with it their present state. I exhorted the husband to make a garland of all his sins and evil inclinations, as he had formerly done of flowers, burn it with sincere repentance before the Mother of God on her feast, and then leave the country as quickly as possible. I shook him by the arm; he awoke and aroused his wife. Both were deeply affected and related to each other the same dream. The slave had already placed the light before the picture for the feast.

I had to return several times and urge the husband to depart, as it was a severe trial to them to leave their houses, their gardens, and all their wealth; but the last night I went I found them all ready to go. They took with them gold, more than sufficient for their wants, left all the rest, and embarked in a large ship for India. The gentleman chose that country, as he had heard that religion was highly prosperous on one of the islands. And so the good slave got back to his own country again.

I saw shocking misery in the island they left (Sicily), the inhabitants living in mutual distrust. I saw also the wife of the man who had fled into Sardinia. She was furious enough to kill him, for it was principally owing to her that he had joined the conspirators; but he was now thoroughly converted. He visited all the shrines in spirit on his journey, and went to confession as soon as he arrived in Sardinia. It seems strange, but I have been told that he will visit our country and I shall, perhaps, see him!

*October 14th*: I saw the family with the old Indian slave landing on the island for which they had set sail. They were well received.

*September 2nd*: I saw the feast of St. Evodius, in Syracuse, and a pious man earnestly invoking the saint. He was in great anxiety respecting the troubled times and he wanted to leave the country; but he had a large family and his wife refused her consent. I was commissioned to tell him to go. It was evening when I entered the courtyard of his house, where he was walking, troubled and anxious. He asked not who I was. We conversed together, and I told him he must go even without his wife; if she would not accompany him, she would follow him before long, and so he went.

*October 13th*: Last night I met on the sea a vessel without oars or sails, tossed about by the tempest. It was full of refugees from Sicily. My guide gave me a blunt iron bar to push the ship forward; but the bar kept slipping off, and so I thought it ought to have been pointed. He told me, however, to go on pushing in spite of trouble and fatigue, that it must be done in that way. Pointed instruments are for worldly affairs, and only too many of them are now in use in Sicily. The ship reached land in safety.

## A Theft Prevented

I WAS in a little town, a hundred leagues distant, and I saw in a church a picture of Mary surrounded by silver offerings, which three men had planned to steal the following night. I recognized one of them. I had given him a shirt just before he left home. He used to be a good young man; it was hunger and misery that had driven him to sin. I pitied him, but for the others I had no such feeling—perhaps they were not Catholics, and I could not pray for them fervently. They argued thus: "We are starving, the picture has need of nothing," and so they thought they were robbing no one.

The poor parents of the one I knew had, on bidding him adieu, recommended him to Jesus, Mary, and Joseph, and I was now charged to dissuade him from the robbery. They had planned to enter the church that night through a window by a ladder. The one of whom I speak was to keep watch while the others despoiled the shrine; the whole affair was repugnant to him, but hunger pressed. Fortunately, just at the moment for the evil deed, a poor woman came to pray before the church. She was the mother of a large family. Her wretched husband had abandoned her, leaving her deeply in debt. Her little household effects were about being seized and in her distress she had recourse to the Mother of God. Her presence frightened the unfortunate men, who put off their design till next morning. I prayed for the poor woman (and here Anne Catherine earnestly begged the pilgrim to unite with her in prayer for the miserable husband).

At noon next day I saw the three comrades sauntering along and deliberating upon their projected theft, but the young man wanted to have nothing more to do with it. He said that he would rather pull up potatoes and roast them when hungry than rob the shrine. His two companions threatened to kill him if he did not join them, so he promised; but he left them, resolved to take no part in the affair. The church stands on the outskirts of the town.

Once, years ago, I had to frighten a young man and thus prevent his committing sin. Later on he married and I often had occasion to advise him and his wife. There was not much blessing on their union, and the husband was tempted to rob. More than once I saw him by night lurking around ovens, a sack on his back, with the intention of stealing bread of which he really had no need. I used to make a noise or frighten him off in some other way, and thus I had the happiness of several times preventing his thefts. One night I saw him stealing into the house of one of my friends, who had a batch of bread in his trough. I was as if spellbound, I could not stop him. He had already filled his sack with dough when the owner, awakened by the barking of dogs, got up to strike a light. Now, if he did this, the thief would be detected and his family forever disgraced, for in order to escape he would be obliged to pass the owner of the house. Not being able to prevent the theft, I sought to screen the thief that he might reform; consequently, I gathered up strength and slammed the door several times. The light went out, and the fellow escaped with his sack. Some weeks after, the good man who had lost the dough came to see me and related the whole affair. He knew not, he said, why he had not seized the thief, but he felt a sort of pity for him; perhaps it was just as well that he had not discovered him, for he could now amend, etc. He spoke very wisely. The thief's wife also came to see me and, as she reminded me that I had before her marriage preserved her from sin, I took occasion to speak to her of the facility with which one falls from small faults into great ones. She wept bitterly, for she knew of her husband's doings. Both have made restitution and corrected. I acted thus by the direction of God.

On January 22, 1820, I was suddenly called by an earnest prayer, and I saw on the shore across the sea an old man praying, in great trouble. The country was covered with snow; there were pines and similar trees with prickly leaves growing around. The man wore a large fur coat and a rough cap trimmed with fur. He lived in a large house that stood by itself in the midst of smaller ones. I saw no church, but some buildings like schools. He seemed to be truly good. His son, who led a very disorderly life, had left the house in a violent passion and gone to sea in a ship richly laden with silver and merchandise. The father had a presentiment of the great dangers he would encounter in a tempest and dreaded his son's being lost in his present state; therefore he began to pray, and dispatched his servants in all directions with alms and requests for prayers, while he himself went to a wood where dwelt a holy solitary in whose intercession he placed great confidence.

All this I saw across the sea; and on the stormy waves I saw the ship in imminent peril, tossed hither and thither by the tempest. It was an enormous ship, almost as large as a church. I saw the crew climbing and scrambling and shouting; few of them had any religion, and the son, I saw, was not good. Things seemed desperate. I prayed to God with all my power and, in various directions, I saw others in prayer for the same intention, especially the old man in the forest. I prayed fervently; I presented my petition to God boldly and persistently. I was perhaps too bold, for I received a rebuke; but I thought not of it. It seemed as if I were not to be heard; but the distress before me was heartrending. I ceased not to pray, to implore, to cry, until I beheld the ship enter a harbor in safety. The father received an interior assurance that calmed him, and I felt that the son would reform, for all which I thanked God. I did know the whole history of the widowed father and his son, but I have forgotten it.

I had to make a long journey (*on July 16, 1820*) with my guide to a city of the north where lived in a small isolated house a poor, miserable couple, seemingly farm tenants. They were expecting to be driven from house and home and reduced to misery, though why I know not. They had confidence in me, and in their distress they thought of me, that I might intercede with God for them. Some of their children were quite young. In a distant country they had grown ones: a son, a fine young man, who traveled on business, and a daughter who seemed to be in my vicinity and pushing me on to her parents. The husband had not always been good, but he had reformed; his wife seemed older than he. They drew me to them by prayer. I had to go to them, and my guide ordered me to follow him. I carried something with me, what, I no longer know; it may have been real or only symbolical. I came to a steep rampart on the way, over which to all appearances I could not possibly climb. I thought of the words of Jesus that faith can move mountains and, full of this truth, I set about penetrating it, when the steep mountain was leveled under my feet. I passed through the country where I had once seen the father of a family saved through prayer from a tempest that threatened his life. I saw in a mountainous district St. Hedwiges on my right, and I met other saints, patrons of the countries wherein their relics repose. It was night when I entered the cottage of the people to whom I had been called. The husband was up, roused by some noise, I think; the wife lay in bed weeping. I no longer remember what I did for them or what I took to them, but they were relieved and consoled; the danger was passed when I left them. I was taken back by a different road more toward the west. I performed many tasks on the way; among them I prevented a robbery.

*On March 2, 1822, a large sum of money had been stolen from a poor tax collector, a Protestant, who had in consequence lost his situation, so that his family was in need of the necessaries of life. The pilgrim recommended the case to Anne Catherine, who very willingly undertook to pray for him. Having done so several times, she remarked:*

It is singular how one can effect so little for such people by prayer! I see such tepid Protestants in a very strange state groping about in the dark, in a fog, perfectly blind and dull! They are as it were in the midst of a whirlwind whose gusts strip them naked. I know not whether God will help in this case or not!

I found myself (*on October 16, 1820*) in a large city with suburbs, smoke, and heaps of coal, where are many students, learned men, and Catholic churches. I saw in a public house a man who had nothing good in his intentions. He sat at table; around him frisked a strange-looking black dog that seemed to be the devil. The man wanted to cheat the landlord and to get off without paying his bill, so he made his escape by a window while the latter was waiting for him at the door. I saw him afterward in a fir forest attacking a harmless foot-traveler who, to save his life, delivered to him a little roll of money and fled. The robber had a knife concealed at his side and he tried to run after the poor man to stab him in the back, but my guide and I obstructed his path. On whatever side he ran, there we stood before him; at the same time the money became so heavy that he could no longer carry it. He was terror-stricken, his limbs trembled, and he cried out: "Friend! Friend! Wait! take back your money!" and then he found himself free to advance. The traveler paused. The robber ran up, restored the money, told him all, even of his design to murder him, but that the sight of two white figures had terrified him, and he resolved never again to commit such a crime. He was a student and had several accomplices whom he warned to follow his example and amend their life. He continued his journey with the traveler, who promised to take an interest in him.

## Assistance in the Kingdom of Siam

I WENT (*on November 12, 1820*) to a vast wilderness and saw a man and woman savage and miserable, on their knees and crying to God. I approached them and they asked me what they should do, for that I was surely the person who, in answer to their prayers, had been shown them in a dream as the one who was to comfort them. I do not remember whether I had seen their distress in vision or whether I learned it from themselves. They were thus abandoned in this desert in punishment of a great crime for which they would have had to undergo mutilation, had not their guards in pity allowed them to escape. Their great misery took the place of penance, but they knew nothing of God.

During their stay in the wilderness they had prayed earnestly for instruction. Their angels had told them in a dream that God would send them someone, and what they were commanded, that should they do. They dwelt in a cave. A great hunt was annually held in these parts. To avoid discovery, the outcasts covered the entrance of the cave with brushwood and before it laid a carcass whose stench drove the sportsmen from that quarter. In conformity with an ancient tradition, such places are regarded as impure, and so the poor creatures remained undiscovered.

Distress and want had rendered them almost savage. I gave them such instruction and consolation as God inspired. I told them especially that the criminal connection in which they lived was an abomination in the eyes of God, and that they must henceforth abstain from such intercourse until they had been instructed in the Christian faith and lawfully united. The poor creatures could scarcely understand me; compliance seemed to them very difficult. They had become like wild animals. I pointed out to them how they might reach a place in which I had seen Christianity making great progress and to which I had sent many persons from Sicily. There they could be instructed. I do not remember any more of this vision.

I went also to that island in which the Christians are so well received by the pagan population, and there I saw many new buildings. The French gentleman from Palermo and his family were there; he had built a house for himself and was preparing another for priests. Catholic missionaries are, unhappily, but few, while the heterodox are numerous.

On this journey I met in the open sea a ship in great distress; it was unable to advance and was in danger of sinking. I saw crowds of evil spirits around it. A Sicilian family was on board, grandfather and grandchildren. At the time of the pillage, they had appropriated immense treasures belonging to the Church for the erection of grand houses in the country to which they were going. This was the reason the vessel could not proceed on its course. I was commissioned to tell them that they would surely be lost unless they restored their ill-gotten goods. This they hardly knew how to do without betraying their guilt. I advised them to deposit the treasure on the shore, addressed to the rightful owners, where it would be found and taken back by some other ship. I knew that God would take care of it. When they had done so, they were able to continue their voyage.

## Labors for Convents

I HAD to go (*on August 13, 1820*) to a distinguished ecclesiastic who allowed many very pressing affairs to lie neglected, to the great detriment of all concerned. His whole interior was shown me—good judgment, humility, apparently a little exaggerated, but great negligence. I saw that once, in some business matter connected with a convent, he received letters from the superioress which he threw among other papers and entirely forgot, thus giving rise to much confusion. I saw too that he took not sufficiently to heart the present state of the Church. I could hardly believe that I was to admonish so distinguished a man as he, one so humble. I looked upon it all as a dream; I was perfectly incredulous. Then Thomas suddenly appeared before me and spoke against incredulity. I had several visions of him. I saw how he had doubted from the very first; but his disbelief of Christ's miracles had led him to Jesus and had ended in the conviction that made of him a disciple. I saw many other incidents of his life.

Then I was taken to the priest for whom I had to pray. He lay in a large room, reading by the light of a taper. I saw that he was anxious; his many oversights were like a weight on his heart. He arose, looked in his secretary for the long-neglected letter of the superioress, and began to read it.

I had also work to do for some future nuns. I saw over thirty young girls conversing together in a convent. They had not yet embraced the religious life. They seemed to belong to three different classes: some to two institutions still existing, devoted to the education of the young and the care of the sick, but which were to be reformed; the others were destined for a third not yet founded, whose object would be manual labor and education. It pained me to see that these girls allowed so much disorder around them. There was one among them destined to be a superioress, and some who wanted merely to be lay sisters, although they appeared to be of as good standing in society as the others. My guide said to me: "See! these girls are all hesitating, they will and they will not! They say, 'This is God's will, that is God's will, where is God's will? If it is the will of God,' but at the same time they are full of self-will! They have outdoors some wild horses which you are to tame," and he took me out.

I saw a herd of wild horses, symbolical of the passions of those aspirants to the religious life, as also of some others—secular persons who were opposed to the establishment of the convent. They were all bound together by these passions and both parties concurred, though in different ways, in marring the success of the undertaking. The horses were almost equal in number to those inside. They went raging around the house, as if about to attack it. It reminded me of the summertime when the cattle, tormented by flies, try to run into houses. It seemed strange that, weak as I was, I should be appointed to tame these animals; besides, I had never been accustomed to them, excepting when as a little child I used to bring my father's horse to him at daybreak. My guide said to me: "By spiritual means you must mount and tame them." But I thought: How could that ever be done? He said: "You can do it and you will do it, but only by prayer and patience, by bearing calmly and meekly what is still in store for you! You will have to begin again and again. Have you not so often declared you would begin anew a thousand times? Now, so begin that at every instant you may be ready to endure new sufferings. Think always that as yet you have suffered nothing, accomplished nothing, and thus you will tame all those horses; for until you have mastered them, these young girls will remain imperfect. In this way also you will influence all around you. You are the spiritual superioress of these young plants of the spiritual life. By spiritual means must you cultivate them, purify them, urge them on in the spiritual life!"

I replied that the task seemed absolutely impossible, as some of the animals were perfectly furious; whereupon my guide said: "The owners of those horses will become the very best, the strongest, columns of the nuptial house. They have superior talents; they will be very influential when their horses are tamed." Then I went out and began to chase the herd before me. They fled in all directions, and I saw all around me pictures of those who, wittingly or unwittingly, opposed the success of the house. Among them were the malevolent and the good, people with a good enough will, but with little judgment; and, to my sorrow, I saw these latter doing even more harm to the undertaking than the former. There were some very respectable members of the clergy among the ill-affected.

Again I had to pray for the re-establishment of a convent of women pointed out to me by two deceased nuns. I saw the convent, and the meadow in which the linen was washed and bleached. There was more than enough linen for a wash, but all in the greatest disorder. At one end of the garden ran a cool, limpid, sparkling stream; but the nuns made no use of it, they went rather to a muddy pool nearer the house. My companions remarked: "Notice how difficult a task it would be to arrange all this disordered linen! A much more difficult one will it be to restore regularity in the community. Try if you can do it!" I set to work at the linen and found it full of rents and old stains; it will give me much trouble, and take a long time.

## Prayer for Greece

ALL last night (*July 31, 1821*) I worked at a singular task, praying for innocent Christians who endure such misery in Turkey, and I had to repel the attacks of the Turks. I invoked Ignatius of Loyola, who gave me his staff and taught me how to use it. I hovered above a city situated tolerably high on a bay toward the west. Numberless ships lay before the city like a forest of masts, and many of the citizens took refuge in them. I saw in vision the holy martyr Ignatius of Antioch brought there in chains on his way to Rome and receiving the visits of other bishops.

The city was surrounded by Turks trying to enter it, sometimes at one point, sometimes at another, by the gardens or by breaches in the wall. All was confusion. I hovered in the air as if I were flying, and when I rose a little I did indeed fly. I gathered my robe around my feet, and holding Ignatius's staff in my hand I flew to meet the assailants. I repulsed them at every encounter, the bullets whizzing around me. Troops of white-robed figures accompanied me, but they often remained behind and let me go on alone. I was at times very much afraid of getting entangled in the high trees, which bore great, broad leaves and black fruit shaped like grapes. I often thought: "It is well that my folks cannot see me now flying in this way! They would certainly think me a witch."

While I fought now here, now there, I saw multitudes hastily leaving the city, bag and baggage, and fleeing to the ships. These vessels were surrounded by galleries from which little bridges reached to the shore; they were full of citizens. All night did I thus labor. I saw the Greeks also, and they appeared even more savage and cruel than the Turks. In a vast field, far away to the north, I beheld numerous troops marching to the rescue of the city, and I felt that, if they arrived, things would go still worse.

Then I had a picture in which it was shown me how widely the Greeks are separated from the Church. I saw it as a running river, and the sight pained me greatly. The Turks when thus invading a country look not like regular soldiers; they wear no uniform, but go half-naked in all sorts of rags.

## Labors for the Parish of
## Gallneukirchen, Austria, Corrupted by Sectaries

I HAVE had more and very fatiguing work to do in this parish. My father's blessing was necessary, and to get it I was obliged to make a most painful journey beset with a thousand obstacles. But I found him at last in a lovely garden surrounded by beautiful dwellings. I spoke to him of my eldest brother's sternness toward the youngest one, and he replied that he knew from experience how grievous such a thing is. He gave me his benediction, and I ascended to a higher region and into a spiritual church. There I found holy bishops of the early ages who had evangelized the country in which lay the infected parish—Maximus, Rupert, Vital, Erhard, Walburga's brothers, and some pious parish priests who had died there.

From them I received a large blessed candle which, through many difficulties, I had to carry lighted into the parish. The way was long, and each instant I thought my light would be extinguished; but I succeeded at last. I placed the candle on a candlestick in the center of the parish, whence it diffused all around rays as bright as the sun. Now, there was a dirty old oil-lamp hanging near the ground from the end of a long pole. It cast around only a dull, dingy glare; it looked more like a hole in the ground than anything else. This I had to remove, though not without great trouble. I could not keep it at the end of the pole.

The road was hilly and full of stones and rubbish. I hurt myself, bruised my knees, soiled my clothes with the grease, and became so tired and impatient that at last I ran to my mother. I found her lying in a beautiful bed in a fine house. She tried to console me, but as I still wept, she told me to put the lamp down, that I could not manage it, for it had to be twisted and hung out of a beam in the hall. Then the thought came to me that it could not be twisted, for it was made of iron, whereupon my mother commanded me to try, and I found I could twist it just like lead. I hung it out of the beams in the unfinished hall, and my mother took me into bed with her and bound up my feet. Then I saw all in the parish gathering around the light.

The two pastors labored earnestly among the people in union with a third, a very zealous man from a distance. I saw also the rector of the parish about a quarter of a league away; he was a little stiff. I saw Rupert, one of the holy apostles of the country, giving instructions with his spiritual voice, and the light increasing wherever he went. The stranger priest was enraptured. He asked the rector if he did not think the sermon admirable. The latter answered that he did not hear a word of it. But his two assistants heard it and led him up nearer to the preacher, when he could hear a little. Things are better now in that parish.

## Conversion of a Rabbi at Maestricht

ON *February 26, 1821, the pilgrim began to read a letter to Anne Catherine containing the news of the conversion of a Rabbi of Maestricht. But she interrupted him:*

I know all about it. I have seen him several times. Once I saw him in a mail coach with some devout persons who spoke of the Mother of God and of the miracles they had just witnessed before a miraculous picture, Our Lady of Good Counsel, I think, which they had just visited. The Jew interposed: "Mother of God! Mother of God! God has no Mother!"—and he mocked their faith. The good people were saddened. They prayed and asked the prayers of others for the Jew's conversion through Mary. All my life I have felt great compassion for the Jews, and through God's mercy many things have been shown me in vision for which I had to pray; consequently, I saw this man also and prayed for him.

After the incident related above he was shown me more frequently, and I perceived that he was unable to drive the thought of

Mary from his mind. I used to see her approaching him and presenting the Infant Jesus to him with these words: "This is the messiah!"—I know not whether he really saw her, or if his inmost thoughts were thus shown me symbolized, as I am accustomed to see consolations and temptations. He looked upon them as temptations and struggled against them. He used to find out where processions of the blessed sacrament were to be made, for the sole purpose of attending them, thus to excite in himself disgust and to mock at them in his heart. I saw him on such an occasion, I think it was Corpus Christi, fall involuntarily upon his knees. I know not whether it was through some inexplicable emotion, or whether he saw what I did—that is, the Mother of God in the sacred host holding toward him the infant Jesus. Straightway he became a Christian. I am sure, were he questioned on the subject, he would say that the thought of Mary pursued him constantly. I have heard nothing of this conversion, and indeed I thought it only a dream.

## An Infanticide Prevented

ON *the evening of February 27, 1821, as Anne Catherine lay in prayer, she suddenly cried out:*

O it is well that I came! It is well that I came! The child is saved! I prayed that she might bless it, for I knew she could not then throw it into the pool. A wretched girl was about to drown her child not far from here. I have prayed so much lately for innocent babes, that they might not die without baptism, for the martyrdom of the innocents again draws nigh, we have no time to lose! I have just been able to save both child and mother. I may, perhaps, go again to see the child.

*Such were the words just after the fact accomplished in vision, of which she gave a detailed account the next day:*

I saw a miserable girl of Münster give birth to a child behind a hedge, and then carry it in her apron to a stagnant pool with the intention of drowning it. A tall, black spirit stood by her from whom radiated a sort of sinister light. I think it was the evil spirit. As I approached the girl and prayed, it withdrew. Then she took the child in her arms, blessed it, kissed it, and had not the heart to drown it. She sat down weeping bitterly, for she knew not what to do. I consoled her and suggested to her to go to her confessor. She did not see me, but her angel told her. She seemed to belong to the middle class.

## Assisting a Dying Jansenist

LAST night my mother appeared to me, telling me to go to a castle she pointed out in the distance, where I was to assist a dying lady. These apparitions of my mother puzzle me. I cannot understand why she is so brief in her words, why she is so strange toward me; perhaps it is because she is a spirit and I am not.

I set out with my guide over a difficult road, to the Netherlands, I think. When we came in sight of the castle we met two roads leading to it: one smooth and pleasant; the other wild and marshy. My guide bade me choose between them. I was at first very undecided and, being very much fatigued, greatly inclined toward the good one; but finally I took the other for the sake of the poor souls in purgatory. The castle was old, dilapidated, and surrounded by trenches; but the land was fertile, and there was a fir forest near. I was at a loss how to enter. Again my mother appeared, and showed me an opening in the wall like a window, through which I climbed. Inside I found a noble old lady in a most pitiable condition. She was at the point of death. She was a most disgusting object, covered with filth and sores. She lay off in a deserted part of the house, abandoned by everyone excepting one old domestic who had been appointed to wait on her. By her, on oblong porcelain plates, lay several small slices of buttered bread. Not one in the house gave the poor lady a thought.

The young people lived in another part of the castle; they were just then having a feast, celebrating a birthday I think. The poor old lady had no priest, for they were no longer Catholics. An ecclesiastic, who had once attended her, had become a Jansenist, and she had followed his example.

Here I was shown something connected with the history of the Jansenists which, however, I do not remember very well. Their first separation from the Church was caused by an ill-regulated desire of greater piety, and they ended by becoming a sort of Calvinists. I saw also that that pious sect lately formed in Bavaria will very likely fall into similar errors.

At my guide's command, and to overcome myself, I had to kiss the poor old lady. As I entered, she seemed quite changed, sat up, thanked me joyously and heartily for coming, and expressed her desire for a Catholic priest. The nearest was three leagues away, but he was brought to her secretly by the old servant. She confessed, received the sacraments, and died in peace shortly after her return to the Church.

*As Anne Catherine was conversing on August 28, 1822, with Father Limberg, her confessor, she suddenly paused and fell into ecstasy, her countenance becoming unusually grave. When she returned to consciousness she exclaimed: "I was called by my angel to pray for a man belonging to the middle class, who was just then dying in a fit!" Such cases were of frequent occurrence.*

# Affecting Death of a Converted Sinner in Münster

I SAW (*on September 2, 1820*) a poor, God-fearing man dying in sentiments of deep contrition, the Blessed Virgin and the infant Jesus at his bedside. Then I saw his whole history. He belonged to a distinguished French family. At his birth he had been dedicated to the Blessed Virgin by his parents, who were I think afterward guillotined. He grew up, became a soldier, and deserted; but, because of his secret veneration for the Blessed Virgin he always escaped the greatest dangers. At last he joined a band of robbers—or rather assassins—among whom he lead a debauched life; but as often as he passed an image of Mary, he was seized with shame and fear.

For some crime or other this man was sentenced to imprisonment for life. His comrades found means to procure his escape, and he afterward led a wandering life until again committed to prison for robbery in a certain city. On an invasion of the French, he recovered his freedom. He again enlisted in the army, once more deserted, took foreign service, received a wound in his arm, and then settled down peaceably on his pension. He married and devoted himself to the care of the sick and similar charitable offices. He was again tempted to commit a robbery at Überwasser; but the Blessed Virgin appeared to him, told him of his consecration to her at his birth, and exhorted him to amend his life. He entered into himself, reflected upon God's patience toward him, and began a new life, a life of rigorous penance, passing his nights in sharp disciplines and prayer. I saw him die last night in peace and joy, assisted by Jesus and Mary. He had often changed his name during his wild career.

*On November 28, 1822, Anne Catherine, though very ill, related the following*:

I have had much to do in the Low Countries. I was with a pastor who lay dying miserably. One could do nothing for him. He was a Freemason, and a crowd of the brethren gathered around him like a strong chain, the padlock of which was another parish priest who lived a scandalous life with a certain person. He too was a Freemason, and in such disrepute that the faithful would not receive the sacraments from his hands. He was now called upon to prepare his friend for death, the latter being fully aware of his evil life.

It was altogether a villainous affair. The chain was fast locked, but the two went through the ceremonies with as much pomp and gravity as if it were a saint assisting a saint. With difficulty I pushed my way to the dying man and, by prayer, obtained that he should live till the morrow and perhaps repent. This nest of impiety must be cleared out. I had business also with the bishop and his affair at Rome. I went likewise to five Beguines who are full of self-conceit, who live perfectly at their ease. I had to send to them a devout man to rouse them up and make them change their life.

*Next day she continued*: The pastor is still alive and even getting better. He confesses all—many things will now come to light! (Anne Catherine was herself very ill at this time.) The other will also confess and amend his life, and the persons seduced by him, as well as their children, will receive a support.

*For several nights Anne Catherine's sufferings were very in-tense, on account of the miserable state of this unhappy priest.*

## A Church Profaned
## and a Sacrilege Committed

I WAS in an agony all last night at seeing a robbery committed in a church of this place, and I had no one to send to prevent it. It was between one and three o'clock. There were five or six men, three in the church, the others keeping watch outside. The watchman passed twice, but the robbers hid. I saw two go by here, and I think one remained concealed in the church to open it. For about two hours and a half I saw them busy rummaging and breaking. In the street back of the choir was a woman on watch and another near the doctor's house; a boy, only eight years old, was stationed near the post office. Once they had to interrupt their work because people were passing through the cemetery. They had planned also to break open the canon's house, and they watched their chance a long time. It is the same party that robbed the dean. I think the mother of one of them lives here.

As they poured out the hosts on the altar cloth, one of them said: "I will lay our Lord on a bed!" They did something also behind the main altar—the sight was horrible! I saw a devil by each of the robbers helping him; but the evil spirits could not approach the altar, they had to remain far off. I saw them running up to one another, and it looked to me as if a devil does not know of what his fellows are thinking. At times they flew to the miserable wretches whom they were instigating to crime and whispered something into their ears. I saw angels hovering over the Body of the Lord, and when the robbers broke off the silver from the large crucifix I saw Jesus in the form of a youth whom they struck and buffeted and trod under foot. It was horrible! They did everything boldly, carelessly; they have no religion. I cried out to Jesus to work a miracle, but received for answer that it was not the time. My heart was rent with anguish!

*On December 30, 1821, lying in ecstasy in the evening, Anne Catherine began to recite gaily the following nursery rhyme:*

> Down yonder, by the Rhine,
> Stands a barrel full of wine,
> Without bung, without tap—
> Now, tell me what is that?

218

*The pilgrim thought she had suddenly recalled some childish sport, and when she returned to consciousness questioned her as to the meaning of it. She seemed at first not to know to what he referred, but after a little reflection remembered having been on the shores of the Rhine, where smugglers had concealed a cask of liquor and then hid from the customs officers:*

I had to go there and pray that they might not be caught. I saw what trouble they would get into if they were taken. I stood by the cask near the Rhine, and I almost froze in the storm. It was a large cask, and I thought: "What a pity! It will go to waste! O if the Father only had it in his cellar!" Then that childish riddle came to my mind, and I recited it shivering with cold.

www.ingramcontent.com/pod-product-compliance
Lightning Source LLC
Chambersburg PA
CBHW022006080426
42733CB00007B/495